NICHOLAS JONES

Soundbites and Spin Doctors

HOW POLITICIANS MANIPULATE
THE MEDIA – AND VICE VERSA

INDIGO

First published in Great Britain 1995
by Cassell plc

This Indigo edition published 1996

Indigo is an imprint of the Cassell Group
Wellington House, 125 Strand, London WC2R 0BB

© Nicholas Jones 1995, 1996

A catalogue record for this book is
available from the British Library.

ISBN 0 575 40052 8

C218550499

301·154

CE

Printed and bound in Great Britain by
Guernsey Press Co. Ltd,
Guernsey, Channel Isles

96 97 98 99   10 9 8 7 6 5 4 3 2 1

Contents

Preface

*T*HIS BOOK explores the pursuit of publicity by politicians and examines their day-to-day dealings with journalists. My aim has been to provide an insight into the way political information is conveyed to the public through television, radio and newspapers. In an attempt to achieve that objective I have illustrated my text by describing situations in which I have been involved personally and by explaining the background to the incidents and conversations which took place. Where I have considered it helpful to the reader I have reproduced exactly what was said to me at the time.

My account of the events and relationships which I describe is based on my contemporary diaries and notes. In presenting this material in the form of a book I have not sought the approval of people whom I have quoted by name. Politics are never constant: the facts about what happened on any given occasion can be hard to determine, and I accept that differing interpretations can be placed on the circumstances surrounding almost any political event. However, I have tried to relate my experiences as honestly and faithfully as I can. The people I have quoted without their knowledge seek to exploit the news media so as to publicise political parties or to promote the government of the day. I hope readers of my investigation into the often private interplay between journalists, politicians and their advisers will obtain an insight into the hidden world of media manipulation. I hope too that I will not be considered to have been unfair or unkind in my disclosures. Many of the incidents which I have described involve situations where my own judgement as a journalist could be questioned. My blow-by-blow accounts are intended to illustrate the pressure under which political journalists work and thereby, I hope, will illuminate the processes through which political information reaches the public.

Introduction: *The Hunters and the Hunted*

Politicians are rightly fearful of the power of the news media. There are many celebrated instances of when the pace and outcome of political events have been influenced and even determined by the way they were reported. Ministers and MPs have their defences: the soundbite and the spin doctor. Carefully worded answers are prepared before any interview to encapsulate their thoughts; public relations experts and other political propagandists then seek to explain and promote the meaning and implication of their replies. Yet politicians are nevertheless regularly caught unawares. Sometimes they realise too late in the day that a story seized on by the newspapers and by television and radio is developing a momentum of its own. On occasion the pressures generated by journalists can be so strong that governments and political parties have to give way to them.

The parliamentary recess of Christmas 1993 was to provide a telling illustration of the awesome forces which can be unleashed. Along with other political reporters I had a part to play in fuelling what American commentators have described as 'the feeding frenzy'. The media pack were about to taste blood. Within a matter of days there would be another ministerial resignation. My contribution as a BBC political correspondent was to ambush the party chairman: just when the story appeared to be faltering some rather contrived but unexpected questions during a radio interview succeeded in reigniting the controversy.

Our quarry that Christmas and New Year was the environment minister Tim Yeo. The Boxing Day edition of the *News of the World* revealed that he had fathered a 'secret love child' during an extramarital affair. A year earlier relentless publicity had forced the resignation of the heritage secretary David Mellor after his affair with an actress. Yeo's confirmation that he was the father of an illegitimate child appeared to make a mockery of what had become known as the Prime Minister's 'back to basics' campaign, launched at that October's Conservative party conference amid a welter of criticism of single mothers.

Instead of playing for time, or trying to brazen out the *News of the World*'s disclosures, Yeo had issued an immediate and explicit statement

1

through his solicitor Peter Carter-Ruck. As it was a holiday period there was a dearth of political news; by his own courageous action, Yeo had turned his affair into a mainstream political story, ensuring that it attracted maximum attention and gained a far wider audience than if it had remained solely the preserve of the tabloid newspapers. In his statement Yeo said his wife and family were aware of the extent of his extra-marital affair. The unmarried Conservative councillor who was the mother of his five-month-old daughter had made a conscious decision not to identify him publicly and she strongly resented that, in order to 'put an end to speculation in some quarters of the media', she now found it necessary to reveal that Yeo was the father. He regarded his relationship with her as an entirely private matter which had no bearing on their respective political duties. However, in the light of the 'continuing intrusion of certain representatives of the press' he had notified his government colleagues of the situation.

By issuing a detailed statement so quickly Yeo hoped to avoid the drawn-out and titillating exposure which had dogged Mellor before his resignation and which had almost forced the departure of another minister, Steven Norris, whose private life was attracting considerable publicity. Initially the tactic seemed to work. The next morning's national newspapers reported that ministerial colleagues were rallying to Yeo's support. He seemed to have retained the confidence of his constituency party. The *Sun*'s headline put it rather more succinctly: 'Cheating Minister Told: Your Job's Safe.'

But, by lunchtime, the tide appeared to be turning. On-the-record confirmation that a minister had fathered an illegitimate child was too tempting a target for at least one publicity-conscious Tory MP. David Evans, newly elected to the Conservatives' backbench 1992 committee, told BBC radio's *The World at One* that if ministers could not adhere to the 'moral standards they are preaching at us every day' then they ought not to stay in office. 'You don't go knocking off everybody. You just have to set the example. If you do it and don't get caught, fair enough. If you get caught, goodbye.' Evans' strictures were backed by Dr Adrian Rogers, director of the Conservative Family Institute, who said the party's grass roots were pretty moral. If the government was talking about the need for a return to basic family values this was not the moment for a minister to be creating a new single family.

However, there was little else to sustain the story. By now Yeo and his family had departed for a holiday in the Seychelles, where he refused to make any further comment about either his marriage or his political future. My own conversations with Conservative press officers confirmed the line taken by the newspapers. Tory Central Office thought Yeo was safe both in his job and in his constituency. He was considered to have handled the disclosures 'fairly well' with the least possible damage to the government.

The following day I had an opportunity to put this relaxed approach to the test. Sir Norman Fowler, the party chairman, had issued a New Year message which consisted largely of an attack on the then Labour leader, the late John Smith, for being 'trapped in a 1970s timewarp'. One phrase in the press release had caught my attention. Fowler predicted that during 1994 'the government's standing will rise.' Although copies of the statement had been made available to that day's newspapers (and I had reported Fowler's message in radio news bulletins that morning), the BBC and ITN were invited to interview the chairman so that he could repeat his criticism of Smith for the benefit of the television news bulletins. I tagged along as the duty radio correspondent, ostensibly to do a follow-up interview in case Fowler said anything new. Party officials and my colleagues were unaware of the fact that I had prepared a sequence of questions on the Yeo affair, pegged rather loosely to the chairman's prediction that the government's standing would rise.

I was pretty sure that Fowler was only too well aware that there might be attempts to force him, against his wish, to answer questions about Yeo. I thought he would almost certainly fob me off politely with a ready-made answer to the effect that he could not comment on such a personal issue. Nevertheless I knew that many newspaper political correspondents would relish the chance to throw an unexpected question, and in order to maintain an element of surprise I waited until last.

Fowler was in an expansive mood, suggesting rather rashly that I could ask him what I liked. He was clearly looking forward to another opportunity to repeat his attack on Labour. After some opening questions about his views on Smith I challenged him directly on whether the government's standing would be damaged by Yeo's disclosures. Fowler denied this, insisting that everyone would regard the affair as a purely private matter. The implication of his reply was that he would go no further. Therefore there would be no point in my asking further questions. If pressed in such circumstances politicians usually repeat their initial answer, often ad nauseam, until the interviewer changes the subject. As a BBC political correspondent I would be expected to take the hint. The interview had been arranged to discuss Fowler's New Year message, not Yeo's personal life.

Undeterred I ploughed on, suggesting that the chairman's answers would not satisfy the outspoken MP David Evans. By now Fowler was looking rather perplexed. He chided me for 'going down a curious road' with my questions. But, instead of sticking to his original answer, he opened up, claiming that the general public did not share Evans' views and that there was no evidence of there being more extra-marital affairs among Conservative than Labour MPs. There was no pressure, he said, in either the party or the country for a resignation and Yeo had not only the support of himself as party chairman but also that of the Prime Minister. Unexpectedly, and perhaps unintentionally, Fowler had given the story a significant new twist. This was the first official confirmation of John Major's support for his beleaguered minister. Major had been severely criticised for standing by Mellor initially before the heritage minister's eventual resignation the previous year. I realised that Fowler's remarks would be seized on by those newspapers which had been so critical of what they considered to be Conservative hypocrisy on family values.

The moment my tape recorder was switched off Tim Collins, the Conservatives' director of communications, who was present during the interview, protested at my conduct. There had been no advance notification from me about my line of questioning and, he said, it was clear all along that Fowler had only intended answering questions about his New Year message. I regarded this as the usual line of attack from a press officer caught off guard. It was Collins' responsibility to warn the chairman about surprise or possibly sneaky questions. If he was so concerned he should have taken the precaution of warning me before the interview started that the Yeo affair was off limits. I mumbled something in reply and then directed my comments to the chairman, defending myself for having asked perfectly proper questions. Fowler also protested at the lack of notice. He would have liked more time to think through his answers. I said that if he had any doubts about his replies I would readily play back the tape. If he was dissatisfied we could do the interview again. Surprisingly he agreed to this. Listening to the tape being replayed Fowler looked troubled. At one point he groaned and appeared to hold his head in his hands. He said that if the interview was going to be used he wanted to be more forthcoming and more supportive of Tim Yeo. Yes, he would like me to ask my questions again. He clearly felt great sympathy for the embattled minister but obviously had not thought through how his answers might be interpreted. Nevertheless he knew he could not retract what he had said.

As a former journalist himself Fowler would have realised there was no point in even trying to persuade me not to report his remarks. I had first made his acquaintance in 1968 on joining *The Times* as a parliamentary reporter. He was then the paper's home affairs correspondent. More recently I had interviewed him quite frequently in his years as a minister and secretary of state and subsequently as party chairman. If he now wanted to harden up his support for Yeo still further, I said, I would be only too happy to give him an assurance that his first, rather more hesitant, replies would not be broadcast.

The second time round Fowler kept his word, becoming far more forthright. What had happened to Yeo was a private matter. The position of two private individuals should be respected. 'It would be a great mistake if we went down the course of trying to pillory people for their own private lives... I actually believe that we should have compassion and understanding, if you don't mind me saying so... I do not believe it is part of our role, and I don't think it is part of the media's role either, to go into the private lives of individuals, unless it has a dramatic effect on the role that the minister is carrying out.'

We parted amicably but I was somewhat perturbed. I feared Fowler would soon regret what he had said and that either he or Collins might complain to the BBC and suggest that the way the chairman had been interviewed was unfair and amounted to a set-up. My conduct had been rather risky and might be frowned upon. It had been a rather blatant fishing trip. Instead of carrying out a structured interview based solely on Fowler's New Year message, I had, without prior notice, reeled off my questions hoping to get a bite.

Needless to say, once they heard the broadcast, newspaper correspondents in the House of Commons press gallery were delighted by my handiwork. After giving his interviews Fowler departed immediately for his New Year celebrations and did not repeat his remarks. My exclusive interview, broadcast that lunchtime by *The World at One*, was widely quoted next morning, with Fowler's plea for compassion featured strongly by most newspapers. The *Sun*'s treatment of the story was an indication of what lay in store. Above an introductory paragraph detailing how the party chairman thought 'ministers who cheat on their wives should be forgiven not sacked' there was a graphic headline: 'Carry On Bonking, Fowler Tells Tories'. The following day the *Sun* awarded Fowler its 'Poppycock of the year award' for having suggested that the press should keep its nose out of cases where ministers committed adultery. Voters based their judgement on the public image of MPs. 'That's why so many politicians include happy family photos on their election literature. And that's why MPs don't like the press spilling the beans when they're caught not practising what they preach.'

By now the weight of media attention was beginning to dictate events. Yeo and his family found themselves besieged by reporters at their holiday hotel in the Seychelles. Instead of staying for a week he left unexpectedly, providing in the process a textbook example of what a politician should not do when being pursued by reporters. Once the *News of the World* published its story Yeo was a marked man. The last thing he should have done was to have gone on holiday to an exotic location by way of international airports where he would inevitably find himself on public display. Departure and arrival shots of celebrities are the stock-in-trade of newspaper photographers; and because there is public access, reporters also get the chance to throw the unexpected question.

Major airports like Heathrow do have air-side entrances and exits specially reserved for VIPs from which the media can be excluded. The Seychelles either lacked such facilities or had little experience in handling a media scrum. However, in an attempt to provide Yeo with a speedy exit the British High Commissioner John Sharland had laid on his official car. Nevertheless he could not prevent photographers taking shots of the minister arriving at the airport with his family. The most damaging picture showed Yeo crouched on the back seat of the car hiding his face in their luggage. 'If You Don't Look ... It Might All Go Away' ran the *Daily Mirror* headline across the top of nearly a page of pictures illustrating how the 'disgraced minister played an elaborate game of cat-and-mouse across the Seychelles in an attempt to hide his shame'.

Yeo had not only provided some spectacular photographs but had also given the newspapers another angle to the story. An inquiry was being demanded into the way 'taxpayers' money' had been used to take Yeo and his luggage to the airport. The High Commissioner confirmed that assistance was provided because of the circumstances in which the minister had found himself. There was further controversy when his flight arrived at Gatwick: instead of having to walk through the arrivals hall, the Yeo family were met by a car at the aircraft steps, thus avoiding the waiting reporters and photographers. George Foulkes, Labour's former foreign affairs spokesman, said it was unacceptable for Yeo to use the privileges which went with his ministerial position for private purposes. Later a government spokesman insisted that no public expense had been incurred in the 'practical assistance' which had been given in the Seychelles and at Gatwick.

Unnamed Conservative MPs were quoted by some newspapers as expressing alarm at the way Yeo tried to hide himself from public view. They thought his conduct very unwise, given the public support he had received from Major and Fowler. The scene was now set for the final and decisive twist to the story.

By stating publicly that he and the Prime Minister stood by Yeo, Fowler had in fact made a judgement on the minister's conduct. In rebuking the media he had also invited retaliatory attacks from the leader writers. Although it had been a pretty action-packed week already on the Yeo front, the Sunday newspapers were determined to give the story fresh impetus. The *News of the World* reprinted its front-page splash headline from the previous Sunday with the comment that the environment minister had 'crept back into the country' showing 'all the spine of a jellyfish'. It concluded that Yeo's future must now be in serious doubt after receiving Norman Fowler's 'vote of confidence'.

Of greater concern to the embattled MP for South Suffolk was that all the Sunday newspapers quoted comments from a prominent constituent calling on him to resign from his ministerial position. Mrs Aldine Horrigan, a Conservative association vice-chairman and the Mayor of Haverhill, the largest town in the consituency, had written to Downing Street asking Major to reconsider his support for Yeo. She disagreed with Fowler's conclusion that this was a private matter because Yeo was a public figure whose actions affected 'the honour of his constituency'. She was supported next day in a letter to *The Times* by Dr Rogers of the Conservative Family Institute, who said Fowler's plea for compassion was misjudged because 'immoral politicians' were 'potentially untrustworthy'.

Yeo could not have had a more formidable opponent than Mrs Horrigan. When interviewed subsequently by BBC television news she wore her mayoral chain, thus lending even greater authority to her request that the Prime Minister should denounce their MP for behaviour which she said the Conservative Party would not tolerate. In a radio interview that Sunday for *The World this Weekend* Major gave the clearest possible signal that the public support proffered by Fowler had in fact been withdrawn. All he would say was that he was not going to get drawn into the cases of individual ministers. Although he was pressed no further, the implication was all too apparent. If Major was still standing by his minister this would have been the moment to say so.

Next morning the newspapers were virtually unanimous in predicting a resignation within days. Most printed the full text of Mrs Horrigan's letter to Major in which she stressed that it was time Conservatives practised what they preached. Later that day the South Suffolk Conservatives' chairman Mrs Patricia Fitzpatrick announced that the constituency officers would meet the following evening. Yeo spent his last full day as a minister insisting he would not be driven out of office by 'media attacks'. He acknowledged that he had acted 'very foolishly', but he believed that the government's position on family values, 'which is certainly one I share, is not jeopardised by anything I have done'.

Arriving that evening at the constituency meeting which he had been asked to attend he expressed his 'deep regret' at the embarrassment his actions had caused. At ten o'clock the next morning Mrs Fitzpatrick read a terse statement calling on Yeo to reflect on the 'widespread disappointment' which party members had expressed. Constituency officers acknowledged his parliamentary service to South Suffolk, and they hoped he would continue to serve as their MP, but they failed to back him as a minister. That evening Yeo tendered his resignation, telling Major that although he considered his personal life had never in any way prevented him from discharging his duties as a minister of state, he believed he had no alternative to stepping down.

Conservative MPs were divided about whom to blame. The former minister Peter Bottomley, wife of the health secretary, Virginia Bottomley, claimed that the real hypocrisy lay in the media, including 'quality journalists and broadcasters', rather than in the politicians. Sir Geoffrey Johnson Smith, vice chairman of the backbenchers' 1922 committee, thought Yeo was right to take note of his constituents' views. Among the newspapers, the *Guardian* expressed sympathy, saying that nowadays no errant minister could survive for more than three days on the front pages. When the tabloids had announced two days earlier that Yeo would go, long before a decision had been taken, they were 'celebrating anticipatorily their power to destroy, not reporting an actual event'. Under the headline 'Pushed Out By The People' the *Daily Mail* said the minister was forced out after a 'dramatic display of Tory grass roots power'.

Inevitably I reflected on my own part in giving the story fresh life and possibly hastening a ministerial resignation. While I was concerned that my action might have added to the distress caused to the women and children caught up in the affair I had no particular sympathy for Yeo. He belonged to a political party which, like its opponents, sought to exploit and manipulate the news media. When we were briefed on the Prime Minister's 'back to basics' speech at the October 1993 conference the guidance of the Conservatives' media officer Tim Collins was that Major was intent on rolling back the permissive society.

In a more general sense, too, the Conservatives had prepared their own bed of nails. During the 1980s they had unleashed and encouraged unparalleled competition between newspapers, television and radio. These commercial pressures had inevitably had an impact on editorial standards. In my thirty-five years as a journalist I had experienced many changes in the demands which proprietors and managers made of their staff. In some ways the greatest transformation occurred in what constituted permissible conduct for journalists. During the same period there had also been signs of a marked shift in what the public considered to be acceptable behaviour on the part of reporters. As well as offering an insider's view of the hidden pressures on, and motives of, the hunters and the hunted in the quest for political news, my book seeks to explore how the rapid expansion in media outlets, and the accompanying alterations in professional values, have affected the relationship between politicians and journalists.

I

Rules of Engagement

When WINSTON CHURCHILL resigned as Prime Minister in 1955 he was still refusing to give interviews for television. His wartime radio broadcasts had been a source of inspiration for the country; but Churchill was not sure he could master the new techniques which he felt were required for television. In contrast, many of his Cabinet colleagues were trying enthusiastically to update their broadcasting skills, taking their first tentative steps towards using a medium of communication which, within less than a decade, was to replace daily newspapers as the public's principal source of political information. The mid-1990s produced a comparable milestone when Tony Blair became the first British political leader to be chosen, in the view of many party activists, largely on the strength of his superiority as a television performer.

Almost a million party and trade union members participated in Labour's first leadership election to be conducted by the enlarged franchise of one member, one vote. One of the commonest reasons given afterwards for supporting Blair was a belief that in the all-important political battleground of the news media he would come across to the electorate, especially in southern England, as the most likeable leader and the best equipped to take Labour to power. Party and union activists remarked on how he seemed to be in total control of himself when being interviewed for news bulletins and current affairs programmes. He appeared to be saying only what he wanted to say and what he believed to be true. They felt this augured well for his chances of reaching Downing Street.

Two possible rival candidates for the Labour leadership, both of whom decided against mounting a challenge, were forced, somewhat reluctantly, to acknowledge their rival's supremacy. Gordon Brown, the shadow Chancellor, was seen as lacking Blair's fluency and friendly spontaneity on television whereas Robin Cook, then Labour's trade and industry spokesman, was not considered to be sufficiently telegenic to become leader, having been described by some political commentators as resembling a garden gnome. Never before had flair and expertise in communicating through television been identified so clearly, and by such a large proportion of the party membership, as a prominent, perhaps the deciding factor in their selection of a potential Prime Minister.

The capacity of television to shape political events derives from its ability to penetrate almost every household in the country. In its role as the leading news provider, television has had a profound impact on political reporting. Newspapers now devote less space to politicians' speeches. The quality press does not always provide a daily record of political events, leaving much of the step-by-step coverage to the broadcast media in order to allow extra space for detailed analysis and informed speculation. In popular papers, much of the coverage tends to concentrate more on personalities, and on purveying a diet of gossip and scandal.

These changes in the dissemination of political news have also been hastened by commercial pressures. Of all the legacies bequeathed by Margaret Thatcher one of the most troublesome for the Conservative politicians who have succeeded her is the virtual free-for-all which has developed in the ownership and control of news media outlets. As a result of the free rein given to newspaper proprietors during the 1980s, allowing them to expand into television and radio, the broadcasting services have been subjected to the same kind of competitive forces which took the popular press even further downmarket. The constant battle for readers, listeners and viewers has had a profound effect on news-gathering and especially on the coverage of the daily happenings in Whitehall and Westminster.

When Mrs Thatcher was Prime Minister she had a powerful hold over the proprietors. If Tory-leaning newspapers stepped out of line, pressure could be exerted behind the scenes. There was a common bond of self-interest which reasserted itself at election times. Under John Major those traditional links have become weaker. His administration has been derided by the Conservative press in a manner which would have been unthinkable under a Thatcher government. Tory MPs have also had to come to terms with the relentless exposure of their private and business lives. They have received a taste of the punishment which was dished out so systematically to Labour politicians and trade union leaders during the 1980s.

However much broadcasters might try to distance themselves from such influences, the excesses of the tabloids do colour their news judgement and are reflected in their treatment of politics. Newspaper exclusives about the salacious or dubious activities of politicians tend to get followed up by television and radio, even if only obliquely at first. The various sections of the media feed off each other. In part this is the result of a great expansion in editorial space and air time. Newspapers have spawned countless supplements and magazines. Hardly a year goes by without the opening of yet more radio stations or the prospect of additional television channels. Technological advances in printing and broadcasting have also helped quicken the pace of change.

My own career is an illustration of the speed and extent of the evolution which has taken place. When I joined *The Times* as a parliamentary reporter in 1968 a fast shorthand note was the essential tool of the trade. I was one of a team of twelve journalists who produced a closely printed broadsheet page packed with verbatim reports from both Houses of Parliament on the questions, answers and speeches of MPs, ministers and peers. The broadcasting of parliamentary proceedings, first by radio, and subsequently by television, put the newspapers at a serious time disadvantage. Their detailed reporting became redundant because readers with an avid interest in parliamentary news had usually either seen or heard the key passages the day before – the day on which they were uttered.

I am now one of seventy journalists employed at the BBC's studios and editorial offices in Westminster. We are responsible for producing hour upon hour of parliamentary and political reporting for the national television and radio networks, regional programmes, local stations and the BBC's radio and television world services. Our output has expanded enormously, as has that of the BBC's competitors, because in agreeing to the recording and televising of their proceedings the parliamentarians have provided the broadcasters with an almost limitless resource of topical material. Perhaps not surprisingly, the number of journalists employed at Westminster by the broadcasting organisations is on the point of equalling if not exceeding the combined political and parliamentary staff of the newspapers. Indeed, there are so many television and radio journalists seeking access that they cannot all be given passes.

Twenty-five years ago the front row of the House of Commons press gallery was usually fully occupied, whatever the hour, by reporters from rival news agencies and national and regional newspapers. Nowadays when MPs look up from their green leather benches they remark on the empty seats above them and complain about the absence of journalists except for Prime Minister's questions or important front-bench speeches. Much of the monitoring of parliamentary business is now done across the road from the Palace of Westminster at the main broadcasting centre in Millbank, where journalists and producers sit observing the proceedings on small television sets built into their desks.

The gradual disappearance of the parliamentary reporter, and the introduction of new technology, have combined to change the face of the press gallery. Many of my old haunts are silent now. Journalists no longer stand in the long rows of phone boxes dictating their stories to copy typists in Fleet Street. Instead they have desk-top computer terminals. In years gone by *The Times* used to require so much parliamentary copy that it had to be sub-edited at Westminster. Messengers walked the majestic corridors between the House of Commons and the House of Lords collecting by hand the freshly typed pages as soon as they were finished.

There was a clear distinction then between parliamentary and political journalists. The former, who sat in the press gallery having to listen to even the dullest of debates, were a breed apart from the political editors and correspondents who stood in the members' lobby, talked to MPs and attended the off-the-record lobby briefings held either in Downing Street or in the privacy of the lobby room high up in one of the twin towers overlooking the terrace of the House of Commons. I well remember being rebuked in my early days for daring to sound out MPs in the hope of finding a story: my job was to report what was said in the chamber and at no stage should I attempt to do the work of a lobby correspondent.

Some of the older MPs still hanker for the days when there was every likelihood their speeches would be reported next morning in *The Times* or the *Daily Telegraph*. A few have failed (or refused) to come to terms with the electronic age, but the vast majority of MPs relish the opportunities afforded by the wider exposure available on television and radio. They realise that however thoughtful or well-crafted their speeches might be, they should always try to include in their remarks a provocative or forceful punchline in the hope of achieving political impact and attracting the attention of the television and radio producers. In their pursuit of publicity even the humblest and most obscure MPs have had to become slaves to the soundbite, capable of encapsulating their arguments in a few short, sharp sentences suitable for inclusion in a broadcast news bulletin.

Television cameras were finally allowed into the House of Commons in the autumn of 1989 as a result of pressure which had built up over the preceding two decades. There was no certainty even then that the televising of parliament was going to be permanent; all that MPs had agreed to was a six-month experiment, and that was only approved by a majority of fifty-four votes. Margaret Thatcher had fought a last-ditch campaign against the cameras. She told MPs that the televising of their proceedings would 'damage the reputation' of the Commons. But for her opposition the broadcasters might have won the day much earlier. Neil Kinnock, the then Labour leader, was fond of remarking that the Prime Minister seemed to be afraid of 'moving pictures'.

By refusing for so long to allow television access to their deliberations, MPs had made themselves something of a laughing stock. The House of Commons was almost the last parliament among the leading industrialised countries to be televised; even the House of Lords had allowed the cameras in in 1986. Radio broadcasts from the Commons had been permitted since 1978, and until MPs and ministers finally relented their disembodied voices would occasionally emerge in the middle of television news bulletins and other programmes. So great was the desire of producers and editors to illustrate political reports with actuality from the Commons that a radio soundbite was considered better than nothing. A photograph and name caption would appear on the screen to identify the MP who was speaking. In the years before even radio recordings were permitted journalists used equally archaic devices to enliven their broadcasts. One of my first duties on becoming a BBC correspondent at Westminster in the early 1970s was to listen to Prime Minister's questions, prepare a summary of what had been said and then rewrite my report in the form of a two-way conversation. My main outlet was the *PM* programme on BBC radio. The then presenter, the late William Hardcastle, would ask an agreed set of questions allowing me to recount what had happened in the liveliest possible manner. By injecting some rather contrived spontaneity into our conversation we hoped to recapture some of the cut and thrust of question time.

In the summer of 1975 I joined the BBC team which worked on the first experimental radio broadcasts. The Speaker's opening refrain of 'Order, order' was on its way to becoming a national institution. In one important respect the early radio broadcasts were probably responsible for delaying the televising of parliament. The jeers and shouts of MPs tended to get amplified by the microphones. Television pictures would have put the noise into context, showing a chamber crowded to capacity. With only the sound of raucous behaviour to guide them, listeners felt they were eavesdropping on the proceedings of a beargarden. Mrs Thatcher considered the rowdiness had done MPs a disservice. When challenged in 1988 as to why she was still resisting the introduction of television cameras she said that ten years of radio broadcasting had not enhanced the reputation of the House of Commons.

Despite another year's delay the broadcasters were finally supplied with pictures on 21 November 1989. The state opening of parliament that morning was televised as usual; then, in the afternoon, the newly installed cameras in the Commons chamber were switched on for the first time. The Speaker, Bernard Weatherill, called the House to order. An indefatigable Labour parliamentarian, the late Bob Cryer, had the distinction of being the first MP to be seen speaking on television when he challenged a parliamentary order. The opening speech was made by the late Ian Gow who moved the loyal address to the Queen. The choice could not have been more apposite, for Gow was a long-standing opponent of the televising of parliamentary proceedings. Standing slightly hunched, with his black-rimmed spectacles and bald head glistening under the much improved lighting, Gow entertained his colleagues with a bravura performance. Apparently, like many other MPs, he had been approached by a firm of image consultants who said they could guarantee to improve his appearance. A new hairstyle might be required; or perhaps they could suggest the type of glasses which best suited his face? Amid general merriment he told the House he was beyond redemption on both counts. Gow also had a serious point. He had been taken aback by the calculations supplied by the consultants. They estimated that 55 per cent of the impression which people made when appearing on television derived from their image. Voice and body language accounted for 38 per cent. Only 7 per cent depended on what the person was actually saying. He felt this was preposterous.

Neil Kinnock, who opened for the opposition, said that like Gow he had not been to a television charm school for grooming. Instead, he had come prepared with one of the sharpest asides of the afternoon. He mocked Mrs Thatcher for being so isolationist. When it was eleven to one against Britain at a European summit, or even forty-eight to one against Britain at a Commonwealth conference, she had apparently said she felt sorry for the majority. Kinnock continued: 'When I hear the Prime Minister feeling sorry for the rest of the world, I understand why she has taken to calling herself "we" – it is less lonely.' His joke was used in television news reports that evening. Parliamentary sketch writers had a field day. Simon Hoggart, writing in the *Observer*, congratulated the Labour leader for having coined the first soundbite of the televised proceedings.

Mrs Thatcher was one of over 100 MPs who had gone to the trouble of attending briefings and rehearsals laid on by the supervisor of parliamentary broadcasting, John Grist. She had also taken the precaution of having her speech notes prepared in a larger type than usual. She enjoyed her first outing in front of the cameras, resolutely ignoring their presence. Unlike previous speakers she avoided any reference to the significance of the occasion. However, she realised the power of the television pictures and showed her mastery of speaking at the despatch box. She allowed a total of thirteen MPs, all eager for televisual exposure, to interrupt her speech on the loyal address. Next morning the Prime Minister's press secretary, Bernard Ingham, told political journalists that she was in her natural habitat when being challenged in parliament and she was well satisfied with her first performance. He even agreed with one newspaper which said that the way she came across during the televised proceedings made her appear almost human for once.

One noticeable change in parliamentary behaviour was the tendency of MPs to cluster round a colleague who had been called to speak. The practice is known as 'doughnutting' and was already a well-established technique in other televised legislatures. Not only do these parliamentary extras hope to be seen on television; they also have a useful supporting role. Their presence reinforces what is being said and, by looking attentive, they give their colleague's remarks even greater weight, especially as the House might be almost deserted, as it so often is for low-key debates. Nevertheless the practice does invite ridicule. Ministers frequently squash themselves in together on the front bench when the Prime Minister is speaking, so anxious are they to appear supportive. After Mrs Thatcher's first televised appearance the *Sun*'s headline was hardly complimentary: 'The government front bench is like the rear window of a Cortina...full of nodding dogs.'

In these early days, some MPs were not quite sure where to look. Cabinet ministers had tended to peer down, across the despatch box, when addressing their remarks to the shadow ministers sitting opposite them on the Labour front bench; now they were instructed to look up when replying, so that they would be full face to the camera. Soon MPs started paying attention to the camera angles, working out which speaking positions suited them best. There was also a marked improvement in their general appearance. The Liberal Democrat Matthew Taylor was taken by the *Today* newspaper to meet Mary Spillane of the Color Me Beautiful image consultancy. At £150 a go she was reported to have advised forty MPs on how to make themselves more telegenic. She considered that Taylor, who at twenty-six was then the youngest MP, looked like a 'boring old fogey'. She recommended that he wore a charcoal suit with a pale lavender shirt, a red and blue tie, and a red pocket handkerchief.

One woman MP who needed little encouragement – or, apparently, advice – was Teresa Gorman, whose colourful, eye-catching outfits marked her out instantly on the Conservative benches. She disliked being doughnutted by her fellow MPs and started speaking from the back row, where, instead of having the distracting heads of other MPs in the background, she was framed by attractive oak panelling. Her preoccupation with the cameras was revealed inadvertently two months into what was still being regarded as an experiment. At one point in a speech Mrs Gorman said: 'People watching this programme may well say...' Amid the ensuing laughter, the Labour MP Andrew Faulds shouted across the chamber: 'This is not a programme, this is a debate in the House of Commons.'

When, in July 1990, MPs voted by an overwhelming majority to continue the televising of their proceedings they also ensured the continuation of the new programmes which had been launched to feed off the coverage. *Westminster Live* on BBC2, featuring Prime Minister's questions on Tuesday and Thursday afternoons, had built up the largest audience.

Each morning a report on the previous day's business was supplied by the BBC2 programme *Westminster Daily*, while Channel Four transmitted daily footage in *The Parliament Programme*. Weekly programmes on the networks and in the regions complemented the daily reporting.

One consequence of this great expansion in political and parliamentary programming was that MPs found they were being invited to take part in many more interviews, both live and prerecorded. Producers had discovered that there was a limit to the amount of parliamentary footage which they could replay without losing the interest of viewers. Apart from confrontational exchanges at question time, and important frontbench speeches, many of the debates were considered to be either too pedestrian or too parochial to be of interest to national audiences, and detailed consideration of most parliamentary bills was regarded as being far too technical. Among many broadcasters, if not MPs, there was an unspoken acknowledgement that the televised proceedings on their own were rarely sufficient to sustain full-length parliamentary programmes. In order to liven up their output, and help explain the issues at stake, producers felt it was far better to follow up the business of the House by talking directly to those involved.

College Green, across the road from the Palace of Westminster, had already established itself as the most favoured spot for television interviews. Its great advantage as a location is that both Houses of Parliament and Big Ben are in the background, providing a marvellous backdrop which can be used for a great variety of camera angles. Now, with the increased demand for interview footage as a much-needed contrast to the rather static and sometimes boring shots of MPs speaking in the chamber, College Green quickly became a hive of activity, and MPs soon found themselves trooping out of the Commons chamber in ever greater numbers. On busy days four or five television crews, plus reporters and producers, could be seen at work; at times of high political drama there might be double that number. Judging by the fascination of passers-by, who started to cluster round to listen to the MPs being questioned, the parliamentary dialogue on College Green began to emerge as a weekday alternative to the soap-box oratory of Speakers' Corner in Hyde Park.

After an initial burst of enthusiasm, when a wide range of news stories were being illustrated with shots of backbench MPs speaking or challenging ministers, the editors of the peak-time news bulletins also became rather bored with pictures of the chamber. As a result they too tended to become more sparing in their use of parliamentary footage. Unless Prime Minister's questions produced a spectacular bust-up, or there was a significant ministerial announcement or an unexpected outburst, run-of-the-mill parliamentary coverage rarely made its way into the news.

In part, this disenchantment stemmed from the strict rules imposed on filming and coverage from the beginning by the Commons Select Committee on Broadcasting. All news outlets were supplied with an identical feed of pictures. Broadcasters had no choice in selecting the material they could transmit. The standard shot of an MP speaking had to be head and shoulders or alternatively a wide angle. Bulletin producers complained about the lack of movement and the sameness of the pictures, and three months into the experiment the committee eased the rules slightly to allow an occasional zoom in or out and group shots showing MPs reacting. It was also agreed that a second television feed, supplying a continuous picture taken from the end of the chamber looking towards the Speaker's chair, should be made available for editing purposes. But the restrictions continued to prevent any lively or imaginative filming.

Most MPs still believe that if camera crews were ever given a free run of the House of Commons they would poke fun at the proceedings and undermine the standing of parliament. Therefore tight guidelines remain in force: if there is grave disorder on the floor of the House, or other unparliamentary behaviour, the picture being transmitted must always focus on the Speaker; shots panning along empty benches are forbidden; and interruptions or demonstrations in the galleries cannot not be televised. These stipulations are perhaps understandable; where the rules do seem unnecessarily petty and restrictive is in the limitations they impose on what might otherwise be regarded as illuminating footage. For example, the cameras cannot pick out the government officials sitting in the box at the Speaker's end of the chamber or film them when they occasionally pass notes to ministers; nor may they show the House of Commons clerks giving advice to the Speaker. There is even a ban on something as mundane as a split-screen shot.

Even after considerable experience in having their proceedings televised successfully, however, MPs have shown no wish to be more flexible or to do anything to encourage more informative parliamentary coverage – despite the first signs of what could perhaps become a long-term decline in the use of parliamentary footage, especially in network programmes. Initially surveys indicated a dramatic increase in the interest being shown by the networks. *Cameras in the Commons*, a study published by the Hansard Society in May 1990, found that in the first three months of the experiment the reporting of the Commons on national television news had increased by 80 per cent. Yet four years later MPs were publicly criticising the broadcasters for allowing coverage to fall off even in the specialist programmes. Frank Dobson, a former shadow Leader of the House, claimed in June 1994 that parliamentary reporting on both television and radio had reached 'an all-time low'. But research commissioned earlier in the year for the *Six O'Clock News* on BBC1 had revealed that among a survey group of viewers politics was regarded as the least interesting of the main topics being dealt with in the news bulletins. Many of those questioned considered political and parliamentary reporting a turn-off. A commonly held opinion was that as politicians could not be trusted there was no point in even watching or listening. Viewers were also critical of MPs for using unfamiliar language when speaking in the House. Some television news producers shared the sense of disenchantment: they too had come to regard the very sight of green leather benches and oak panelling as something of a switch-off, regardless of what MPs might be saying in the chamber.

Channel Four was the first to act, replacing *The Parliament Prgramme* with *House to House*, which was based on an interview format and was given a much wider political remit. Some months later BBC2 introduced a new programme, *The Midnight Hour*, which had a team of four presenters and aimed to provide a lively round-table review of the day's parliamentary news. In February 1995 the late-night show was relaunched as an early-morning phone-in called *Westminster On Line*. Ministers and MPs faced live questioning from viewers who could put their questions by telephone, fax, video phone or the Internet. In addition to the new programme, which was described as the BBC's first regular political access show, BBC2 continued broadcasting *The Record*, a daily round-up of the events in the two Houses of Parliament. The emphasis on live discussion rather than on broadcasting more of the televised proceedings was deplored by one regular BBC presenter, Sheena McDonald. In a letter to the *Guardian* in December 1994 she said that if the BBC could provide ball-by-ball coverage of a cricket match on the other side of the world then it should be able to find time for speeches, debates and committee meetings in the House of Commons. In her opinion MPs should at least have equal time to that enjoyed by 'the pundits, spin doctors and purveyors of flannel whose agitations presently win air time'. But the parliamentary programmes were reflecting a trend which had been gathering pace for some years throughout the broadcasting industry. Increasingly in current affairs programming there had been a move away from straight reporting and the use of prerecorded material towards a far greater involvement of programme presenters and many more live interviews.

Ever since the launch of Independent Television News in 1955, and its decision to use journalists rather than professional news readers, the programmes have seen all too clearly how their viewing figures can be affected by the popularity of their presenters. The great expansion in television and radio services, which has now continued unchecked for nearly forty years, has undoubtedly encouraged the cult of personality.

High-profile presenters can easily earn three or four times as much money as many of the highly experienced journalists whose specialist knowledge forms the backbone of any news-gathering operation. Six-figure salaries are commonplace, reflecting the fact that presenters are in many cases all-powerful: their ability to pull in viewers and listeners can make or break a television or radio programme.

Of the various factors currently influencing the way politics are being reported, presenter power is in my view probably having the greatest impact. Recent technical advances, including the use of satellites, have revolutionised broadcasting. A live television link-up can often be established in less time than it takes for an interview to be prerecorded and for the tape to be transported back to the studio by a despatch rider. Presenters are no longer tied down to having to write and read introductions to prepared material. Instead they can now be offered an almost limitless range of interviewees. They get every opportunity to demonstrate their presentational flair, and also their skill in questioning, when tackling prominent public figures.

Politicians have been among the principal beneficaries of the growth in presenter-led reporting. If need be they can be interviewed live in their offices, homes or constituencies rather than in a studio. However, their ready availability is aiding and abetting an insidious form of political manipulation. Competition between rival television and radio channels for what is inevitably a finite supply of ministers and leading political figures is now so intense that on most days government public relations officers and party fixers can take their pick from a wide array of competing bids. So many requests were made to interview Mrs Thatcher after international summits that her press secretary estimated that it would have added at least another hour to her working day if she had agreed to do them all. In his autobiography *Kill the Messenger* Bernard Ingham said the proliferation of broadcasting services 'made for indigestion': although many programmes and their presenters regularly 'tried their luck with a bid' he always attempted to limit Mrs Thatcher's interviews on such occasions to six.

Programme editors and producers anxious to line up an important political interview can find themselves subjected to all sorts of pressures and blandishments. Ministers frequently demand guarantees about the likely line of questioning before agreeing to take part; senior politicians often try to pick and choose their place in a programme's running order so as to get a peak-time slot; and they can even attempt to exercise a veto over the choice of other studio guests. Programmes which step out of line are easily punished. Politicians will refuse to appear if they dislike the presenter or if they feel they have been offended or slighted in the past. Government information officers and the media staff of political parties can make life difficult for individual programmes or producers through a surreptitious withdrawal of cooperation.

Most politicians prefer live interviews. They like being in control, knowing that their remarks cannot be edited in any way. They also enjoy having the last word. Nothing annoys them more than finding that a lengthy prerecorded interview has been reduced to one fleeting answer or even perhaps just a sentence, sometimes lasting no more than a few seconds. Therefore, if invited, and if at all possible, they will invariably go direct to a studio or agree to a live link-up with a programme presenter. Because of this television and radio reporters based at Westminster find they are frequently denied the opportunity to conduct their own interviews for news purposes. Ministers and MPs know the potential pitfalls only too well. A specialist correspondent would be more likely to concentrate on a single issue or event and would have the time to conduct a more detailed interview than would be possible in a live programme.

Newspaper political correspondents have become vociferous critics of this, as they see it, blatant manipulation. They believe that when politicians are in difficulty or are having to make sensitive announcements they deliberately opt for what in all probability will be the simplistic questions of a live appearance, so as to avoid being forced into holding a press conference where they might be subjected to far tougher and more sustained questioning. Most ministers and MPs make no secret of this, finding news conferences often extremely tiresome. They dislike the way some reporters hammer away at a minute point of detail or alternatively are only looking for quotes to fit a predetermined story line. Another source of irritation are the attempts by journalists from the opposite end of the political spectrum to score points rather than keeping their questions to the subject at hand.

If ministers or party spokesmen do use television or radio interviews to reveal a delicate shift in policy, or perhaps to make a limited but nonetheless potentially significant on-the-record statement, journalists will be referred subsequently to a transcript of what was said. In this way politicians feel they have satisfied the need for disclosure and public scrutiny under what they hope will have been controlled circumstances. Most programmes will readily provide a platform for a newsworthy politician in return for an exclusive live interview. The trade-off is that the interviewee can usually impose some constraints on the scope of the interview. There is often discussion beforehand on the likely range of questions and usually at least some understanding about the likely severity or length of any interrogation.

The growth in live broadcasting has inevitably brought about a subtle shift in editorial influence. Presenters and their producers have realised that they are now having to shoulder far more responsibility for the journalistic thrust of the news coverage on television and radio. When programmes do get the opportunity to make the news and not just report it, the production teams are anxious to demonstrate that their editorial standards have not been compromised and that they did not shy away from posing tough and embarrassing questions. Inevitably, then, as the demand for live interviews has increased, so has the need for improved back-up within the programmes. A presenter's reputation counts for a lot with the public. Many viewers and listeners have built up a warm affection for those who front the programmes which they see and hear regularly. Presenters are admired and respected for their ability to ask questions on a wide range of complex issues. It is thus all the more important that on fast-moving stories, which can break when a programme is on air, they are updated constantly. They also have to be briefed beforehand, and at length, on the background to those subjects which are of public interest but which their interviewees might wish to avoid.

Competition for guests shows no sign of slackening. Producers are occasionally desperate to provide a credible line-up for their programmes, even to the point where sometimes the likely content and value of what might be said seems to get overlooked. All too often the overriding objective appears to be the need to ensure that the presenter, on trailing the contents of the programme, is able to hold out the prospect of at least one or two significant interviews, preferably a live encounter with a minister or other senior politician.

One worrying consequence of this growing dependency on live interviews is that politicians have found ways to bypass the often stricter disciplines which have to be observed by correspondents working for the television and radio newsrooms. Ministers, party leaders and backbenchers alike have grown accustomed to dealing directly with the staff of individual programmes. Producers are encouraged by editors and presenters to build up strong working relationships, and as a result they can end up being on far friendlier terms with individual politicians than some political journalists would either contemplate or tolerate. Both sides benefit. Production staff get rated on their ability to pull in high-calibre interviewees, so they are obviously anxious to please; and politicians find that although they might be ignored by the bulletins, because of a more rigorous judgement on what is considered to be of news value, they can still secure widespread exposure on television and radio because of their friendly connections with other programmes and their presenters.

My first experience of the shift in power from specialist reporters to programme presenters occurred during the hectic industrial disputes of the early 1980s. These were boom years for broadcasting. Within a decade the amount of air time allocated to television news and current affairs had quadrupled. The launch of breakfast television, additional news programmes, extended bulletins and hourly summaries gave birth to an army of new presenters all anxious to prove themselves in the art of live interviewing. Aggressive questioning of trade union leaders became the norm. An on-air confrontation with the miners' president Arthur Scargill seemed at that time to be the ultimate goal of every presenter.

As labour correspondent for BBC radio throughout the 1984–5 pit strike I would have relished an opportunity to quiz Scargill live on air; but, just as in the other big disputes of the period, the presenters felt, quite justifiably, that this was their prerogative. Scargill was a seasoned performer. He was far happier in a television or radio studio facing up to the general and perhaps more predictable assertions of the programme presenters than finding himself cornered by labour and industrial correspondents. He knew only too well that the vast majority of presenters lacked any detailed knowledge of the intricate internal politics of the National Union of Mineworkers and that his evasive or incomplete answers would in all probability go unchallenged.

The priority for most presenters was to tackle Scargill about the lack of a pithead ballot and his continued failure, as the strike weakened, to consult the NUM membership. In this respect the production staff believed they were acting in the public interest: television and radio programmes were somehow calling the miners' president to account. But the correspondents who were reporting the strike felt this was a sterile area of debate. They knew that as Scargill could deliver a string of well-rehearsed answers such interviews were unlikely to get anywhere. They would have preferred an opportunity to question Scargill about the intricate, detailed issues on which he was becoming vulnerable, like the growing split with miners in South Wales and Scotland, the legal challenges by working miners and the unexplained movement of NUM assets. The value in such circumstances of live interviewing is the element of surprise which, when backed up by expert knowledge, can prise loose previously undisclosed information. Presenters not equipped with this ammunition were unable fully to exploit their opportunities in interviews. As the newspaper correspondents kept reminding me, as the dispute drew wearily to its conclusion, it was the press and not the broadcast media which had done most to expose Scargill's exploits.

While the pit strike had shown that there was no way the Thatcher government could either restrict or deny trade unions access to television and radio during a damaging industrial dispute, there were ways of lessening the impact of their message. Ministers helped to achieve this by refusing to take part in studio debates with union leaders and by insisting, if there was a live discussion, on always having the last word. Their aim was to marginalise the union voice. As the years progressed I was constantly reminded of the effectiveness of this tactic. Union leaders would tell me how invitations to participate in live debates with ministers and other government spokesmen had been withdrawn at the last moment without adequate explanation. Later on the same evening they would see the relevant minister being interviewed live, on his own, without any opportunity for the union to reply.

Nigel de Gruchy, general secretary of the National Association of Schoolmasters/Union of Women Teachers, first became aware of the pressure which ministers could exert during the 1985 teachers' pay dispute. Although the then Secretary of State for Education, the late Sir Keith Joseph, was prepared to argue his case in live interviews with the unions, de Gruchy noticed that Sir Keith started insisting, as a precondition, that he must be given the last word. When Kenneth Baker replaced Joseph as education secretary in January 1986 the unions found that even stricter conditions were imposed. Ministers would refuse to debate issues face to face, demanding that they should be interviewed separately. They would even decline to take part at all if they found union leaders were being invited to appear on the same programme. Producers and reporters told de Gruchy of instances when they had personal knowledge that he had been stood down from television and radio interviews as a direct result of government pressure.

Programme editors considered they were in an invidious position during the big disputes of the 1980s. They needed a ministerial interview to balance their coverage. If they had not given way and agreed to allow the minister sole access their refusal might have jeopardised an entire report about a particular strike. Unless the government was allowed to reply to the report then the whole programme or news bulletin might have appeared unbalanced, thus rendering the editorial team vulnerable to accusations of bias.

In subsequent years Labour politicians have proved to be just as adept as Conservative ministers in dictating terms to the broadcasters. At the height of the 1990–1 Gulf War the then shadow Foreign Secretary Gerald Kaufman played an astute hand. He refused to allow members of the front-bench team to appear on programmes alongside those Labour MPs who were critical of Neil Kinnock's support for the allied troops fighting Iraq. Kaufman's objective was to prevent damaging divisions in the party being aired on television and radio in the run-up to a general election and reawakening accusations that Labour was weak on defence. He would rather pull out of a live appearance than allow himself to get drawn into confrontation with Tony Benn or Labour's other anti-war MPs.

Kaufman could be quite intimidating when laying down conditions and he would be quite unforgiving if he felt programme staff were going behind his back. Benn appeared frequently on his own, arguing the case against the allied operation, but the party would not budge in its refusal to take part. Although an explanation of Labour's official position regularly went by default, Kaufman was able to justify his tactics because party unity was maintained, despite several resignations by peace campaigners from the lower ranks of Labour's front-bench team. Kaufman won many Tory plaudits for his firm resolve. Gillian Shephard, then financial secretary at the Treasury, and a close friend of John Major, told me Kaufman deserved a medal for the way he had helped maintain cross-party consensus for the allied war aims.

Kaufman's attempts to starve the anti-war faction of publicity had one unexpected repercussion. When Labour turned down requests for interviews, the Liberal Democrats' leader Paddy Ashdown was only too eager to step forward. His frequent appearances, and the authority with which he could speak as a former marine commando, prompted a telling line in a *Spitting Image* sketch on the Gulf War: 'Over now to our assembled experts. . .and Mr Ashdown.' Indeed, on the morning the land offensive began, Ashdown had already given three live interviews before Major emerged to make his statement on the steps of No. 10. Kinnock preferred to observe protocol, waiting for the Prime Minister to speak before giving his own response. In order to make the most of the opportunities with which Labour were inadvertently providing them, the Liberal Democrats pulled together a team of diplomatic and military advisers to prepare daily briefings for their leader. Occasionally Ashdown slept in his office in order to be available at a moment's notice. His staff said that one day Major telephoned to compliment him on a television interview in which he had correctly predicted the government's next move.

Assessing the strength of competing interview bids, and working out each day's news priorities, can be a full-time task for those advising ministers and their Labour shadows. In his early years as Mrs Thatcher's press secretary, Bernard Ingham transformed Whitehall's response rate to media inquiries. Government departments were told in no uncertain terms that opportunities to put the government's case must not be overlooked or ignored. Ministers were advised that whenever possible they should do their utmost to respond if they were asked to appear on television or radio programmes. And, Ingham always insisted, it was the responsibility of departmental information officers to make sure that the government had something positive to say.

A decade later Ingham's strictures sound somewhat dated when set against the burgeoning demands of the broadcasters and his own subsequent acknowledgement that ministers had become overwhelmed by interview bids. But at the time he was responding to Mrs Thatcher's wrath when she discovered that the government's case had gone by default. Ingham's successors do face a daunting problem. The amount of air time being offered to the government is so vast that the task of managing ministerial exposure, on both television and radio, has become an extremely complex one. At exceptionally newsy times the pressures are so great that they appear to overwhelm the government's public relations machine. Whitehall's information officers regularly return home after an exhausting day to find themselves besieged by interview bids and inquiries from a fresh wave of reporters, producers and researchers who, having just started work, are full of enthusiasm, preparing for next morning's breakfast programmes. The television and radio services deploy massive resources, and twenty-four-hour broadcasting can impose tremendous demands. Some advisers and party officials think it is time for a reappraisal: that governments must consider how to control or lessen these pressures if ministers are not to find that their effectiveness in running their departments has been impaired.

Douglas Hurd, the Foreign Secretary, gave an insight into the burdens placed on ministers by the demands of the broadcasters when he spoke to the Travellers' Club in September 1993. He described how, on becoming Home Secretary in 1987, he found that the staff in his private office were catching trains home almost exactly an hour later than they had five years earlier when Lord Whitelaw was doing the job. The additional workload in the Home Office was due entirely to the need to communicate: more time was having to be spent dealing with the news media, preparing for television and radio interviews, issuing statements and answering parliamentary questions. Hurd concluded that the demands of the media had added an extra dimension to the business of government. Previous administrations had realised that the need to work with the media must be part of their strategy, and an ability to relate to journalists was an essential skill for every politician. However, after forty years, the Whitehall publicity machine had changed beyond recognition. As an example of the importance attached to the presentational side of a Cabinet minister's work, Hurd described the commitments which have to be fulfilled immediately after a ministerial statement to the Commons. Typically there would be requests for five or six separate interviews, usually four for television and two for radio. In addition the minister would have to brief the press. If any of these were neglected, he said, then 'critics and commentators will fill the space'.

He acknowledged that openness, and the need to take account of public opinion, had become almost as vital to the success of any policy as the sensible construction of that policy in the first place. There were now almost no subjects, except perhaps interest and exchange rates or defence operations, on which it was good enough to say 'no comment' without that in itself becoming a news story. If the media were against a government, public opinion could turn the same way; so ministers had to take professional advice and recognise that the news media had to be part of their strategy and not always an obstacle to it.

Where Hurd took issue with journalists was over the way he thought they were becoming actors as well as spectators in foreign affairs. The searchlight of media coverage was not the 'even and regular sweep of a lighthouse' but patchy and determined by editorial whim. Bosnia had been selected by Europeans from among the world's tragedies for television coverage and it was there that journalists from the BBC, *The Times*, the *Independent* and the *Guardian* had become founder members of the 'something must be done' school. They had all become enthusiasts for further military intervention in Bosnia, whether by air or on the ground. Reporters and commentators, said Hurd, had a different angle of vision from those who had a responsibility to decide and to act; and they should not fancy themselves as generals or members of the Cabinet any more than governments should be seduced by the apparent lure of favourable media comment.

Rarely before had a minister spoken so openly and so constructively about the transformation which has taken place in the relationship between journalists and politicians. In examining the media's impact on foreign affairs Hurd had illuminated one corner of a much wider canvas. The opportunities which exist for improved presentation by governments are also open to their political opponents. Therefore politicians cannot afford to relax. They have no alternative but to find ways of responding to the fast-changing demands of the media. There can be no permanency about the rules of engagement.

2

Slaves to the Soundbite

EFFECTIVE POLITICAL communication has always relied on easily understood slogans and phrases aimed at promoting and justifying the policy decisions of governments and their opponents. Radio, and subsequently television, provided politicians with an opportunity to explain their objectives to a mass audience in a personal and friendly way. However, those with a message to get across have been forced to acknowledge that the attention span of listeners and viewers can be very limited; indeed, according to political research in the USA, it is becoming progressively shorter. Therefore the most important point in any speech, broadcast or interview has to be delivered briskly and summarised as concisely as possible. Politicians want the public to remember their punch line.

American television and radio journalists first used the term 'soundbite' in the late 1960s. They recognised, just as did political managers and publicists, that there was a degree of self-interest on both sides in trying to persuade politicians to encapsulate their arguments in brief, self-contained statements or answers. News reports on television and radio are prepared under tight time constraints. Long, rambling replies or discursive extracts from speeches cannot be accommodated. Equally, politicians, desperate to publicise their hopes and aspirations – the aims of their party or government – know that if they want to achieve maximum political impact they have to supply the broadcasting organisations with what they want.

Although the art of political phrase-making and sloganising has been refined and improved out of all recognition since the earliest days of radio and television, soundbites have remained a highly individualistic form of expression. At their most effective they not only convey political messages but also say something about the person who utters them. The most memorable seem to reinforce already well-known personal characteristics. Others just happen to highlight endearing idiosyncrasies or perhaps unwelcome traits.

Close to the top of any soundbite hit parade would have to be The Lady's Not For Turning, Margaret Thatcher's strident refusal to change course when faced by a deepening recession and rising unemployment. Her speech-writer, the playwright Sir Ronald Millar, adapted the title of Christopher Fry's 1948 play, *The Lady's Not For Burning*, to supply the Prime Minister with an unforgettable line which was to enter political folklore: 'To those waiting with bated breath for that favourite media catchphrase, the U-turn, I have only one thing to say. You turn if you want to. The lady's not for turning.'

Five of the national newspapers used The Lady's Not For Turning as the splash headline on their front pages next morning. In later years, Millar told me that when he wrote such lines for Mrs Thatcher he always had in his mind their possible use as a soundbite or basis for a headline: he never did better than this in more than a decade of contributing to Margaret Thatcher's speeches.

Mrs Thatcher used her speech to the Conservatives' 1980 conference to deliver two messages. She was telling the country that despite the government's difficulties and unpopularity she intended to continue the policies which she believed would wrench Britain out of economic decline. Her other target was the so-called 'wets', the Cabinet ministers who were so critical of what they considered was her doctrinaire monetarism. On both counts, Millar's soundbite could not have been more effective. He had also helped to reinforce what would prove to be an abiding image. Of all the catchphrases of the Thatcher era, The Lady's Not For Turning seemed to sum up best of all the Prime Minister who would not give way.

An ill-judged or badly worded soundbite can prove equally enduring. Harold Wilson's The Pound In Your Pocket did him incalculable political damage. In his ministerial broadcast after the 1967 devaluation of the pound he tried not to sound too unnerving, seeking to reassure the country: 'From now on the pound abroad is worth 14 per cent or so less in terms of other currencies. It does not mean, of course, that the pound here in Britain in your pocket or in your purse or in your bank has been devalued.' The words rebounded on the Prime Minister. His opponents regarded the broadcast as an example of his deviousness for trying to kid the British people into thinking that the devaluation would have no effect on their lives.

One important similarity in these two soundbites was that they emerged from key moments in the Wilson and Thatcher governments. Both were aimed at shoring up public support for momentous shifts in economic management. The criticism levelled at the soundbites of the 1990s is that all too often they are written and delivered in the absence of policies. Instead of working out their objectives or taking the necessary harsh decisions, politicians prefer, so the argument goes, to put presentation before policy, to think up the soundbite rather than work out the solution.

Nor have the news media escaped criticism. Journalists have been accused of allowing themselves to be seduced by the soundbite, of letting the politicians dictate the news agenda with empty words and meaningless phrases. Here broadcasters face a continuing dilemma. Soundbites cannot be ignored because they often form the very crux of a speech or interview. The words which were used were probably chosen with great care; they could well have taken weeks of internal Cabinet or party discussion to agree and were presumably intended to convey a significant political message, perhaps a strong commitment to a particular policy or a clear rejection of it. Indeed, politicians and their publicity advisers complain vigorously when a much-signposted soundbite in a speech or at a news conference is ignored. They cannot understand why television and radio journalists insist on going over the same ground by way of an interview. Ministers and their opposition shadows get even more annoyed when broadcasters push the point even further by attempting to refine or make more explicit what was obviously a carefully drafted statement or answer.

The conflict seems certain to continue. For politicians there is no alternative. They cannot be expected to forsake the opportunity of using well-prepared soundbites when speaking in public, nor can they afford to be caught off guard during interviews by falling into the trap of making loosely worded policy pronouncements. For their part, television and radio journalists want to hold the attention of viewers and listeners and therefore will always tend to illustrate their reports with the clearest pledge, the sharpest rebuke or perhaps the pithiest comment, even if such remarks were all carefully thought through beforehand.

While soundbites may have their detractors, they have become part of the lifeblood of daily political journalism and are of as much interest to newspapers as to television and radio. Lists of the best quotes of the day or the week are a regular newspaper feature, a point not lost on the politicians. However, many soundbites owe their existence not to political phrase-makers but to journalistic persistence and ingenuity. Broadcasters are naturally pleased with themselves when they succeed, perhaps against stiff competition, in teasing out an unexpected answer which then makes the lead item in the news bulletins. Newspaper correspondents are equally delighted when an exclusive quote which they had the initiative to obtain, again perhaps after a great deal of patient coaxing, suddenly tops the news agenda. Indeed, most reporters will reel off tales about their most topical soundbites and quotes as readily as they will try to talk up their latest scoop.

Among the soundbites which have the greatest impact are the unexpected. A routine assignment can suddenly take off when, out of the blue, something is said which transforms an event: perhaps a vicious attack on an opponent, a threat to the government or an abusive aside. Such remarks are not the premeditated soundbites of politicians but a sudden burst of passion or anger which somehow encapsulates an important or dramatic moment. Late one November night at the height of the 1984–5 miners' strike I was one of several reporters standing outside the London headquarters of the Trades Union Congress. Two leaders of the National Union of Mineworkers, Mick McGahey and Peter Heathfield, were in the process of making a short statement on the possibility of fresh negotiations. Suddenly a man wearing a black leather jacket, whom we had seen waiting around, emerged out of the darkness and rushed forward saying he had a court order for McGahey. I was standing right beside the NUM vice president holding out the microphone of my tape recorder. On being challenged by the writ server McGahey could not have been more contemptuous: 'You have an order? I have an order for you – get out of my bloody road. Cheerio pal.'

McGahey carried on down the steps of Congress House. Ray Buckton, leader of the train drivers' union ASLEF, was waiting with his car to take the two NUM leaders to their hotel. As McGahey got into the rear seat the court bailiff threw the writ into the car through the open door. The court papers were immediately thrown out again through the car window and landed at my feet. I quickly stuffed them inside my coat, hoping no one else had noticed. Some weeks later Buckton told me in hushed tones how he had asked his driver to throw the writ towards where I was standing. He said he saw me pick it up and even claimed that he and the policeman who was on duty outside Congress House exchanged a thumbs up sign on seeing me retrieve the documents.

By chance I had been in the right place at the right moment. I had secured a soundbite which marked one of the defining moments of the pit dispute. In my news reports next morning for BBC radio I explained how the court order was designed to stop McGahey, Heathfield and Arthur Scargill withdrawing money from a Swiss bank account. The writ had been obtained by the sequestrators appointed after the NUM had failed to pay a £200,000 fine for continuing to declare that the miners' strike was official despite the lack of a pithead ballot. I made sure, of course, that the documents were returned to the sequestrators' solicitors later that day.

Because I had been standing so close to McGahey I had the only clear recording of his curt dismissal of the writ server. The sound had to be dubbed across film for use in television news bulletins. The quote was also reprinted in full by the newspapers. McGahey could not have been more forthright. His deep, gravelly voice and thick Scottish accent added to the drama of his brief outburst, which, although it lasted only a few seconds, could hardly have been surpassed as a signal of the NUM's defiance of the courts.

The McGahey soundbite was a princely reward for the endless hours I had spent, as have most other reporters, photographers and television crews, hanging around on countless doorsteps. We all know from years of experience that public figures can be at their most vulnerable on their arrival at and departure from meetings and other engagements. Therefore there is always the possibility that a mundane assignment might become headline news – although in these circumstances politicians, union officials, employers' negotiators and the like are usually on their guard: after all, they know the routine only too well. Sometimes they appear bright and breezy on arrival, happily giving a jokey or upbeat answer when asked about the likely prospects for the meeting ahead of them. On other occasions they remain, as reporters like to say, tight-lipped, refusing to make any comment when faced by a barrage of questions. A repeat performance can follow the conclusion of their discussions. All too often if they do feel like being at all communicative they will readily trot out the same non-committal answers.

Although the whole exercise might seem like a terrible waste of time it does perform several valuable functions, even in the absence of the news-making line. In the first place, film of the arrival and departure of key participants is an essential requirement of television news. Sensitive political meetings or pay negotiations are invariably held in private, so there will probably be very few alternative shots available during the rest of the day. Therefore every frame of the arrival footage might well have to be used. Newspaper photographers, too, know that they will probably get only one chance to take pictures. As arrivals are of such importance, advance information about the start time of meetings and their precise location is of the greatest value to the news media. Moreover, while the majority of the comments made during doorstep encounters must strike the public as banal in the extreme, for broadcasters with an eye to future developments they are nonetheless a valuable news commodity. Optimistic remarks or asides may suggest a positive mood to the meeting, perhaps producing a result; glum faces and downbeat answers are a pointer perhaps to a long and fruitless discussion. And however short or simplistic they may be, such replies do help illustrate and break up otherwise complex and rather predictable television and radio reports about industrial disputes. The prospect that at the end of the day there might be a decent soundbite or a good quote does help sustain those assigned to these interminable vigils.

One all-night wait during negotiations about the 1982 train drivers' strike over flexible rostering ended most fortunately. No official comment was being made about the outcome of the meeting but, shortly before 7 a.m., Sir Peter Parker, the then British Rail chairman, emerged bleary-eyed from the offices of the Advisory, Conciliation and Arbitration Service. Parker was a skilful self-publicist. Seeing me standing there on my own with my tape recorder he walked across and turned in a perfect soundbite. Yes, he said, he was optimistic and was off to have his breakfast with 'my egg sunny side up'. I already knew from the information I had gleaned from TUC leaders and ACAS officials that a formula was likely to emerge later that day to end a two-week rail strike; Parker's answer was tantamount to official confirmation of my story.

No doorstep assignment can be more time-consuming or taxing than Downing Street. Michael Heseltine's dramatic walk-out from a Cabinet meeting in January 1986, at the height of the row over the future of the Westland helicopter factory, taught television and radio journalists a much-valued lesson: at moments of political crisis television cameras *always* have to be at the ready, trained on the Prime Minister's front door. In his book *Live From Number 10* Michael Cockerell describes what for any doorstep foot soldier is a nightmare scenario: 'The press and television photographers who had filmed the cabinet arriving an hour earlier had all gone for coffee; only a BBC news cameraman was left. "I have resigned from the cabinet," the blond bombshell announced to the camera, "I will be making a statement later this afternoon." '

Heseltine's readiness to play to the cameras, even though on this occasion apparently only one was actually turning, has become the bane of many a political correspondent's life. They dread stake-outs in Downing Street, considering them an awful waste of time. On the other hand, television newsrooms believe, quite rightly, that if a defence secretary can resign and walk out of a Cabinet meeting then there can be no question about the need for constant vigilance.

Downing Street is also a good training ground for acquiring another useful attribute of a successful doorstep reporter: the ability to shout questions. Tightened security has meant that journalists, photographers and television crews are now kept behind barriers on the other side of the road to No. 10. The opportunities to ask questions are severely limited and those that are asked can be drowned out by other noise. Ministerial cars often pull up right outside the front door, enabling the occupants to be inside within seconds. The chances of attracting a target's attention are somewhat improved when ministers walk slowly up the pavement to No. 10 or if, once their cars have been parked, they casually cross the road. While all Downing Street reporters obviously hope their questions might one day produce usable answers, the shouting itself is not without its purpose: the television crews and photographers are just waiting for some kind of acknowledgement, even if it is merely a smile or wave at the camera, as this puts life into an otherwise featureless arrival shot.

As there is often the chance to raise only one topic, reporters sometimes try to work out an agreed question which they can all shout in unison. 'Are you going to resign?' is a favourite when a minister's pet project is reported to be at risk. Eight years after his celebrated walk-out Heseltine was greeted by precisely that question when the Cabinet abandoned plans for Post Office privatisation in November 1994. On arriving at the Millbank studios, the President of the Board of Trade faced a barrage of 'Will you resign?' Heseltine greeted reporters with a cheerful smile but walked straight past the television cameras.

Joy Johnson, a former producer for Independent Television News who became political news editor for BBC Westminster and subsequently Labour's campaigns director, built up a fearsome reputation for asking the most threatening questions she could think of. Her aim always was to surprise Cabinet ministers in the hope this might provoke a response. Ms Johnson told me how she changed tack for the July 1989 Cabinet reshuffle, shouting 'Are you happy?' as each minister emerged from No. 10. Any response was of value, as the list of new appointments was not due out until after the teatime news bulletins and there was unlikely to be another opportunity to question ministers that evening.

On this occasion the late Nicholas Ridley was the first to emerge from his interview with Mrs Thatcher. As Ms Johnson had hoped, he responded, with 'Yes, I'm always happy.' Later it was announced that Ridley had been moved from environment to be the new trade and industry secretary. Chris Patten, who took over at environment, smiled broadly as he too delivered the appropriate answer: 'Yes, I'm always happy.' John Gummer was the next minister to appear. Having just been told that he had won promotion to the Cabinet as Minister of Agriculture, he hardly needed any prompting. Gummer looked particularly pleased with himself and was word perfect for Ms Johnson, replying: 'I'm always happy.' But when Kenneth Baker, then education secretary, left No. 10 he replied less convincingly: 'Yes, it is a nice day.' Ms Johnson said the cameramen and photographers knew instantly that Baker could not have got the top Cabinet job he had been hoping for. He had in fact been shifted sideways and appointed party chairman. The most poignant moment was the departure of John Moore, who was sacked from his job as social security secretary. Ms Johnson shouted: 'Have you got a job?' Moore replied: 'I'm going to enjoy myself with my family.' What might have seemed a routine assignment had been turned into pure drama; but if Ms Johnson had not shouted her questions the harvest would have amounted to no more than what the television newsrooms might have considered a few wallpaper shots.

The question-and-answer session which Ms Johnson felt was her most effective earned her a £1,000 bonus from the ITN chairman Sir David

Nicholas. She was on duty at the 1987 Labour conference where Neil Kinnock's speech as party leader prompted speculation about the imminent abandoning of Labour's commitment to unilateral nuclear disarmament. When she succeeded later in tackling Kinnock about a likely switch in policy he got red-faced and annoyed, and her persistent questioning of the Labour leader provided dramatic television footage which was exclusive to ITN.

As Kinnock walked through the conference hotel Ms Johnson challenged him over a speech to be delivered that evening by the left-wing MP Ken Livingstone, who was predicting civil war in the party if Labour abandoned unilateralism. Kinnock repudiated Ms Johnson's interpretation of Livingstone's speech. He then made the mistake of attacking her on camera: 'Why don't you just stop trying to make trouble...There is a strong spirit of unity...The misfortune for you as an interviewer is that on this occasion I have read the speech.' At this point Kinnock was walking away from Ms Johnson with his back to the camera. She shouted after him: 'So you are not going to abandon unilateralism?' Kinnock turned to face her: 'We are maintaining the non-nuclear defence policy and you know it. I said it yesterday.' Kinnock had ended up contradicting the impression he had given the day before, and ITN had exclusive film of this major development.

Earlier that year, during the 1987 general election campaign, Ms Johnson embarrassed the then Conservative Party chairman, Norman Tebbit, by holding up a tape recorder replaying a tape of what he had previously said about unemployment. In a radio interview a few years earlier Tebbit had conceded that if unemployment was still above three million at the time of the 1987 election, the Conservatives would not deserve to win. Tebbit was furious that his photo-call had been upstaged in this way. Instead of ignoring her he tried to stop the tape recorder and kept saying: 'We don't need that tape to be played.' Ms Johnson also made an impact on John Major in his first few months as Prime Minister. After discovering that she worked for one of the television organisations, Major asked ITN's political editor Michael Brunson if he knew who 'that woman' was who kept shouting at him in Downing Street.

Major took his revenge on the Downing Street shouters in his Cabinet reshuffle of July 1994. To the surprise of waiting reporters, fewer ministers turned up than expected. Apparently the Prime Minster had felt for some time that it was unfair and hurtful to ask those who were being sacked to run the media gauntlet on their way into and out of No.10. Therefore on the day of the reshuffle he called in only those ministers who were being promoted or who he knew would be happy with the changes he was announcing. Journalists had expected to see the outgoing education secretary John Patten, but he was one of four Cabinet ministers who were called in privately the night before to be told they were being dropped. Patten was spared what would have been a long, humiliating and televised walk to the gates of Downing Street. Major's press secretary Chris Meyer confirmed to me afterwards that the Prime Minister made the change out of humanity for his former Cabinet colleagues.

I discovered for myself a few weeks after Major's accession to the premiership in November 1990 that he was not always at ease himself with the shouted question and the instant soundbite. My doorstep assignment was to stand outside the church near Chequers where the Majors were spending their first Christmas. Torrential rain and a biting wind across the Chilterns had already taken the gloss off Christmas morning. Water was dripping down my neck as I wracked my brain trying to think of a suitable question to shout from my vantage point, which was across the road from the path leading up to the church. Lacking inspiration, I fell back on an approach which had always worked well with Mrs Thatcher during the war with Argentina over the Falklands when any enquiry about 'our boys' always did the trick and brought an instant response.

My aim in asking a soft first question on such occasions is to engage a politician's attention. Once they stop and walk over there might be a chance to ask all sorts of tougher supplementaries or perhaps move on to more sensitive political issues. Ministers and MPs can easily take fright and, while the blunderbuss technique suits the Downing Street doorstep, I felt it would be entirely out of place on my Chequers assignment. As British forces were at this time being deployed in the Gulf, following Iraq's invasion of Kuwait, I used a variation of the Thatcher question, shouting out: 'Prime Minister, what's your Christmas message to the troops in the Gulf?' Major and his wife Norma ignored me completely, not even bothering to turn to look at the television cameraman at my side. A *Daily Mail* photographer who was with us said the pictures were hopeless. He had been hoping for a family shot including the Majors' son and daughter James and Elizabeth, and perhaps the Prime Minister's mother-in-law as well. Our spirits sinking, we stayed on until the end of the service. I tried the same question again as Major walked to his car and this time he did respond: 'Christmas is the message to the troops and to everybody. Thank you very much. Have a nice day.'

I did have a soundbite of sorts, but it was hardly what I expected. Back in the television newsroom the editor of the day was in no doubt: Major's answer was so innocuous that it failed to warrant a place in the teatime news which, sandwiched between *ET: The Extra-Terrestrial* and *Only Fools and Horses*, had probably the biggest audience of any Christmas Day news bulletin.

Three weeks later, by chance, I met Major at a social engagement where he struck up a conversation about our Christmas morning encounter. He remembered it clearly and said that, hearing my question on the way into church, he had mulled it over during the service. He had found it difficult to know what to say and had been conscious of the need not to cause offence by giving a political answer. He felt people would be divided on the issue. Half the country would not want to hear a political message on Christmas Day and the other half probably would not mind. I explained how an article I had written for the *Guardian*'s media page, giving an account of what happened at the church, had provoked correspondents' letters which described my question as fatuous and had praised the Prime Minister's measured response. On hearing this Major showed that he could indeed produce the instant soundbite: 'what next, letters of support in the *Guardian*? Don't tell the chief whip, otherwise I'm finished.'

Major had been in No. 10 for less than two months and he was surprisingly frank about the thought he was giving to the challenge posed by the questions being shouted at him on doorsteps. Trying to think up snappy replies was proving much more difficult for him than coping with a structured interview. He told me he still could not decide whether it was best to dismiss them with a wave, give a flip answer or respond properly to what had been asked. Major seemed so concerned, and had been so open with me, that I felt it would be unkind to explain to him that most doorstep reporters would probably relish hearing news of his dilemma. The only consolation for them for the hours spent in Downing Street is the prospect that one day the Prime Minister or one of his Cabinet colleagues might be caught unawares. The revelation that Major was still taking each question as it came would be seen as highly encouraging.

Politicians around the world face the same dilemma. As television output expands so does the demand for arrival and departure footage; the shouted questions seem to get louder and more persistent, and inevitably ministers and government officials become increasingly concerned at the impression they are making. They have come to realise that the doorstep soundbite is a critical form of political communication. When public figures are shown walking along or getting out of their cars viewers almost expect to see or hear some sort of acknowledgement. Nor is the demand for speech alone: body language can be as important as words. Politicians who are always offhand with waiting journalists, and who fail to observe common courtesies, run the risk of damaging their reputation not only with the news media but also with the viewing and listening public.

Jacques Delors, the former President of the European Commission, who was a prime hate figure among some sections of the Conservative Party and the Tory press, became extremely adept at using his televised doorstep encounters to improve his image in Britain. Journalists, producers and television crews based in Brussels noticed that he went out of his way to smile, acknowledge their presence and say a few words in English. He had obviously realised there was every likelihood that a soundbite delivered on the move would be used, sometimes in preference to more formal answers given at news conferences. By being cooperative he gained a valuable platform for simple, positive messages about the Commission and its work and in addition he became a great favourite of the media pack.

An even more significant conversion to the value of the doorstep soundbite took place in South Africa in the months leading up to the first non-racial elections in April 1994, where John Harrison, the BBC's Southern Africa correspondent until his death in a car crash in March 1994, is credited by television cameramen and sound recordists with having brought about a transformation. Years of white majority rule, and a necessarily compliant news media, had provided a degree of protection for local politicians, who were accordingly not accustomed to the full rigours and aggressive questioning of the media scrum. As a former BBC chief political correspondent, however, Harrison had no hesitation, on his arrival in South Africa in the autumn of 1991, in applying the Downing Street treatment to President F.W. de Klerk. On the first occasion he was challenged unexpectedly de Klerk gave a rather hesitant, muddled answer. The convention had always been that ministers were interviewed formally and not thrown questions on the doorstep. The President's aides were furious and immediately rebuked Harrison, saying he had no right to embarrass de Klerk in that way and should refrain from such conduct in the future.

Those who witnessed the argument which followed were taken aback by Harrison's audacity. He told de Klerk's advisers in no uncertain terms that he would go on asking questions whenever and wherever he saw the President in public. Their job was to advise de Klerk on what he might be asked, not to prevent journalists gaining access to a politician. Within a matter of weeks de Klerk was quite happy to be questioned when confronted by television crews, and would even seek out the BBC's correspondent. Nelson Mandela, then President of the African National Congress, was challenged in exactly the same way and responded equally positively: if he saw Harrison and his television crew being held back by his bodyguards, he would intervene and beckon them over, responding readily to his questions.

John Major found that his own qualms about appropriate doorstep techniques were soon dispelled by force of circumstance. There is no substitute for experience and, as events in the Gulf War gathered pace in the winter of 1991, the Prime Minister found he was having to make two or three statements a day in Downing Street, most of which were broadcast live on television and radio. His preferred approach was to write down the main points on small cards which he checked one last time before leaving No. 10 and starting his walk from the front door towards the waiting microphones. By dispensing with a written statement or notes he could appear relaxed and concentrate on his delivery.

A year later, in the run-up to the 1992 general election, Major reverted to a political prop of his youth to help counter adverse publicity about his lacklustre speeches and Dalek-like delivery. One of the opening salvoes of the Conservatives' campaign in March 1992 was a party political broadcast entitled *John Major: The Journey*. It described how, during his teens, Major had addressed passers-by on the political issues of the day from a soapbox in Brixton Market. Halfway through the campaign, when the Prime Minister, at a shopping centre in Luton, was surrounded by demonstrators from the Socialist Workers' Party, his minders opened up the luggage compartment of his armour-plated coach and dragged out a stout wooden document box. Mounted on this, gripping a loud-hailer, while police officers struggled to form a cordon around him, Major saw a chance to exploit the SWP demonstration by comparing it to the protests in the so-called 'winter of discontent' in 1979; and, like the street-corner campaigners of old, he found that the soundbites were there for the making: 'Can you hear? Don't let the people who take to the streets take your vote away . . . This is not the sort of country that will put the mobs back on the streets like before in 1979.' A child in the crowd was suddenly up with the Prime Minister on his soapbox: 'This is the boy the future's about. This is what the election's about. . .this boy's future.'

Major showed the same dogged persistence in mastering Prime Minister's questions. Commentators and sketch writers who had been sharply critical of his parliamentary performances during the early years of his premiership started becoming more complimentary as he continued to grapple with Conservative splits over Europe and survived repeated speculation about a possible challenge to his leadership. By the autumn of 1994 the new Labour leader Tony Blair and the Liberal Democrats' leader Paddy Ashdown had both been through some bruising exchanges with Major, who was increasingly using the tactics of a street fighter – and, moreover, relishing the verbal pugilism: having survived over two hundred question time appearances, the Prime Minister had come to enjoy his spats across the despatch box. Sir Graham Bright, who was his parliamentary private secretary until the July 1994 reshuffle, told me that Major had become much more confident because he was finding that all his careful preparation was paying off. Three to four hours would be spent getting ready for each fifteen-minute session. He usually started work the night before looking through briefing papers on the twenty to thirty new subjects which his advisers thought might be raised each week. Then, on Tuesday and Thursday mornings, there would be meetings with officials and another two hours' preparation.

Arriving in the chamber to answer questions, Major could always be seen carrying a ring-binder file. This held the information he might need. There were little markers at the top of each section. Each page was laid out with two columns of typescript, and from the press gallery it looked as though there were usually about a dozen possible answers to each page, some highlighted in yellow. As MPs tried to surprise the Prime Minister by asking supplementary questions on issues about which he had not been given notice he would have the file on his knees and could be seen flicking through it quickly to find the page containing the relevant notes and answers.

Major's detailed homework made all the difference as he fought to re-establish his authority after the government's defeat in December 1994 over the doubling of value added tax on domestic fuel. Blair, already buoyed up by his success on this issue, had seized on news of a 75 per cent pay increase for the chief executive of British Gas. Major hit back immediately, suggesting the Labour leader should improve his own lines of communication because Labour's Treasury team were saying that pay was a matter which should be left for negotiation between unions and employers. When Blair came back at him a third time, Major flung his ring-binder on to the despatch box with such force that it thumped against the microphone. Ashdown was given an equally brusque answer when he criticised British indecision over Bosnia. All the Liberal Democrat leader had ever done, Major said, was 'undersell and undermine' the role of British troops. 'He has done nothing but grandstand on this issue.' Ashdown looked put out; but, unlike Blair, he had no right to ask a supplementary question.

Major was at his most daring at the Conservatives' 1994 conference in Bournemouth where he outlined his ideas for a world of 'grown-up politics' free of windy rhetoric and pious clichés. Jonathan Hill, the Prime Minister's political secretary, assured reporters that the speech had been written 'single-handedly by Major himself, from beginning to end'. Casting aside the teleprompter used by other ministers, and the rest of the props on the conference platform, Major stood on his own at a microphone placed towards the middle of the hall, and as on his soapbox in the general election campaign, was ready to be himself again. He said he would stick to his core beliefs, ask for patience and realism in others and put his trust in results. 'The glib phrases, the soundbites, the ritual conflicts – all these may be the daily stuff of life for the upper one thousand of politics. But to the fifty million other people in this country, they are utterly irrelevant. My interest is with them.'

Most of the party representatives in the audience seemed captivated by what was obviously a heartfelt declaration of his aims and values. Despite the unpopularity of his government, which within days was hit by further ministerial resignations amid the controversy over allegations that Conservative MPs had taken cash for asking parliamentary questions, Major still seemed secure in his own position. In 1992, when the odds were stacked against the Conservatives, his soapbox oratory had helped him look and sound both assertive and sympathetic. Standing outside in the wind and the rain, displaying dogged determination in the face of adversity, he presented a peculiarly British image which could prove very appealing. A similar impression was conveyed by the self-effacing delivery and plodding presentation of his 1994 party conference speech. Many of the commentators described it as a compelling performance when viewed on television. Major had taken a risk; but in doing so he had proved, at least to the party faithful, both in the hall and watching at home, that he still had a sure touch when speaking to the public.

Major had spoken of his determination to be himself when he became Prime Minister in late November 1990. However, within days of taking office, the sketch writers had doubted this would ever be possible. After hearing him twice at question time they were convinced that he had lowered his voice. The *Guardian*'s Andrew Rawnsley was sure Major had spent his first weekend as premier attending elocution classes at Conservative Central Office: he had dropped a couple of octaves and was producing 'a huskier, deeper, gravelly sound'. But Quentin Letts of the *Daily Telegraph* considered that Major's 'deeper timbre lends authority to Prime Ministerial pronouncements'. When asked that weekend by BBC Radio Peterborough whether it was true that he was lowering his voice and adding some colour to his grey hair, he denied making any changes. 'I am what I am and people will have to take me as I am. Image makers will not find me under their tutelage. I shall be the same plug ugly.'

In my own article for the *Guardian* in January 1991, in which I referred to Major's difficulties in coming to terms with the demand for soundbites, I recommended that as a New Year resolution he should make up his mind whether he was going to continue giving the impression that he had 'come upon fame by chance and thereby deserves an easy ride from reporters' or acknowledge that 'Prime Ministers probably have no alternative but to seek publicity.' My strictures struck a chord with Tony Blair, then Labour's employment spokesman, who stopped me next day to discuss my suggestions. Blair was as usual polite and charming but also quite adamant, saying: 'Let's hope the Prime Minister doesn't take any of your advice.'

In subsequent months I was to have several conversations with Blair about the merits of soundbites. While not as frequent as I would have liked, they were nonetheless of great interest to me because, unlike many politicians, he could talk about his television and radio appearances with a welcome degree of detachment. He also seemed to be developing an acute grasp of the mechanics of the role of political journalists and broadcasters. Armed with his inside appreciation of the finer points and potential pitfalls of political interviewing, Blair was no pushover. A bruising encounter I had with him the previous summer had taught me to approach him with care.

Blair's great accomplishment in his early years as a front-bench spokesman was to steer the party towards a new era in their relationship with the trade unions. Within weeks of being given the employment brief in November 1989 he announced that Labour would accept European Community legislation banning the closed shop. In the following months he worked behind the scenes, meeting union leaders, as the party prepared for the launch in May 1990 of its new policy document *Looking to the Future*. This put beyond question Labour's acceptance of much of the Conservatives' employment legislation, including provisions on secret ballots and the sequestration of union funds, restrictions on secondary action and the ban on mass picketing.

As the launch date approached I was commissioned by BBC television's *Breakfast News* to prepare a report on Labour's likely plans, most of which had already been well trailed in the newspapers, and to examine the scale of any possible opposition. A prerecorded television interview had been arranged with Blair but, on the day this was to be conducted, his office indicated that he wished to withdraw. I made the point that we had been relying on his contribution and, rather reluctantly, he agreed that he would walk across to College Green with Peter Mandelson, Labour's campaigns and communications director, who would discuss it with me. Mandelson was maintaining an exceptionally firm grip on interviews about the policy review. I knew he had a particularly close relationship with Blair. I feared the worst.

Mandelson got straight to the point, saying he saw no advantage to the party in participating in what he knew from observing my work would be 'one of my usual knockabout reports on Labour and the unions'. I made it clear that I was not proposing a lengthy interview; that I realised Blair could not answer detailed questions about the new policy document; and that the only issue I was seeking to put to the party's employment spokesman was that Labour appeared to be on the point of announcing a new accord with the unions. After a short discussion between the two of them Blair said he would give me an answer, but Mandelson insisted he would hold me to my promise of asking only one question.

Blair's reply omitted all reference to the party's relationship with the unions, concentrating instead on Labour's commitment to training and their plans to meet the skills shortage. It was an answer I had heard many times before, and I expressed my disappointment; but I realised there was nothing more I could do. Before the interview started Mandelson had demanded to know the names of the other interviewees in my report. I saw him frown as I mentioned the name of Leslie Christie, general secretary of the National Union of Civil and Public Servants, who was one of the sponsors of the newly launched Campaign for Free Trade Unions which was seeking to persuade Labour to allow workers to retain the right to 'picket effectively'.

Once I had completed my short interview with Blair, Mandelson rebuked me for proposing to include Christie in my report. He said that as I was a former labour correspondent I would be well aware that although Christie's union belonged to the TUC it was not affiliated to the party. Therefore my report would be a serious misrepresentation and as far as he was concerned it proved his point that my contribution to *Breakfast News* was going to be 'the same old story of Neil Kinnock being kicked around by the unions'. I pointed out that Christie was acting as the spokesman for a group of general secretaries whose unions were almost wholly Labour-affiliated and therefore his inclusion could hardly be grounds for criticism.

At this point I asked Blair, who had been smiling at my attempts to defend myself, if he would walk with me across College Green so as to provide a walking shot of the two us in case I needed it when editing my report. Blair could not have been friendlier. He explained that it was extremely difficult trying to answer questions ahead of the policy launch and said I must understand that there was considerable pressure within the party against him saying anything at all. The whole question of the union relationship was the biggest problem they faced. As we ambled back towards Mandelson I realised I was in the company of what was beginning to feel like a formidable political double act. I was not sure what was coming next, but sensed the curtain was about to go up on another scene in their hard–soft routine. Mandelson looked me in the face: 'I don't trust you. Once a labour correspondent, always a labour correspondent. Never trust labour correspondents.' With that the two of them marched off back to the House of Commons.

Mandelson's dislike of former labour correspondents like myself who have switched to political reporting has deep roots. Unlike many of our colleagues at Westminster who have not had experience of reporting trade union affairs, we are likely to have a wide range of contacts throughout the labour movement. These additional sources can be of great value at times when the party is reluctant to provide journalists with information. In addition, ex-labour reporters tend to be more questioning over developments affecting Labour's link with the unions and less prepared to accept the party line at face value.

Though I had stood my ground over the need to include Leslie Christie's remarks in my *Breakfast News* report I knew Mandelson was unlikely to let the matter rest. As I expected, I heard within days that he had made an official complaint direct to Ian Hargreaves, then the BBC's director of news and current affairs. Hargreaves in his reply conceded that two reports that week on *Breakfast News* about Labour's policy review fell short of the BBC's normal standards, identifying the problem with both items as that they set themselves objectives which were far too ambitious and as a result veered between 'specific allegation and broad generalisation' in a way which was neither illuminating nor convincing. However, Hargreaves noted Mandelson's acknowledgement that senior party figures had felt 'unable to comment' ahead of the policy document and therefore Hargreaves considered the 'fairness of intent' of the correspondents involved was not in question.

Several months elapsed before I had a chance to discover whether Blair's reaction to my report matched Mandelson's. I had already heard at the TUC conference in September that many union leaders were pleased with the way the party leader had defused the whole argument over employment law. When we met at a union reception shortly before Labour's annual conference the following month I found him in an expansive mood. Blair had not seen my *Breakfast News* report but assumed it had been the subject of a complaint. I remarked rather ruefully that Mandelson had certainly needed no advice on how to penetrate the BBC's bureaucracy, because he had ensured that his complaint went right to the top. Blair gave me one of his by now famous grins, replying: 'That is precisely why Peter Mandelson is a star.'

My next stand-off with Blair over a question-and-answer session took place in the run-up to the 1992 general election. The first opinion poll of the year had given Labour a five-point lead and I was assigned the task of seeking out reactions to the finding. As it was a Saturday morning there were few shadow Cabinet ministers in London, and Blair was put forward as the party's spokesman. We met as arranged on College Green. As the camera crew got into position I gave him an idea of the kind of questions I intended putting. Blair looked puzzled, saying he had no intention of allowing himself to be interviewed. He simply intended giving me a comment on the latest opinion poll. I explained that as it was the start of what looked like being a significant political year I intended raising a number of other issues. He just laughed at this, saying it would be a ridiculous waste of time for him to answer such questions when it was obvious the BBC would only use a fifteen-second soundbite.

When I refused to accept any restriction on what I might ask, it became evident that Blair had thought through his position with great care. He said that if he was being invited by a current affairs programme to take part in a lengthy interview he was quite prepared to undertake the considerable preparation which that might involve. However, if all a news bulletin needed was one quick quote then it was unreasonable to expect a politician to have to think through replies to a host of potentially difficult questions when the answers might never be broadcast. I accepted that it was rather futile for reporters to persist in conducting lengthy interviews when it was obvious only one short soundbite would be used, but insisted that there was nevertheless a point of principle at stake: interviewers had a duty to test the validity of any statement or answer by a politician and therefore there should be no automatic ban on supplementary questions. We agreed to proceed on that basis.

My first question produced the answer which Blair had obviously prepared in advance. This was to the effect that Labour's opinion poll lead reflected the popularity of their strategy in calling for increased investment in public services and industry rather than the tax cuts favoured by the Conservatives. I then put my additional questions. Blair, polite as ever, merely repeated his initial answer. Again, there seemed no real point in persisting. Because it was a Saturday I knew I was on weak ground: there are far fewer news outlets at weekends, with the main bulletins on Saturdays only half the length of those on week-days and hardly any Saturday current affairs programmes. Therefore, even if I had obtained a newsy or confrontational interview it stood little chance of being used. I realised that Blair would be aware of this, giving him added justification in resisting my additional questions and sticking to his short soundbite. Unlike Sir Norman Fowler, who had unwisely allowed me to range more widely in my questioning during the Tim Yeo affair, Blair was not going to be enticed into departing from the point he wanted to make.

Throughout our conversation Blair remained pleasant and unflustered, as he had done during my equally unwelcome interview on Labour's approach to employment law. I found myself beginning to admire his steely determination. He was not only making sure that his exposure on television and radio took place on the terms he dictated, soundbite or interview, but also revealing a refreshing take-it-or-leave-it attitude towards the news media. He was not oblivious to the details of the impression he made: on our meeting that morning on College Green he had been rather agitated to begin with about his hair, having forgotten his comb, and we trailed back to the BBC office to retrieve one from my briefcase before rejoining the television crew. But notwithstanding that one concession to presentation Blair struck me as being remarkably free of the all-consuming desire for publicity which can be so corrosive of a politician's judgement and standing.

The apparent effortlessness with which Blair appeared able to make the most of the access which he granted to journalists presented a marked contrast to the frenetic activity of his long-time friend and shadow Cabinet colleague Gordon Brown. No senior Labour frontbencher had applied himself to this task with more diligence. However, the greater Brown's efforts to use and cultivate the news media, the more elusive seemed his goal of achieving a durable and fruitful relationship. His activity in the pursuit of publicity was phenomenal, especially when compared with some other members of the shadow Cabinet, but it tailed off noticeably after he stood aside for Blair in the 1994 leadership election. It may even have worked against his leadership ambitions: one reason given by some senior Labour politicians for his failure to mount a credible challenge was his very dependency on the soundbite. They considered that he had fallen victim to the lure of a quick fix appearance on television or radio when he should have spent more time devising and then projecting a believable alternative economic policy for the party.

Blair, however, went out of his way to praise Brown's undoubted talent for summarising complex policy proposals and presenting them in a way which is understandable to the media. In an interview for the *Sunday Times* shortly before he was elected leader, Blair acknowledged the debt he owed for the patient instruction he had received: 'My press releases used to read like essays before Gordon showed me how to write them.' He was equally fulsome in his tribute to Brown for his help in speech-writing and for teaching him the difference between a talk to a seminar and a piece of polemic. As a political correspondent I endorse that tribute wholeheartedly: Brown had been more responsive and co-operative than any other politician I had encountered. His unerring news sense and his sharp turn of phrase owed much to the time he had spent at Scottish TV, as a presenter and editor, before becoming an MP in 1983. Perhaps his one failing, as a former journalist, had been his inability to shake off the deeply ingrained tendency which, once acquired, seems to condemn many journalists, whether they like it or not, to a perpetual compulsion to relate their lives to the news of the day.

At some stages in his front-bench career Brown's slavish application to the daily news agenda bordered almost on the fanatical. He regularly left Labour's publicity staff trailing in his wake, unable to keep pace with his press releases, newspaper articles and non-stop television and radio appearances. Attempts to lighten his burden were frequently rebuffed. He seemed oblivious to warnings from fellow MPs that his efforts could become self-defeating. The more Blair started to wean himself off the need for a daily dose of publicity, the more anxious Brown became in his desire to chase the next news bulletin.

Brown was propelled to the forefront of Labour's Treasury team in the autumn of 1988 after John Smith, who was then the shadow Chancellor, had his first heart attack. He quickly became a rising star within the parliamentary party, turning in some devastating performances against Nigel Lawson, then Chancellor of the Exchequer, and that November he topped the poll in the shadow Cabinet elections. My first clash with him occurred, as so often seemed to be the case, because of a dispute about a soundbite. Brown, then shadow Chief Secretary to the Treasury, visited Richmond during the by-election campaign in February 1989 on the very day I had been commissioned to compile a radio feature examining the significant military presence in the constituency, which included Catterick Camp and RAF Leeming. As Brown was Labour's visiting front-bench spokesman I approached him for a comment on the likely impact locally of the government's defence policy. Much to my surprise he refused point blank, arguing that as a member of Labour's Treasury team he could not comment on defence matters. I protested as forcibly as I could, saying that as it was a by-election campaign, and as he was the only shadow Cabinet minister in the constituency that day, it seemed an entirely appropriate request. Mo Mowlam, Labour MP for the nearby constituency of Redcar, who was assisting in the campaign, intervened on my behalf without success. She told me later that Brown had insisted on asking for a ruling from Peter Mandelson. Ms Mowlam assured me that no slight had been intended: Brown's overriding concern had been his wish to observe party discipline and ensure that as a member of the shadow Cabinet he did not speak out of turn. However, I noticed that in subsequent by-elections visitors from Labour's front bench were encouraged to consider themselves as jacks of all trades, capable of fielding a broad range of questions.

The following autumn I again found myself involved in discussions with Brown after he turned down another request for an interview. As the political correspondent on duty on the Saturday after the 1989 Wall Street crash I had approached him for a comment for use in the main television news bulletin. He refused, saying that he had to defer to the shadow Chancellor. So I rang John Smith, who was in no mood to have his weekend interrupted and promptly put the phone down. As an alternative I tried Bryan Gould, then the trade and industry spokesman, who was only too delighted to do the interview. Several days later I related this sequence of events to Brown, commenting that I was surprised he had missed an opportunity to appear on prime-time television. Saturday evening bulletins, I reminded him, regularly attracted some of the largest news audiences of the week. After listening to my account of what had happened he said somewhat ruefully that he would definitely have done the interview had he known all the circumstances.

The following month Brown obtained his own front-bench brief on being promoted to shadow trade and industry secretary. Now there was no stopping him in his efforts to secure publicity. He was often at his busiest at weekends, when newsrooms can be a soft target for exposure-hungry politicians. Newspaper offices and television and radio stations grew accustomed to receiving his Saturday morning news releases faxed from his home in Scotland. Broadcasters on weekend duty would express their amazement at his readiness to drop everything for a television interview, even if it meant he would be late for an important rugby fixture or might possibly miss the game altogether. Party workers for their part marvelled at his skill in fashioning news stories even on the quietest bank holiday weekend. John Underwood, who briefly succeeded Mandelson as Labour's director of communications, spoke frequently of his surprise on finding Brown in his room at Westminster hard at work at his computer screen, busily drafting statements for the media. Underwood considered it was his job as press officer to be writing the news releases, and he thought a shadow Cabinet member of Brown's standing would have been better employed on long-term strategic thinking.

As his efforts to make use of the media increased, so Brown's output became more prolific. In addition to preparing articles on Labour policy for the national press he was also a regular columnist, writing not only for a Scottish morning newspaper, the *Daily Record*, but also for the trade union journal, the *T&G Record*. Film of Brown typing furiously on his keyboard, looking for all the world like a journalist with a deadline to meet, was used in the BBC's political programme *On The Record* in its report on his rapid rise through the party.

Brown has always appeared to enjoy the company of journalists. At social gatherings he would take the trouble of enquiring which reporters were next on duty and would offer to run through the likely publication dates of forthcoming statements and policy documents for their benefit. He was an invaluable contact, always returning calls and making himself available. One New Year weekend when I discovered he was at home with a cold he insisted on ringing back with a quote. If a news story broke unexpectedly he would do all he could to provide background information. In July 1992 he arrived at the BBC studios in Millbank one Friday morning expecting to comment on a reorganisation of the Department of Trade and Industry. Instead, at a few moments' notice, he agreed to give his response to an account leaked to the BBC of the government's plans for the future of the Eurofighter project. His comments were used throughout the day on television news bulletins.

It seemed that there was nothing more that Brown could possibly do to assist the media. However, when it came to putting across his own message he was in one sense handicapped by his preference for economic briefs. As trade and industry spokesman, and more recently as shadow Chancellor, he had no shortage of news pegs on which to hang press releases and interviews, the rush of economic events meant that he was in constant demand. But frequency of appearance on radio and television is no guarantee of commensurate impact: many of his responses had of necessity to be based on statistics, and facts and figures do not always provide the basis for compelling interviews. All too frequently his answers were not conversational enough, sounding rather as if they had been written by a journalist trying desperately to pack in too much information. A typical Brown soundbite would open in a familar fashion, starting perhaps on the following lines: 'With three million people out of work, Britain urgently needs a new economic approach . . .' or possibly: 'With redundancies at an all time high . . .'

Aware of criticism that his delivery could be stilted and that he some-times had a wooden appearance, Brown went to inordinate lengths to inject vitality into his answers. During a hectic round of interviews in the week of the 1992 autumn spending statement, a television studio tech-nician observed the care with which he practised what was obviously the key sentence of his reply, repeating it a dozen times before deciding which words should get most emphasis. Such assiduity had its disadvan-tages: once he had memorised a soundbite, Brown had a tendency to keep repeating it whatever the subsequent questions. Some programme editors grew reluctant to accept his contributions, claiming they were predictable and repetitive. For a time producers on the BBC's *One o'Clock News* were told to do their utmost to find other Labour voices: Brown was considered to have become over-exposed.

Other journalists were also taking aim. They considered that once Brown had been appointed shadow Chancellor he should have spent more time on policy issues. Michael White, the *Guardian*'s political edi-tor, was perplexed by Brown's habit of remaining 'poised over his fax machine, restlessly seeking exposure by soundbite'. Stephen Castle, writing in the *Independent on Sunday*, observed how, in an attempt to manipulate television and radio journalists and force them to use the soundbite he wanted, Brown would 'shamelessly repeat the same line over and over again until the interviewer gives up'. Milton Shulman, television critic of the London *Evening Standard*, concluded that the shadow Chancellor's repertoire of answers had 'the repetitive consis-tency of a speaking weighing machine'.

Nor were these criticisms confined to media circles: political col-leagues and opponents alike had their reservations about Brown's near-obsession with media coverage. Some among the Conservatives found his preoccupation with publicity, and the seriousness with which he delivered his soundbites, just too much to take. In 1991, the then trade and industry secretary, Peter Lilley, started describing his Labour shadow as Ron Glum and said that like his namesake in the radio series *Take It From Here*, Brown could brighten a room merely by leaving it. A year later, Lilley claimed, Brown still seemed to be 'overdosing on gloom'. Sketch-writers and commentators joined in the fun. After one clash between Brown and Lilley across the despatch box, the *Guardian*'s Andrew Rawnsley chid the Labour spokesman for 'constructing an entire speech on nothing but soundbites'.

Among less hostile critics, Brown's closest parliamentary colleagues had been concerned for some time by his failure to heed their advice that he should concentrate more on longer-term policy considerations. They pointed to his success in the Commons in savaging Norman Lamont during the latter's tenure as Chancellor and argued that by giving fewer but more thoughtful interviews he could restore his credibility with the media. They found his reliance on statistics particularly exasperating. One Scottish MP said that to reinforce their point he would ring up at weekends after hearing yet another soundbite and would challenge the shadow Chancellor on his statistics – but Brown would rarely see the joke.

But Brown was not impervious to the pressures of his self-imposed thraldom to the news industry. On occasion he could appear plagued by self-doubt. After one television interview he looked particularly miserable, saying he thought he had failed even his walking shot. Jibes about his inability to smile when appearing on television must have been some of the most wounding. He made great efforts, but it seemed an uphill task. In a 1992 election broadcast directed by Hugh Hudson he appeared jovial and relaxed, prompting political reporters who saw the preview to compliment him on being so natural. Afterwards Brown told me that his mother had been telling him for years to smile more often. However, a year later, in March 1993, when he recorded his broadcast responding to the budget, there were a number of retakes after he was told he looked uncomfortable and should try to smile.

The morning after that recording I saw for myself the considerable strain imposed on the shadow Chancellor by the constant demands of the media, especially in budget week. Labour were busily attacking the government over the announcement that value added tax was to be imposed on domestic heating fuel. I had seen Brown trying without success to ring out while waiting to be interviewed live by the *Today* programme. I walked over and showed him how to obtain a line on the newly installed telephone system. Once the interview was finished he immediately picked up the phone and started dictating a statement to Chris Moncrieff, political editor of the Press Association news agency. At the very same moment the housing minister, Sir George Young, plus entourage, swept past on their way to the studio. Young was accompanied by an adviser and a press officer whose task it was to smooth out any difficulties and make sure that the minister's interview went without interruption. Yet there was the shadow Chancellor struggling with the phone, dictating his own press statements, obviously overburdened by his do-it-yourself drive for publicity.

Within a year Brown's media relations had been transformed. By the spring of 1994 the shadow Chancellor had suddenly stopped dealing with every journalist's enquiry himself. His news releases were no longer stacking up unwanted at the fax machine, and he had halved his appearances on television and radio. When interviews did take place the arrangements were closely supervised and there was a detailed discussion beforehand about the likely line of questioning. Brown had finally acquired a filter and a minder, having recognised at long last the value of appointing a press officer capable of providing him with the front-line defence which he needed so badly against the daily onslaught of the media.

His choice of Charlie Whelan, who had previously worked for the Amalgamated Engineering and Electrical Union, was an astute one. As an established trade union press officer Whelan was already well versed in many of the potential pitfalls in publicising Labour politicians. He had a reputation among Labour's media staff for single-minded determination in pushing the party line once it had been agreed. On taking up his appointment in January 1994 he tried to ensure that Brown did not waste effort, or damage his credibility, by making statements of questionable news value. He insisted that Brown did fewer interviews so as to give more weight to his appearances. Whelan succeeded where others had failed; and he enjoyed the notoriety of being, as he said, the only Labour press officer whose job it was 'to keep a member of the shadow Cabinet off television and radio'.

There was one setback to Whelan's efforts to achieve a sense of order in Brown's approach to publicity. Shortly before the October party conference the shadow Chancellor had again become the butt of the political writers for delivering a lecture which was ridiculed for sounding like 'gobbledegook economics'. A ninety-one-word sentence, which the *Sun* claimed had baffled even city experts, included this description of one of the ideas in which Labour's new economic policy was said to be rooted: 'the growth of post neo-classical endogenous growth theory and the symbiotic relationships between growth and investment in people and infrastructure'. The Plain English Campaign awarded Brown the title of king of gobbledegook, echoed by the *Daily Express* in its headline: 'Meet Mr Gibberish.' Knowing as he did that his lecture was going to be televised, Brown was asking for trouble in failing to check that it would be comprehensible to the average viewer; parts of it, clearly, were not, as he privately admitted later. However, the incident does raise the question of how complex ideas or detailed expositions are to be put across in a media environment habituated to the relentless pursuit of the soundbite: with political discourse increasingly reduced to a battle of slogans, there is a real problem for anyone who wants or needs to hold the listener's attention for longer than a few seconds.

Broadcasters unable to extract what they judge to be a suitable soundbite from an unexciting speech frequently take their revenge by poking fun at the politician who has thus disobliged them, drawing attention to *longueurs* in the address or to an apparent lack of interest on the part of the audience – and, a habit that politicians find especially exasperating, talking over film of the speech so that television viewers have to listen to the journalist rather than the politician. This practice of 'goldfishing' – reducing the speaker to the status of a guppy in an aquarium, haplessly opening and shutting his mouth in silence – is the source of many complaints to the broadcasting organisations.

It is somewhat ironic that Brown should have been castigated on the one hand for relentless plugging of his own soundbites and also on the other hand for long and unintelligible speeches that resisted all attempts at encapsulation. But not all commentators were infected by the disinclination – or inability – to differentiate between the muddled language that reflects muddled thinking and the complex language that reflects complex thought. One columnist who sprang to Brown's defence was the *Independent*'s Andrew Marr. He said the years Brown had spent 'drenching himself in academic thought' would help provide his party with a comprehensive economic re-education which might win Labour the next election. In Marr's view it was a caricature to describe the shadow Chancellor as a shallow politician addicted to soundbites and self-promotion: 'He is, in reality, a deep and serious man whose personal PR has been catastrophically bad.'

Irrespective of these developments in Brown's extra-parliamentary presence, 1994 ended with the shadow Chancellor winning plaudits throughout the party for having done so much damage to the Conservatives' reputation as a tax-cutting party. Labour's defeat of the government over the doubling of VAT on domestic fuel silenced at a single blow all the criticism there had been of his failure to think through a credible economic strategy. Again, political and media reaction struck the same note. Brown's 'single-mindedness' in pursuing the government was praised by Martin Kettle of the *Guardian*. By relentlessly targeting

VAT on fuel as the embodiment of Tory unfairness, Brown had helped Labour inflict on the Conservatives their 'single greatest parliamentary humiliation in a generation'. Kettle acknowledged that Brown had been criticised 'for caution, for wordiness and for reducing fluid complexities to repetitive soundbites', but after the government's VAT defeat he would always be able to retort that 'he was right on the big one and that his critics were wrong'.

Whelan's own single-mindedness in improving Brown's profile was already having an effect at the time of John Smith's sudden death in May 1994. But although he had gone some way towards repairing the damage to the shadow Chancellor's reputation, the leadership contest reopened the debate about Brown's addiction to soundbites. As the party started assessing the value of the likely contenders, there were powerful voices in the Labour hierarchy who said Brown was too light-weight to become leader.

Tony Blair had spent the two years between the 1992 election and John Smith's death carefully avoiding over-exposure in the media. His appointment as shadow Home Secretary had given him as much scope for generating publicity as Brown; but, unlike his friend and colleague, he chose not to respond to every headline. He cultivated a thoughtful stance by agreeing to far fewer television and radio appearances than Brown. Editors felt there was a certain cachet about having him on their programmes and as a result the interviews which he did give tended to be run at length and be given greater prominence. News producers also detected the same steadfast refusal by Blair to be cajoled or deflected from giving the responses which he thought most appropriate. His answers, instead of sounding as if they had been mentally sub-edited so as to encompass several separate points, seemed more effective in connecting with what people were thinking.

Not all his utterances were well received, even in his own party: one of his soundbites, to the effect that Labour would be 'tough on crime, and tough on the causes of crime' was derided by some Labour MPs on the left as nothing more than empty rhetoric. Nevertheless, Blair proved to be as successful with the home affairs brief as he had been on reposition-ing Labour in relation to the employment laws. His initiatives on tack-ling crime met with widespread praise and he was credited with clawing back Labour's reputation as a party which could be trusted on law and order. On this issue he had the Conservatives on the defensive. At the height of the 1993 controversy over police batons, Blair effectively side-stepped the question and instead used his reply to congratulate the government on adopting Labour's policies.

Brown's position as potential challenger was not helped by a continu-ing debate within the party about its reliance on presentation rather than policy. In the aftermath of their fourth election defeat Labour's former foreign affairs spokesman, Gerald Kaufman, suggested that one reason for their failure was the party's readiness to connive with the BBC and ITN in allowing peak-time news bulletins to debase political discourse by their dependence on soundbites. He criticised the way leading politicians were being allowed only a few dozen words to put their case.

Writing in the *Guardian*, Kaufman explained why he felt a radical socialist case could not be communicated in soundbites and photo opportunities: 'An almost subliminal flash of Labour spokesman X is given equal time with a glimpe of Tory minister Y ... Instead of mutilating its ideas to fit the Procrustes' bed of quick bursts of vision and sound, Labour must force its way to public attention through considered speeches and structured arguments.' His concerns were echoed by Labour's director of communications, David Hill, who said that when broadcasters were packaging their news reports they should at least allow politicians from the three main parties an opportunity to deal with the same point. 'What ought to happen is that three questions should be asked, three answers given and three answers broadcast. That's the direction in which the broadcasters should move. That would provide political balance over a period of time.' Hill's predecessor Peter Mandelson agreed. He thought the packaging of soundbites was leading to the shrinkage of serious coverage. However, politicians had to accept the disciplines and reality of communicating through television and radio and that meant they had to be able to express themselves in a few clear sentences.

Shortly after Blair's election as leader, Kaufman returned to his theme when interviewed by Steve Richards for *Talking Politics* on BBC radio. He repeated his theory that one reason for Labour's last electoral defeat was the party's willingness to 'amputate its policies to fit into soundbites'. He refused to participate any further in the degrading of political discussion and added somewhat cryptically that he could think of 'one politician whose career has been destroyed' by cooperating with the broadcasters. Kaufman did not mention Brown by name, but there was no mistaking whom he had in mind.

Kaufman launched yet another attack on his party's embrace of the soundbite in December 1994 on the eve of a spectacular Labour victory in the Dudley West by-election. Although he was confident Labour's campaign had worked, he had come to the conclusion that thinking up fifteen-word answers for by-election walkabouts was a humiliating waste of time. Writing in the London *Evening Standard*, he said he doubted whether he had ever gained a single vote for Labour by participating in such rituals. Kaufman seemed to have missed the point that politicians knocking up voters during by-elections have to be able to deliver fifteen-second answers as that is often as long as they will get before householders have had enough and want to shut their front doors.

I must probably take some of the blame for Kaufman's refusal to take part in by-election photo opportunities because he provided me with the most celebrated gaffe of the Liverpool Walton by-election in 1991. He was then shadow Foreign Secretary, and he toured the constituency one Saturday morning. I followed him round one of the local shopping centres. Without realising whom he was greeting, Kaufman went up and shook hands with Tony Jennings, leader of the twenty-five-strong broad left group on Liverpool City Council. The broad left were backing a rival candidate in the by-election, Lesley Mahmood, who was backed by Militant and was standing as Walton Real Labour. Jennings immediately attacked Kaufman for supporting the official Labour group on the city council which had brought in a private contractor to handle Liverpool's refuse collection. Kaufman said the privatisation of the service was 'necessary because the people of Liverpool deserved a proper service and it was not being provided'. His endorsement of a privatised council service was not the soundbite I had expected from a member of the shadow Cabinet and it was used extensively that day on BBC radio. Chris Patten, the Tory chairman, congratulated Kaufman for his unequivocal support for privatisation. Kaufman accused me subsequently of sneaking up behind him and recording his answer without his knowledge. He said he wanted to 'wring my neck'. Because he felt my conduct was unacceptable he refused to be interviewed by me ever again. I felt his complaint was hardly justified, as I had been invited by Labour's press office to attend his walkabout. Kaufman had only himself to blame if he had failed to take the obvious precaution of being able to identify the leader of the broad left group on the city council, especially as Liverpool had been the source of so much anguish for the party.

As Labour's debate over the merits of soundbites continued Roy Hattersley, a former deputy leader, joined in, reflecting in his weekly *Guardian* column on the days when he was subjected to 'television tyranny' and recalling his resentment at being bullied into compressing his ideas into ten seconds of transmission time. One Labour politician who tried over the years to turn the tables and impose his own controls on broadcasters was Tony Benn. He developed a much-admired defensive technique, used especially when being interviewed for news bulletins: he would insist on knowing the precise amount of time allotted for his contribution and then timed his remarks to the second, thus hoping to deny producers the chance to edit down his answers. Benn had however a wider complaint: he believed that soundbites were simply being discarded if they did not fit the broadcasters' predetermined news agenda.

'We have become the chessmen of master chess players who can play the game exactly as they wish.'

The possibility of political parties collaborating in a self-denying ordinance to cut down on the plethora of television and radio interviews has been aired occasionally. Charles Moore, writing in the *Spectator*, suggested that modern politicians should restrict themselves to speeches, debates and statements. A few British institutions were still respected because those who were responsible for them, such as 'serving army officers, senior consultants, High Court judges and so forth' rarely gave television interviews. A contrary view was put forward in the Labour weekly *Tribune* by the *Today* newspaper's political columnist Alastair Campbell, who became Blair's personal press officer in October 1994. He argued that it was stupid to criticise soundbite politics. The reason for the opposition's existence was to persuade the public that they could do a better job than the government. The news media were a central battleground for all political parties and therefore it was essential that Labour MPs did all they could to continue getting 'tagged on' to the end of television reports which examined government policy. In response to Kaufman's complaint about soundbites in the Dudley West by-election, Campbell said that Labour's coverage on local television had played an important part in their victory. One of the most successful visits during the campaign had been that of Labour's deputy leader John Prescott, whose resistance to 'soundbitery had made him one of Britain's most popular politicians'.

I do have some sympathy with politicians over their complaint that television and radio journalists increasingly shape the questions they are posing in order to get the answers they want. I think broadcasters have tended to become soundbite junkies. However, we should be prepared to defend our craft. In my efforts to get shorter and less complicated replies, I frequently find myself trying to persuade ministers and MPs to rehearse their answers. I continue to ask them the same question, perhaps with a slight variation, until I am satisfied with the length and content of their reply. Surprisingly, most politicians welcome this and say that when they are asked to respond instantly to the latest political development of the day, they realise that to begin with they are probably trying to cram too many points into their answer. Frequently their initial responses are longer than the duration allotted to the entire item. If a journalist is prepared to advise them on the point in their reply which is most likely to be used they are ususally only too willing to redo the interview in the hope of providing a concise answer which will stand on its own and not need editing. I accept that in taking this approach I may be laying myself open to accusations of collusion, but I see my role when preparing news items for television or radio as being no different from that of a newspaper journalist who might compress or tidy up one of the many quotes recorded in a notebook. I want the politicians I interview to be as clear and as intelligible as possible in the news reports for which I am responsible. The more important tests for broadcasters are those of accuracy and fairness and the need to avoid bias.

Even if there were fewer political interviews, I doubt this would lessen the trend towards ever shorter soundbites. The degree of access in public affairs which is being afforded to television and radio is increasing all the time: therefore the amount of televised and recorded material which is available to broadcasting organisations will go on expanding. At the same time, as competition among broadcasters increases, so will the demand for brighter and slicker news services. If past experience is any guide, these competitive pressures will inevitably go on influencing editorial standards and practices throughout the broadcasting industry.

3

The Love Affair with the Lens

POLITICIANS EASILY outshine most other groups in public life when it comes to thinking up contrived poses or bizarre situations in which to be photographed and filmed. The need to find a suitable photograph for an election leaflet or poster is one of the first tasks which faces every budding politician, and from that moment on many seem to be hooked, remaining forever on the lookout for flattering or newsworthy pictures. Sometimes the temptation is too great. Examples abound of publicity stunts which went horrendously wrong, and promising careers can be blighted in an instant by an ill-judged photo opportunity; yet the political love affair with the camera lens shows no signs of abating. Against their better judgement, or perhaps because of bad advice, politicians can be persuaded – often, it seems, without much difficulty – to participate in all sorts of escapades.

Conservative MPs, ministers and backbenchers alike, have been more adventurous and perhaps more successful over the years than their Labour counterparts in using press photographs and television to publicise themselves. In part this is due to their closer links with the advertising and public relations industry – and also to the Tory leanings of many of the popular newspapers, which tend to commission many more personality pictures than the quality dailies. Years of distrust about the hidden motives of the the news media have made Labour politicians far more cautious. Their memories are imprinted with the occasions when the morning newspapers have splashed over their front pages snatched photographs which were taken without the knowledge of the senior party figures concerned but which caused them the deepest embarrassment.

An apology had to be sent to Buckingham Palace when Labour's then defence secretary, the late Fred Mulley, was pictured on the front pages having dozed off as he sat next to the Queen at an air show marking the RAF's silver jubilee in 1977. Photographs showed him yawning and then slumped on one side, eyes closed, his head resting on his hand. He said he was 'very, very sorry' for the impression he had created which he attributed to a 'momentary lack of attention'. A spokesman for the royal family who was quoted at the time, expressed surprise that anyone could have nodded off during a flypast by 140 planes, including V-bombers, Phantoms, Harriers and Jaguars. Similar fury was vented in the tabloid press when Michael Foot, who was then leader of the opposition, was photographed at the Cenotaph on Remembrance Sunday in November 1981 wearing what some newspapers described as a donkey jacket.

Some of the most hazardous venues offer themselves at party conferences or out on the hustings in election campaigns. The lure of publicity can prove too much for politicians desperate to communicate with their supporters and with the wider electorate. They cannot believe their good fortune when they find themselves surrounded by journalists, photographers and television crews all on the lookout for the unexpected and the unusual. Many an accident-prone politician has found the potential danger of such situations an irresistible attraction. They think they know best, and are wholly confident that events will remain firmly under their control; but invariably the promotional activities devised by the parties bear little relation to the pictures which the media would like to engineer, and damage to political credibility and reputations is all too often the result.

Every political activist has his or her own favourites from a vast miscellany of ill-fated photo opportunities. Lord Hailsham's exploits as party chairman at the Conservatives' 1957 conference in Brighton have yet to be equalled for their sheer verve and eccentricity. He donned flippers and a snorkel before plunging into the sea for a swim. Then, at the end of the conference week, he rounded off his closing speech with the clamour of an enormous ceremonial handbell which he rang by waving it above his head. As he brought the party representatives to their feet at fever pitch he bellowed out the intonation: 'Let us say to the Labour Party: seek not to inquire for whom the bell tolls: It tolls for thee.' Years later Lord Hailsham acknowledged in his autobiography *A Sparrow's Flight* that the two incidents had dogged him for the rest of his political life – although he maintained rather cheekily that he never deserved the reputation he acquired for 'self-advertising publicity'.

Neil Kinnock's ill-fated publicity stunt almost three decades later on that same pebbly beach at Brighton ended with an equally vivid picture sequence which was to acquire a cult following. The newly installed Labour leader is being filmed walking on the shore, hand in hand with his wife Glenys: he trips and, at the very moment that he falls on to the shingle, he is hit by an incoming wave. Kinnock was doubly unfortunate: not only did he fall over but his slip-up was recorded by a television cameraman and then immortalised by being replayed time and time again in the opening titles of *Spitting Image*. He had, in the parlance of the journalistic trade, been 'set up and stitched up'. No wonder that in his years as party leader he remained wary of reporters and photographers.

Kinnock's great adversary Margaret Thatcher was a surer-footed exponent of the art of self-publicity. Her instincts as to what would make a compelling picture were often sounder than the judgements of her media advisers and minders. While out on the campaign trail in the 1979 general election they looked on aghast as Mrs Thatcher picked up a baby calf which she then held up in her arms for the benefit of the photographers. Without needing to be told, she had spotted what turned out to be one of the most memorable images of the campaign, a talent which she was to display repeatedly during her years as Prime Minister – abetted perhaps by an element of good fortune that eluded Kinnock: Labour claimed at the time that on the television recording Denis Thatcher could be heard warning his wife that unless she was careful the Conservatives would end up having a dead calf on their hands.

Even prearranged pictures can turn out to be not only inept but devastating in their consequences, despite often being the product of considerable advance thought and consultation. Those who take part seem to forget that all too often publicity stunts have a tendency to develop a life of their own. Politicians thirsty for attention can find themselves egged on by the photographers and the television crews with their shouts of 'Smile, please' or 'Look this way.' Like the pools winner who says 'yes' to publicity when filling in a football coupon, the participants can precipitate their own demise through over-exposure. Prominent public figures fail to appreciate that a single ill-judged picture can destroy the respect and affection which might have taken them years to establish.

At the height of the 1990 scare about eating beef, due to the emerging panic over 'mad cow disease', John Gummer, then agriculture minister, fell victim to the combined ingenuity of his departmental press office and the *Sun*. In what was then being regarded as one of the paper's more helpful phases in its chequered relationship with Conservative ministers, the *Sun* had apparently been badgering Gummer for some time to lay on an exclusive photo opportunity so that he and his family could demonstrate that they had no fears about consuming British beef.

Gummer had been making great play of the fact that the eating habits of his household had not changed despite the spread of bovine spongiform encephalopathy. Only the week before he had offended vegetarians by claiming they were guilty of 'wholly unnatural practices': quoting from the Bible, he said meat was an essential part of the diet. In an attempt to reassure the public about the safety measures being taken to deal with BSE, he said that roast beef, minced beef and beef burgers were regularly consumed by his four children Benedict, Felix, Leonora and the youngest, four-year-old Cordelia.

Simon Walters, the *Sun's* political correspondent, contacted the Ministry of Agriculture's press office to ask if the paper could take a picture of the Gummer family sitting down to a joint of roast beef with the minister happily carving off the slices. Alternatively they could photograph the Gummer children tucking into beef burgers. The *Sun's* political editor Trevor Kavanagh had chipped in with the idea getting a *Sun* tee-shirt printed with the slogan 'Eat British Burgers'. Much to the annoyance of Kavanagh and Walters, the men from the Ministry took up the idea, but instead of arranging an exclusive *Sun* picture turned it into a general photo call for the rest of the news media as well.

In allowing Gummer to proceed with a personal and highly publicised attempt to restore consumer confidence in beef the Ministry of Agriculture were going against their own internal advice. Research had shown that politicians and civil servants were the last people the public believed at the height of health scares, and in response to concern over pesticides, for example, the Ministry had always favoured using government scientists to give news conferences and television and radio interviews. However, the conventional wisdom on whether or not politicians could be trusted to tell the truth on health issues had already been shattered by Edwina Currie – with unfortunate results for her career. Her assertion as a junior health minister in December 1988 that 'most of the country's egg production' was affected by a salmonella outbreak was believed to such an extent that egg sales dropped by 50 per cent. The resulting outcry from the poultry producers forced her resignation.

Gummer, however, presumably thought he could manage things better. The East Coast Boat Show at Ipswich, which was being opened by the minister and happened to have a handy beef burger stall, was chosen as the location for the photo call. Cordelia was the sole representative of the Gummers' offspring but, true to their word, the *Sun* at least cooperated and played the game by printing a happy family photo next morning showing father and daughter smiling away as they munched their freshly cooked beef burgers. However, Paul Currie, one of the many photographers who took up the Ministry's invitation to attend the Gummer photo call, decided to take his picture from a different angle. He caught the precise moment when Gummer was handing Cordelia her beef burger. In bending over, the minister appears to be almost force-feeding his reluctant daughter. The rest of the cameramen and a television crew are silhouetted in the background of Currie's photograph, underlining the fact that this was a carefully orchestrated event laid on for the media. His picture was widely used by the national press and it was reproduced on the next cover of *Private Eye* with a cartoon bubble out of the television cameraman's mouth saying: 'The public won't swallow this' and Cordelia repying: 'Neither will I.'

Needless to say, the *Sun*'s political team were none too popular with either the Ministry's public relations department or Conservative Central Office. Simon Walters was told by one of the press officers that they hoped he would keep his bright ideas to himself in future. The *Guardian*'s media page awarded Gummer first prize for the most counterproductive image of 1990, declaring: 'The gruesome spectacle of the agriculture minister and his daughter cramming their mouths with what the nation instantly christened BSE-burgers turned over more stomachs than salmonella, listeria and lager-and-vindaloo combined.'

In the aftermath of his disastrous visit to the beefburger stall, Gummer remained cheerily dismissive of suggestions that he had made a hash of the photo opportunity. He told me subsequently that the real trouble had been that the beefburger was too hot for Cordelia and that was why he held on to it for her while she took a bite. Even so, his mishandling of the event, and his failure to think through how the picture might be misinterpreted, was all the more surprising in view of his own connections with the public relations industry. His brother Peter Gummer had founded the Shandwick PR firm and had become an unofficial but nonetheless influential publicity adviser to both Mrs Thatcher and, subsequently, John Major. Peter Gummer told journalists he was not prepared to 'break his cover' and acknowledge publicly the help he was giving to No.10, but by the mid-1990s his advice was widely respected within the Tory party and he was said to be having regular discussions with Major on an almost weekly basis.

A similarly misjudged family photo was arranged in July 1992 by David Mellor, the national heritage secretary, in an attempt to counter adverse criticism about his affair with the actress Antonia de Sancha. Mellor's photo opportunity came to be regarded as an unsavoury testament to the hypocrisy of Conservative ministers on the question of family values. Not content with including his wife Judith and sons Anthony and Freddie, Mellor enlisted his parents-in-law, Professor Edward Hall and his wife Joan, to join them in looking over a garden gate for the benefit of newspaper photographers. Most MPs make widespread use of their wives, husbands and children for publicity purposes, especially in their election literature, but few could recollect an occasion when a politician fending off adverse press comment had taken advantage of a family gathering in such a blatant and manipulative way. Mellor justified the picture on the grounds that it was his way of disproving innaccurate newspaper stories which were suggesting that he had told his wife's parents they would never see their grandchildren again if they continued speaking to the news media. With all three generations lined up beside him outside the West Sussex home of his in-laws, Mellor said the family had resolved to discuss their affairs in private. 'We have put all of the misunderstandings of the past week behind us.'

Amid ever more lurid revelations about his private life, Mellor fought desperately to hold on to his job until finally being forced to resign in September. Political journalists were among those from whom he sought advice as to the best way to deal with what were plainly some pretty far-fetched stories about his alleged sexual preferences. Another person he consulted was Sir Tim Bell, chairman of Lowe Bell Communications, who was a frequent adviser to Margaret Thatcher when she was Prime Minister. Indeed, Bell was credited by some with having thought up the garden gate photograph. According to the *Today* newspaper, Mellor turned to Mrs Thatcher's 'PR guru to polish up his image', and he recommended 'a kiss-and-make-up photograph with the in-laws' as a way of showing family solidarity. Subsequently Bell denied ever having given that advice. He told me that the embattled minister had contacted him frequently to discuss various possible strategies for withstanding what had become a vicious campaign against him by the popular press. 'Mellor rang me at three in the morning to say he was going down to his in-laws and would pose with them to counter the stories that he had banned them from seeing his children. He asked me what I thought of his idea. I said it sounds fine. But I didn't offer him any advice. I just said yes. Don't forget it was three in the morning and I was fed up with his phone calls.'

Mellor's deployment of his family as a weapon in his fight against the tabloids was an act of sheer bravado. At moments of acute stress, when their political careers are at stake, many MPs could do with a public relations minder beside them all the time, and most certainly whenever they emerge into public view and might find themselves being filmed or photographed. In contrast to Mellor's assertive pose, Tim Yeo's action in using his luggage to shield his face on his hurried dash to the airport in the Seychelles reinforced the impression that he was ashamed of himself and had something to hide.

Mellor was not alone in responding to media attacks head-on. Neil Hamilton, the corporate affairs minister who was caught up in the renewed allegations about MPs taking cash for questions, was needlessly provocative when he posed for pictures only five days before he was finally forced to resign in October 1994. After opening an extension at Wilmslow High School in his Cheshire constituency, Hamilton, accompanied by his wife Christine, stood holding up a large biscuit which he had been presented with by the pupils. 'They've given me a reward for coming this morning. I shall of course be registering the biscuit on the Register of Members' Interests.' Hamilton enjoyed his light-hearted badinage with the photographers and reporters and told them they would now have every opportunity to write a corny headline. He even suggested one himself: 'The man who takes the biscuit!'

Hamilton's mistake was to think that the public would automatically appreciate his joke. In a Gallup opinion survey conducted earlier in the month for the *Daily Telegraph*, 61 per cent of those questioned believed the Conservatives were giving the impression of being 'very sleazy and disreputable'. Hamilton, in the process of fighting to keep his job (admittedly he had announced he was starting a libel action, but his position, as events proved, was still extremely precarious), blithely ignored the experience of so many other politicians who have discovered to their cost that there can come a moment, however hard to define, when they lose public sympathy.

The sense of satisfaction which the public can obtain from the humiliation of prominent people, and the perverse pleasure which journalists can sometimes derive from collusion in destroying those whom they may have helped achieve prominence in the first place, is perhaps the least discussed of all the phenomena associated with the modern news media. At various stages in my career I have found myself swept along on what I can only describe as a roller-coaster of news stories which have undoubtedly done incalculable political damage and hurt a great many public figures in the process.

Labour were swept out of office in 1979 after a sea-change in electoral opinion, a tide swollen by years of unfavourable publicity during which the party's fortunes had come to be linked inextricably in the public's mind with widely reported abuses of trade union power. There was something infectious about those days: exposing union malpractices became the great journalistic challenge of the period. The arrogance of union leaders and shop stewards acted as a spur to reporters. During the intense media blitz over the ministerial resignations which accompanied both the Conservatives' 'back to basics' fiasco and the turmoil over the allegations of sleaze I was reminded of how I felt on being caught up in the anti-union fervour of the 1970s.

Labour MPs on the left of the party have been a regular target of the sustained media campaigns which I have described. They would say, perhaps with some justification, that they were in fact hounded by the right-wing press and were subjected, over the years, to what could only be described as a witch-hunt. Nevertheless the behaviour of some Labour MPs, just like their counterparts in the Conservative Party, has on occasion left a lot to be desired. Ron Brown, the maverick left-wing Labour MP for Leith, found that his slide towards deselection was hastened by a damning photo opportunity choreographed by the media.

Brown was already well on the way towards being ousted by his local party when he emerged from Lewes Crown Court in January 1990 after having been fined £1,000 for causing criminal damage to the flat of his former mistress, but acquitted, on the recommendation of the judge, of a more serious offence of stealing a number of items, including jewellery and two pairs of knickers. Brown was delighted by his acquittal on the theft charge. Next morning's newspapers showed him shaking a bottle of champagne and, like a grand prix winner, being showered by the bubbles. He was quoted as saying: 'It's a moral victory.'

His picture made the front page of the *Sun*, which described how 'love cheat Labour MP Ron Brown swigged champagne after being fined £1,000 for wrecking his former mistress's home.' His previous exploits, which included picking up and then dropping the House of Commons mace, had hardly endeared him to the Labour leadership; but nothing could have been more insensitive or politically incorrect than to be seen celebrating the outcome of a court case that had caused deep offence in a party actively trying to end sexual discrimination and tackle the problems of harassed and battered women. Brown was immediately censured by his constituency party, which called for his resignation as an MP. In a letter of apology he said it was reporters and not himself who had used the phrase 'moral victory'. There had been no 'champagne reception'; a bottle of sparkling wine, which was opened by his solicitor, had been supplied by members of the National Union of Journalists.

The precise chain of events which ended in Brown being photographed with his wife May, cracking open a bottle of champagne, was, as journalists might say, somewhat hazy. Sandra Barwick, writing in the *Independent*, was in no doubt as to what happened: 'The press had provided a bottle of fizz and glasses. At the urgent request of photographers, Ron shook it so that it rained champagne on him and May.' Talking subsequently to one of the television crews, I was told that press photographers purchased the bottle three hours earlier and then handed it to him already opened. Some weeks later, when I asked Brown why he had allowed himself to be pictured with what the photographs clearly showed was a bottle of champagne, he claimed he had been fitted up. 'In all innocence I took a sip of the champagne. I was sure it had come from sympathetic journalists. With hindsight it was perhaps foolish. I was caught by the media.'

Being 'caught by the media' is a fear which haunts politicians, and most MPs pride themselves on having the wit to spot the potential pitfalls and avoid being coerced into participating in publicity stunts which could backfire. The advice of Barry Jones, Labour's former shadow Welsh secretary, has always been that MPs should stand back for a moment and think of the possible implications. Whenever he was stopped unexpectedly and asked by photographers to step forward, he tried to keep in mind the advice of 'Professor' C.E.M. Joad, who was a regular panellist in the 1940s on the radio programme *The Brains Trust* and became famous for prefacing his answers with the words: 'It all depends what you mean . . .' Jones said the greatest risk he took was to wear a kimono and hold up a Japanese sword at the ceremonial opening of the Toyota engine plant in his Deeside constituency. He always thought the funniest stunt of all was Denis Healey donning a woolly sweater and climbing an apple tree. This is one picture which is missing from *The Time of My Life*, the autobiography of Labour's former Chancellor of the Exchequer. However, the book does contain photographs of him receiving the Order Against Political Pomposity in 1969 and then, twenty years later, dressing up as Father Christmas for the Epping by-election.

One of Healey's successors at the Treasury, Kenneth Clarke, has displayed the same playful characteristics and has been photographed regularly with a pint of beer, smoking a cigar or playing the saxophone. At the 1994 Conservative conference he merrily boarded the Dotto train which runs along Bournemouth seafront – in contrast to Cecil Parkinson who, at the party conference there four years earlier, when he was transport secretary, had been petrified all week that he might be press-ganged into taking a ride on the same train. He was fearful of newspaper headlines to the effect that he could not run a railway.

Clarke has, however acknowledged, somewhat belatedly, the dangers which politicians face if they respond too readily to the instructions being shouted at them by photographers and journalists. On his appointment as Chancellor in May 1993, after the sacking of Norman Lamont, he posed on the Treasury steps with his Chief Secretary, Michael Portillo. I was one of the journalists in the scrum outside. As Clarke was his usual bouncy self I kept asking him to turn back to back with Portillo, and at one point he did so. My aim was two-fold. First, the photo-call had already turned out to be great fun and I was hoping I might be able to get a shot for my television report showing them looking rather like the comedians Morecambe and Wise. In addition, a shot of them facing in different directions would be an ideal illustration for any script line to the effect that the two ministers had markedly different views on economic policy and would be rivals in any future leadership contest. A year later, in a BBC film portrait entitled *The Bloke Next Door*, the Chancellor made it plain he regretted getting carried away on that occasion and having danced to the tune of the photographers and journalists. His objection to the picture was nevertheless quite unrelated to anything I had intended to portray. He feared that he and Portillo had allowed themselves to 'look like a couple of mafia bosses who had just taken over a night club'.

Anxieties about clothes and general appearance do preoccupy many politicians. If they are photographed or filmed without their knowledge or against their wish they will go to inordinate lengths to make sure the offending pictures or footage are not printed or broadcast. For their part, in return for the access and facilities on which they rely, photographers and television crews do on the whole try to be as accommodating as they can, and to ensure the pictures they take are as fair and as favourable as possible. Of course, while ready and willing to be cooperative, they cannot ignore the unexpected gaffe, and the good-natured badinage of a photo call can evaporate within seconds if a well-planned event unwinds spectacularly and sensational or amusing pictures are there for the taking.

Sometimes, of course, because of time pressures, appointments are missed, undertakings are broken and then the recriminations begin. When a television crew got held up by London traffic and was seven minutes late arriving to film Sir Leon Brittan, one of Britain's two European Commissioners, he said he had no alternative but to cancel the interview. He was running late and had already started changing into his dress suit for Glyndebourne. It soon became evident he had no intention that evening of allowing himself to be filmed wearing a black bow tie. The cameraman offered to frame the interview in a head-and-shoulders shot so as not to reveal that Brittan was already wearing his dress trousers. When he refused, insisting that he could not afford the time, the cameraman left, but waited to get a departure shot. When Brittan finally emerged in his dress suit to get into his car it was obvious he was still troubled by the presence of the film crew. He held a bundle of newspapers up to his neck, covering his shirt so as to disguise the fact that he had not yet put his bow tie on. The resulting picture made him look infinitely more ridiculous than the absence of the tie would have. Shortly after his departure Brittan's press officer was on the telephone saying that the pictures must not be broadcast under any circumstances because the Commissioner had been made to look as though he was 'a villain on the Costa Del Sol slinking away'.

Luckily for Brittan there was no requirement for a departure shot of him that day and the footage was never transmitted. However, it might well have been used despite the protest from Brittan's office. In view of the complaint, the editor of the day would probably have had to take the decision. While the shot might not have fitted in, on its own, into a pacy news bulletin because of the need to explain Brittan's demeanour, a programme like *Newsnight* might well have had time to use the whole sequence and put it in context. Decisions of this nature can be difficult: televisions newsrooms have to be careful not to jeopardise future access while on the other hand not bowing to unjustified attempts to stop the transmission of legitimate news footage.

In similar circumstances other famous politicians would have had no hesitation in being filmed or interviewed wearing a dinner jacket and tie. Even so, few can match the ease and confidence of Michael Heseltine and his family when they have appeared before the cameras either at their

London home in Belgravia or in the splendour of their country mansion at Thenford, near Banbury. During the 1990 Conservative leadership contest there could hardly have been a greater contrast than that between the grandeur of Heseltine's properties and the much more modest home of John Major. Heseltine has maintained what can only be described as a robust relationship with the news media. He has always remained approachable and shown an understanding of the pressures under which journalists have to work; yet at the same time, like other forceful politicians, he succeeded in ensuring that most of the television and radio interviews which he gave were conducted strictly on the terms he dictated. Nevertheless, he did seem oblivious to the resonances of the image he created during the leadership election and the way it might have counted against him. Major's campaign team took care to play up the humble origins of the then Chancellor of the Exchequer and were not averse to making occasional snide remarks about Heseltine's wealth.

I was assigned by BBC television to report Heseltine's campaign. As he spent each weekend in Thenford I spent hours standing at the gates staring up the drive at the magnificence of his country house. We were not allowed to go any further. On one occasion I ventured inside uninvited and was promptly escorted back down the drive by a member of the local constabulary. The media pack were waiting at the gates enjoying the spectacle. I felt as if I had been caught with a couple of Heseltine's pheasants stuffed down my trousers.

Our photo opportunities had been few and far between. However, on the final Sunday of the campaign, a clear November day, Rupert Heseltine informed us that limited access would be granted to reporters, photographers and television crews on condition we stayed in the area designated. There would be no opportunity to ask his father any questions. Mrs Heseltine called the dogs to heel. Never before had I been in such opulent surroundings for a political photo call. As Heseltine walked with his family through the grounds the bright morning sun highlighted their fair hair, giving an almost magical feel to the pictures. Politicians and their advisers spend so much of their time thinking about the impression they are creating that it was refreshing to find the Heseltines only too happy to be themselves in front of the cameras. There was certainly nothing which appeared false or unnatural in their demeanour, which reinforced the impression I had formed that they were a strong and united family.

However, even those who do appear regularly before the cameras are known to be surprised and even shocked from time to time on seeing their own expressions or behaviour on television. Barbara Follett, who has acted as an image consultant for the Labour Party, and who has said in the past that advising MPs on their body language on television was her area of special expertise, was taken aback on seeing herself featured in news reports of the 1994 Labour conference. On the day that delegates voted to continue a quota system aimed at doubling the number of Labour women MPs, Mrs Follett, filmed in the middle of a group of women MPs who were sitting together in the front row, could be seen bobbing up and down in her seat as she joined in the ecstatic applause. As head of the Emily's List group, which raises funds for women Labour candidates, Mrs Follett had been campaigning actively at the conference for her cause. On meeting her two days later I said that the television pictures were so strong and emotive that I had used them all day; she had not realised, she said, until she saw herself in the news bulletins that evening that she had got so carried away. Her husband, the novelist Ken Follett, could not help smiling when I explained that the pictures were particularly powerful because the enthusiasm being shown by his wife was nearly on a par with the unrestrained excitement which accompanied the General Synod's vote for women priests.

Mrs Follett has given invaluable advice to many Labour MPs. Robin Cook, who regarded himself as her greatest challenge, was recommended to wear clothes in autumn colours. Once he began choosing 'browns and oysters' he was surprised at the number of people who came up saying how well he looked. Harriet Harman was another prominent member of the Labour front bench who, as the process came to be affectionately described, was successfully 'Folletted'. Being a member of the party's health team, Ms Harman was in pretty constant demand during 1990, and would sometimes arrive for her next television interview holding a plastic carrier bag. This contained an alternative top in case she changed her mind about the clothes she would wear. Mrs Follett had suggested she wore clean-cut power suits with padded shoulders instead of her favourite flowery and floppy dresses.

Broadcasters have a significant advantage over newspaper reporters when it comes to developing the kind of easy-going relationships in which discussion of everyday concerns likes clothes and appearance does not seem out of place. As part of our job we frequently have to stand or sit with ministers and backbenchers while waiting for television crews and studio technicians to adjust cameras and other equipment. In these situations polite small talk is essential, helping to put the interviewee at ease and giving the sound recordist a chance to set voice levels; but these conversations can also be an invaluable source of background information. They usually provide at least some clue as to the likely mood or reaction of the politician who is about to be interviewed.

Politicians who remain frosty or non-committal during a prolonged warm-up do present a dilemma. Rather than talk about the weather, I prefer to remind them of the need to look at me seriously when the listening shots are filmed. These pictures, which show the interviewee listening to the reporter's question, are needed for editing purposes; when included in a news report they usually precede the answer, but they are almost always filmed last of all, once the interview has been completed. By this stage in the proceedings most politicians are naturally more relaxed and ready for some light-hearted chat, and there is a real danger the listening shot might show them smiling or looking cheerful. As that can look decidedly out of place in an otherwise serious report, most ministers and MPs appreciate a reminder.

Another fruitful topic for discussion during these moments is a politician's preference for a possible set-up shot. The favourite when both interviewee and journalist are in a hurry is the much over-used walking shot, which has become the visual cliché of television news, with MPs regularly seen hurrying along outside the Palace of Westminster or climbing the stairs to the Millbank studios. Some kind of an establishing shot is often as essential as the doorstep footage of arrivals at and departures from meetings. Although newsrooms do have ample supplies of library pictures showing ministers opening their red boxes and perusing their documents, most interviews are conducted under considerable time constraints and producers often have no alternative but to fall back on firm favourites like asking an MP to look at the Commons order paper or perhaps to walk up to a bookshelf and pull down a book.

Polly Toynbee, the BBC's social affairs editor, who switched to broadcasting from newspapers, has come to the conclusion that the 'familiar old set-ups are a weary convention recognised by every viewer'. In an article for the *Radio Times* in February 1993 she described how on looking through archive footage of Sir William Beveridge she was surprised to discover that the only shots of him were precisely the same as those of today's politicians she was commissioning herself, fifty years later. She inquired rather plaintively: 'What else can you ask a serious person to do convincingly?'

By and large politicians are only too happy to cooperate in these well-established rituals. Some do remain self-conscious about their walking shots: instead of bustling along purposefully they persist in looking into the camera, which defeats the object of the exercise and tends to make them look furtive. A few MPs refuse point-blank, claiming they look ridiculous if made to walk along the pavement. I have always found that a useful guide to an MP's likely chances of withstanding the hard knocks of political life is the degree to which they can see the funny side of what they are required to do for television.

From his earliest days as a Cabinet minister John Major demonstrated an ability to engage in casual conversation with journalists and joke about his appearance. This may have been related to the fact that, unlike most party leaders, he had acquired professional experience in handling the media before entering politics. For two years in the late 1970s he was public relations manager for Standard Chartered Bank and established its first press office at the behest of the then chairman, Lord Barber. Interviewing Major at length for the first time in 1990, when he was Chancellor of the Exchequer, I was immediately struck by his friendly repartee. On this occasion he was in North Wales to address a Confederation of British Industry dinner; his speech was considered to be of some significance as he was due to outline the government's latest position on a single European currency. Time was pressing and we had to hurry our interview; once it was finished I was anxious to keep him seated for a few more minutes for the listening shots. I started talking and told him to remain serious and look at my lips. When the cameraman took the reverse two-shot, which meant I had to listen to Major saying something, he reminded me that this was the moment to 'look at the lips of the Chancellor'. Although unaccustomed to his levity I said we would spare him the walking shot, not least because I was sure that now he was Chancellor he was relieved of the indignity of having to traipse across College Green for the cameras. Much to my surprise Major had a ready response: 'Now, as a Cabinet minister, if one really wanted to rejoin one's family, one would really know one had arrived, if one was back on College Green doing those silly walks for the BBC.'

This was an extremely perceptive aside: Major had touched on what can be a raw nerve among ex-ministers. While holding government office they would have been able to command a studio for their interviews, not least on the grounds of security, because they could legitimately fear, if they were being filmed outside, that they might be a target for terrorists or find themselves upstaged or embarrassed by demonstrators such as motorway protestors or animal rights activists. Ministers are therefore usually given priority in studio bookings, and as a result backbench MPs are frequently relegated to College Green, where they might have to wait some time for their turn to be asked questions if the crews are particularly busy. The hidden nuances of this particular political pecking order had been brought home to me rather forcibly only a few weeks before my chat with Major in Wales. In an attempt to clinch an interview with Norman Tebbit, the former trade and industry secretary, who by then had returned to the back benches, I promised his personal secretary, Miss Beryl Goldsmith, that I would make sure a television crew was on College Green on the instant. Miss Goldsmith, a doyenne among MPs' secretaries, was decidedly withering in her reply: 'Mr Tebbit does not do interviews on the Green. He is not one of those rent-a-quote MPs who pops up outside the House of Commons with Big Ben sticking out from the top of his head. His interviews are done in studios.'

Despite his own bravado in North Wales, Major did suffer from one long-standing anxiety. Harsh studio lighting emphasised his five o'clock shadow. Interviews have had to be delayed to await the arrival of a make-up artist if there was no powder readily available to apply to his stubble. After seeing some deft touching up of what was then the Chancellor's chin at the 1990 IMF talks in Washington, a BBC news producer, Lucian Hudson, called in at a Body Shop before setting off for Rome where Major was attending his first European summit as Prime Minister. At the appropriate moment he handed over the powder, brush and mirror to Sarah Charman, a Downing Street press officer, who dusted over Major's chin. By the time it came to the 1992 general election the Prime Minister was making light of the process. In between several set-piece interviews about the Conservatives' manifesto he inquired about his make-up, asking at one point: 'I don't look like Yorick, do I?'

The late John Smith could be equally engaging. Although the least interested of any recent party leader in the art of self-advertisement he enjoyed journalistic banter and would make light of the tiresome technicalities of the television interview. Whenever I reminded him of the need to look serious for a moment he would have none of it, saying he had no intention of being hypnotised by a BBC correspondent. He was rarely flustered by the hitches and delays which seem so endemic in broadcasting. On the day a cameraman turned up at his home in Edinburgh without a reporter Smith commandeered his wife Elizabeth to ask the questions. Joking about this shortly before his death, he said he expected one day to find a robotic camera knocking at his front door. In fact, because of cost-cutting, one-man crews have become commonplace. If there is no reporter available the cameraman asks the question and simultaneously holds out his free hand, to which the interviewee is asked to direct his answer, imaging that he is speaking to Sooty, or some other appropriate puppet. Concentrating on the cameraman's hand enables the subject to avoid staring straight at the camera, thereby ensuring a more natural eye-line. I am confident Smith would have taken such instructions in his stride.

Smith had short arms and a rather rolling gait, and while he came across as friendly and approachable when walking into shot, it was suggested that he did not always appear as authoritative as he might and that he should insist on being filmed in more formal poses. After one party meeting he was interviewed sitting in a deep armchair: this was considered too casual as the chair's high back had the effect of accentuating his short, stocky build with distracting effect. As a consequence, many interviews were filmed across a polished table, either in the leader's office or in the shadow Cabinet room, a setting which suited his serious demeanour and purposeful way of speaking. Mrs Smith and their three daughters were also a strong restraining influence and cautioned him against taking part in any potentially demeaning publicity stunts. Their good taste could not be faulted, as they demonstrated on the day he was elected Labour Party leader when, in a restrained family photo call, they all strolled together across the footbridge in St James's Park.

Party officials would frequently make a fuss about interviewing arrangements, insisting that reporters and camera crews should wait in Smith's office rather than stop him in and around Westminster. They feared he could looked startled and a touch goggle-eyed if pounced on suddenly and then dazzled by the lights of a television crew. However, Smith himself was easily bored by the whole business of media management. He told senior colleagues quite regularly that he thought the value of personal publicity was highly overrated, and he had not felt it necessary to appoint his own separate press officer, relying instead on the party's director of communications David Hill. His laid-back approach won him many plaudits, not only in the party but also among professionals in the communications industry who studied political promotion. Winston Fletcher, an advertising executive, had praised Smith, some months before his death, for being one of the few politicians in history to show 'an impressive disregard for fame and publicity'.

Not everyone, however, approved of the new leader's approach. Among some Labour MPs there was criticism of Smith for not continuing the high-profile campaigning which had been such a feature of Neil Kinnock's tenure. Nevertheless, there was a widespread welcome for what was seen as a new era in the party's relationship with the media. Kinnock was considered to have been far too sensitive about the coverage he had received. Although sickened by the wounding tone which some newspapers adopted towards him, many in the party had grown weary of the permanent antagonism which seemed to characterise Kinnock's relationship with so much of the press. Certainly few contemporary politicians have had to endure anything like the sustained savaging which was inflicted on him during his eight and a half years as leader of the opposition. In important ways this campaign of hostility was counterproductive: Kinnock himself developed an unparalleled degree of resilience to the smears and ridicule to which he was subjected, and political correspondents paid a heavy price for the activities of the Get-Kinnock Tendency among journalists on right-wing newspapers. Access to the Labour leader had become so carefully controlled by the run-up to the 1992 general election that he had almost ceased to engage in the informal question-and-answer sessions which journalists so appreciate with opposition politicians. After years of mounting distrust his advisers had concluded that the potential dangers were too great when so much of the press corps was intent on searching for material to support a well-rehearsed but predetermined story-line that Kinnock was ill-equipped to become Prime Minister. A more controlled and structured approach, they felt, would reduce the danger of the party leader being misquoted or lured into providing material that could be used to his detriment.

The increasing formality of Kinnock's contacts with the news media was the more striking in its contrast with his former practice. Journalists remembered with affection the matiness of the sessions that took place late each Thursday afternoon, when they would assemble in the shadow Cabinet room. At the appointed hour Kinnock would breeze in. Out would come his pipe and tobacco. First, a little pipe-cleaning; sometimes quite a heap of blackened, sticky matches would pile up in the ashtray. Perhaps his political mentors in South Wales had performed identical rituals. Soon blue smoke would be twirling its way to the ceiling. By now Kinnock was in full flow, engaging and amusing. It was a moment to be savoured: the union banners hanging on the wood-panelled walls, the Welsh accent and the fragrance of the pipe smoke conjured up a rich political history.

These weekly briefings for political correspondents, which opposition leaders had maintained for most of the post-war years, were ended abruptly by Kinnock without any real explanation or apology. In his first break with the established tradition of these gatherings, Kinnock insisted that future briefings must be held on his terms: at his invitation and 'on the record'. Party strategists knew that the slightest slip could be magnified out of all proportion. However, this precautionary move failed to take account of a hidden peril for politicians: the pocket tape recorder. Also, the hostile elements in the press simply adjusted their approach. Some newspapers had already intensified their quest for Kinnock contradictions; now, instead of indulging the Labour leader and allowing him to range freely in his observations, their journalists used the briefings to launch into detailed and well-prepared questioning, especially on the economy and taxation.

One such probe appeared to have been prearranged. Out of the journalists' jacket pockets came their miniature tape recorders which were slid deftly on to the shadow Cabinet table. The tiny, tell-tale red lights which indicated that the tapes were recording served as a signal to the rest of the lobby correspondents that their colleagues' objective was to gather direct quotations. A deepening frown on the face of Peter Mandelson said it all: there was no way Labour's communications director was going to allow Kinnock to fall foul of another ambush like that.

Kinnock's forced retreat provided an ideal opportunity for Paddy Ashdown. Media advisers for the Liberal Democrats needed little encouragement before invading any territory which Labour dared vacate, and within no time at all Ashdown was holding his own weekly briefings for political correspondents, promising that he would always permit the kind of no-holds-barred sessions which the other party leaders were too frightened to allow. Ashdown's effectiveness in garnering publicity had been a crucial factor in the Liberal Democrats' climb back from opinion poll ratings of only three and four per cent during the turmoil which followed the break-up of the SDP–Liberal Alliance. His party could not have had a more willing or able student for the tough assault course which faces newly appointed political leaders. As might be expected of a former commander of a marine commando company, he was deadly serious in his early media training. His determination to master the art of presentation was evident from the day he stood for the party leadership; and he learned quickly from his mistakes, knowing he might not get a second chance.

At his first news conference in the summer of 1988 Ashdown read out a lengthy opening statement. His prepared text did not appear to contain a short, clear summary of his position. As there was a tight deadline I interrupted him the moment he had finished and asked why he wanted to stand for the leadership. He looked pained and said that was exactly what he had spent the last five minutes explaining. I realised I had to be blunt. Thrusting my microphone even further towards his face I said I needed a short answer for use on radio. Newspaper reporters get annoyed when broadcasters push in like this to ask simplistic questions, so the difficulty I was encountering caused some amusement. To his credit Ashdown laughed engagingly at himself, but recovered within an instant and delivered a crisp, polished response. I never saw him caught un-awares again by television or radio journalists. Nor did he need another reminder at news conferences that quick-fire questions from broad-casters require punchy answers.

Soon he was thoroughly relishing getting immersed in the tiniest detail of media presentation. One news conference in his newly opened briefing room was delayed for a few moments while he discussed with the television crews the precise positioning of the party's logo. He wanted to know whether it could be seen clearly in the background. The cameramen were only too happy to oblige. Once a trial shot was lined up and recorded Ashdown was invited to view an instant replay. He accepted with alacrity, stepping smartly behind the camera position. To the evident despair of his staff he could soon be heard agreeing with the camera crews that the grey backing of the logo would have to be lengthened.

Ashdown's opportunistic approach paid off: he quickly acquired the reputation of being the most media-friendly of the three main party leaders. If a shadow Cabinet minister could not be provided for a studio discussion, television producers would frequently check out the avail-ability of the Liberal Democrat leader rather than accept a junior member of Labour's front-bench team. As the 1992 election approached he even went so far as to congratulate the media for having been fair in their coverage of his party. He described how acquaintances were expressing surprise that he was never off their television screens. Within weeks Ashdown was to face his sternest test as party leader: after a shaky start he carried off a shrewd exercise in damage limitation.

On discovering that the *News of the World* was about to disclose details of his affair with a former secretary, Ashdown's solicitors secured an injunction to prevent it being publicised by newspapers and broadcasting organisations. Five days later, as rumours about his involvement in a sex scandal continued to sweep Westminster, he took the bold but risky step of confronting the media head-on. The order to prevent publication was obtained from the High Court because a document stolen from the safe of his solicitors had been offered for sale to the newspapers. The *Scotsman* had already reported how Ashdown had taken legal action to 'gag the press', and he was anxious to explain why he intended lifting the injunction. At a crowded news conference he made a short and dignified personal statement: 'It is clear to me that in this pre-election atmosphere, I, my family, my friends and party colleagues, will not be left alone. . .It is my view that this brief relationship of five years ago is, and always should have remained, a private and personal matter of concern only to those involved.'

Ashdown had done what so few politicians seem capable of. He had been prepared to go through the public humiliation of making a personal statement. He had owned up to an extra-marital relationship in front of journalists, photographers and television crews. This openness had its reward. Press coverage next day was far more sympathetic than might have been expected. Senior Conservative and Labour politicians joined Liberal Democrat MPs in agreeing that his disclosures were of no political significance and should not be exploited during the general election.

Five weeks later, when the election campaign started, there was no mention of Ashdown's private life at the Liberal Democrats' opening news conference. His wife Jane sat five rows back from the platform. To start with she looked pensive, holding her index finger to her chin. Straining against the glare of the television lights Ashdown looked for her and they exchanged a smile. Once his interviews had been completed, Ashdown stared intently at the shiny steel framework which had been erected around the platform. 'This contraption is supposed to make our set look modern and urgent. What do you think? Does it look cluttered? I won't know for sure until I see what it looks like on television.' Alongside him, smiling, was the party's senior media officer, Olly Grender. The previous month Ms Grender had kept a cool head on finding herself in the middle of a media circus waiting impatiently to hear Ashdown's admission that he had had an affair with his secretary. Now, hearing him fussing away about the presentational apparatus, she knew he was back on form, concentrated on fighting the election.

By striding so purposefully around Westminster, on his way from one interview to the next, Ashdown encouraged the media's use of military metaphors. He rarely showed even a flicker of uncertainty when passing the massed ranks of television crews and photographers, nor was he thrown by unexpected questions shouted at him in the street. Once he had decided not to stop he appeared to walk even faster, looking straight ahead and taking ever larger strides as he disappeared into the distance. Politicians have to retain their composure in such circumstances. Once they falter or look worried in their walking shots they invite broadcasters to write to the pictures, and if they are facing any uncertainties or difficulties they can, however unwittingly, supply visual confirmation of their predicament.

Labour's 1994 leadership election, and their new leader's first few months in office, provided some telling illustrations of the potential hazards of being caught unawares. While appearing composed and engaging in well-rehearsed interviews and at high-profile news conferences, Tony Blair experienced some awkward and uncomfortable moments during his campaign. He seemed most at risk during his televised arrivals and departures, which admittedly are some of the toughest obstacles for those with less experience of the limelight. Lacking Ashdown's military discipline, and not having acquired the steely but suave shell which party leaders must develop for moments like this, he looked startled and almost nervous on some occasions, and did appear slightly intimidated when having to push his way through a doorstep crush.

Shortly before the leadership election got under way Blair had to attend a meeting of Labour's national executive committee to discuss the timetable for the contest. On the pavement outside the party headquarters there was a sizeable crowd of reporters, photographers and cameramen. Blair arrived together with Neil Kinnock, whose technique if he did not want to be questioned was to approach the assembled media throng at a run, as though preparing for a rugby tackle, and barge his way through. As Kinnock gathered speed ready to mount the steps to the front door, Blair wisely tucked in behind and the two of them hurried in together. On departure, however, Blair was on his own. As the leadership candidates had been told to refrain from campaigning until after the local council and European elections, he ignored questions from waiting reporters: but instead of smiling and dismissing us all with a throwaway line he pursed his lips and tried to walk away. In doing so he appeared annoyed and agitated, which made the film crews all the more determined to follow his progress along the pavement. At one point he stopped completely and just glared.

Luckily for Blair the departure shots were not required. If they had been broadcast they might have given further inspiration to the cartoonists, who could then have added a startled look to their Bambi-like caricatures which had already begun appearing in newspapers and magazines. When asked at the Eastleigh by-election a few days later how he felt on being portrayed as a Disney lookalike, Blair could not have been more dismissive. Without acknowledging what had been asked, he simply said: 'Next question.'

A week later Blair provided further footage which, had it been transmitted, might have provoked ridicule and cracked his image as a supercool television performer. On the first of the one-day strikes by signal staff which led to a summer of disruption on the railways, reporters and crews from BBC, ITN and Sky were waiting on the doorstep of the Millbank studios seeking the reaction of passing politicians. Blair was known to be inside the building. Labour appeared vulnerable over their approach to the dispute and therefore the first day of strike action was seen as the moment to test the position of each of the leadership candidates. Apparently all three contenders, Blair, John Prescott and Margaret Beckett, had been advised by the party's media staff to avoid getting drawn into commenting and instead to leave official comment to Labour's transport spokesman, Frank Dobson.

Blair must have got wind of the fact that television crews were waiting for him at the Millbank front entrance because he left by a rear door. He was nevertheless spotted by reporters and though he hurried away down Great Peter Street he was quickly pursued, ITN's political correspondent Hugh Pym leading the chase and cornering the quarry after a few hundred yards. Although flustered and rather breathless, Blair had the presence of mind to demand that the filming should stop. Needless to say the cameras kept rolling. When television crews are outside in what is after all a public thoroughfare and find they are caught up in a potentially significant confrontation, they fall back on their news judgement and are hardly likely to stop filming. They know that careful consideration will be given after the event as to whether or not the pictures should be used.

In the event footage of Blair's contretemps with the television crews was not broadcast. Untransmitted film of the encounter shows him explaining that Dobson is speaking for Labour on the rail dispute. Pym insists that Blair's views as prospective party leader are important. Sky's reporter asks him why he is running away. On his saying that he would like to check up to see if the other candidates are commenting on the strike, a cameraman offers him the use of a mobile phone. At this point Blair says he will go away and consult. He was observed some minutes later conversing with Dobson, who happened to be nearby on College

Green. After some delay, and further conversations with colleagues which took place off camera round the corner, Blair returned to recite what would become his standard answer: 'I do not think it helpful for the government or anyone else to intervene in the dispute. It should be left to the unions and management to resolve in the normal way.' Although he had declined, as might have been expected, to express a view on the strike itself he had supplied an answer.

Accounts vary as to what took place when Blair retreated to seek advice. Among those alerted to the Great Peter Street confrontation was the party's former communications director Peter Mandelson, who, after being elected MP for Hartlepool in the 1992 election, had become one of Blair's closest advisers. Mandelson was aghast on hearing that Blair was being 'chased around Westminster' and feared that his refusal to reply might develop into a far more damaging story than anything he could conceivably say about the signal workers' claim. From his experience in handling similar disagreements he knew that if lanced straight away with a diplomatic answer the whole kerfuffle would in all probability die down as quickly as it had started. He therefore said Blair should immediately 'stand and deliver' and give his reaction.

Dobson was puzzled as to why there had been any confusion at all. He had supplied the three campaign teams with a detailed brief on the dispute well before the first one-day strike. Therefore he could not understand why Blair had not replied the instant he was challenged. Dobson was more concerned about the competence of those advising Blair. As far as he was concerned it was obvious from the moment the campaign started that Blair should have been travelling around Westminster by car so as to lessen the chances of him being pursued and challenged unexpectedly by reporters.

Subsequently, more care was taken. Members of his campaign team checked to see if reporters were waiting before Blair emerged into the open, and would often try to get an idea in advance of what was likely to be raised. Sometimes they would make it plain that on a particular issue Blair would not answer, even if asked. Occasionally campaign workers would offer to do a deal, promising additional opportunities for pictures in return for an assurance that Blair would not be delayed by questioning. 'Controlled doorsteps', as they have come to be known, are not uncommon. A degree of cooperation can be advantageous to both sides. If the greatest need is for pictures then the reporters might back off and leave it to the television crews and photographers. Alternatively, an agreement might be reached on the form or length of any questioning which allows replies to be given in an orderly fashion without hesitation or interruption.

After his election as party leader by an overwhelming majority at a special conference in July, Blair made doubly sure that the lessons learned during the campaign were not forgotten. He needed no reminding of the way favourable coverage for his predecessors had turned all too rapidly to negative reporting, or of the rigorous self-discipline needed in the face of the requests for statements and interviews with which party leaders get inundated. A casual, off-the-cuff answer or an ill-considered photo call can be regretted within an instant. Accordingly, on returning from his summer holiday Blair proceeded with great caution when confronting the media. When about to be filmed greeting a union delegation representing Swan Hunter shipbuilding workers, he reminded the film crews personally that it was only a photo opportunity; if asked a question he would not answer it. He was well aware that once he agreed to say something, the reporters would not be satisfied with a simple expression of support for the unions but would want to raise more detailed points on Labour's defence and industrial policies. Rather than get involved himself, he said that Labour's defence spokesman, then Dr David Clark, who was at the photo call, would be available for interviews.

It soon became apparent that Blair was still feeling his way. While he would go to great lengths to avoid being hustled into premature comment on events, he did not shrink from taking centre stage once he judged it appropriate and felt he was sufficiently well briefed to be able to handle potentially difficult questions. On the day the IRA announced a complete cessation of violence Blair waited for over four hours before commenting. Several opportunities for Labour to put their case on television and radio were thereby missed, but he was anxious for the confusion over possible clarification from Sinn Fein to be resolved before the party made any response. Blair had also begun work on a new policy statement, which, in taking account of the Downing Street declaration, would balance Labour's long-standing commitment to a united Ireland with the need to ensure that any constitutional settlement had the 'consent of a majority of the people of Northern Ireland'.

Before it emerged that Blair intended making Labour's response himself, the party's Northern Ireland spokesman at the time, Kevin McNamara, had been lined up to give his reaction to the ceasefire. Within half an hour of the IRA's 11 a.m. statement he was sitting in a studio in Hull ready to contribute to either the BBC's live coverage or the *One o'Clock News*. However, he was told by Blair's office to wait. As the time ticked by he went out and bought a book to read. McNamara, who had been criticised by some sections of the party for favouring Irish unity at the expense of the Unionists, later denied suggestions that he was annoyed at having been ordered to hold off from commenting until mid-afternoon. 'If Mr Blair wanted to speak about the IRA announcement then obviously as party spokesman I had to wait. He had to react first and it was entirely right that he did so.' Nevertheless this was an early pointer to the firm grip which Blair intended to exercise when controlling Labour's reaction to controversial issues.

The newly elected deputy leader John Prescott was similarly asked to stand aside on the day Blair announced that he favoured arbitration in the protracted and increasingly bitter signal workers' dispute. Prescott had promised to make an early morning appearance on the *Today* radio programme and was expecting to be asked questions about the continuing strike action. At the last moment he was told by the leader's office to withdraw because Blair intended to give interviews himself that lunchtime before leaving London for the TUC conference in Blackpool. Prescott was annoyed by the sudden change of plan and the unspoken implication that he could not be trusted, that he might have said something out of place and thus embarrassed Blair. In fact the reason his interview was cancelled was because Blair's advisers were determined that nothing should be done to lessen the impact of what would be a carefully stage-managed announcement.

Some trade unionists were critical of Blair for being less than enthusiastic in his backing for the signal workers. Because of this he was having to prepare for a potentially difficult encounter with political and labour correspondents who were waiting for him at the TUC conference. In order to avoid the possibility of a hostile doorstep confrontation, and so as to get maximum coverage for his request that the rail union should accept arbitration, Blair did live interviews for the *One o'Clock News* and *The World at One*. Labour's communications director David Hill said they were convinced a lunchtime announcement in London had the strongest chance of leading off news reports on the dispute. The tactic worked. As they had succeeded in dictating the agenda Blair was in a far stronger position on his arrival in Blackpool and was able to expand on what was already a running story.

For his arrival at Preston, Hill arranged for television crews to film Blair stepping off the train and walking down the platform. He was then held back to give the crews and photographers time to get outside the station ready to take more pictures as Blair got into the car which would take him to Blackpool. The doorstep photo call and interview in the foyer of the Pembroke Hotel was the largest Blair had faced since becoming leader. It could not have gone better. News of his blunt advice to the signal workers had caused a stir but, just as Blair's advisers had planned, they knew in advance that most of the questions to the Labour leader would be on an issue about which he felt strongly and on which he was well prepared. Blair arrived looking confident and relaxed, and fielded reporters' questions with ease. A messy confrontation in which the

Labour leader might have appeared on the defensive had been avoided.

Less carefully staged encounters, however, still revealed potential weaknesses. Later that evening, on leaving the TUC general council's annual dinner, Blair was challenged unexpectedly and asked more questions. As on some previous occasions, he looked uneasy as he walked away ignoring the reporters. Hill, conscious of the need to stop Blair being shown on television avoiding questions, took the precaution of trying to prevent a similar situation developing at a special meeting of Labour's national executive committee shortly before the party conference. He promised television crews that they would get ample opportunity to film departure shots of Blair on condition he had an assurance from myself and two political editors, Elinor Goodman of Channel Four News and Adam Boulton of Sky, that we would not ask questions. Reluctantly we acceded to his request because Hill insisted Blair would not stop for us under any circumstances.

Blair's ability to master the custom and skills of arrivals and departures was proving erratic to say the least, and it was not until the week of the Labour party conference, when he was finally joined by his new personal press officer Alastair Campbell, that he began to take them in his stride. Campbell had built up a reputation as a tough and ruthless journalist who enjoyed nothing more than aggressive doorstep questioning. He was no stranger to the behind-the-scenes arm-twisting which is an everyday aspect of the fraught relationship between politicians and the media, and was therefore the perfect foil for Blair. As he escorted the Labour leader from studio to studio for the inevitable round of conference interviews, Campbell soon became known as a no-nonsense minder, permitting no interruptions. He made it abundantly clear that he would exercise total control over casual encounters between journalists and Blair.

The events of the summer had underlined the need for Blair to remain aware and on guard whenever he was confronted by a television camera, whether or not he intended to say anything. Even greater vigilance is required by Prime Ministers. Downing Street press officers have credited Mrs Thatcher with perhaps the sharpest turn of heel of all in recent years. They say she could get out of her car, acknowledge reporters but avoid their questions, and walk into No. 10 within an instant, yet appear unhurried and in total control throughout the process.

Margaret Thatcher had not only a commanding presence but also a capacity to think ahead as to what the pictures might look like. My suspicion that she could perform for the camera and almost simultaneously look into the viewfinder as well was first confirmed when waiting for her to comment on the Clapham rail disaster of December 1988. Reporters and television crews were assembled in a room containing the No. 10 Christmas tree. We were told that first of all officers of the Grantham Rotary

Club intended making a presentation to the Prime Minister. She would speak to us about the rail crash afterwards. Mrs Thatcher posed with the Rotarians in front of the tree while the official photograph was taken. Once the ceremony had finished she turned towards the television cameras and microphones, and as she did so she began walking away from the tree towards a fireplace on the other side of the room, saying it would be inappropriate at a time of grief to be filmed in a seasonal setting. She seemed to know instinctively that a neutral backing would be more in keeping with the sombre statement she was about to make. We had been caught by surprise at her sudden change of position; she had begun moving across the room before a press officer could possibly have intervened or prompted her to get away from the tree.

Her knack of being able to visualise the effect she might be creating stood her in good stead at times of crisis. In her memoirs, *The Downing Street Years*, Lady Thatcher described how she maintained a 'mask of composure' while she sat on the front bench listening to the resignation speech by Sir Geoffrey Howe which triggered her downfall. Her emotions were in turmoil but she realised that she herself was as much the focus of attention as was Sir Geoffrey. The proceedings were being televised, and up above her were the reporters in the press gallery. When interviewed for the television series which accompanied publication of her memoirs, Lady Thatcher described that fateful moment: 'I knew the press were watching me. I had to keep my face calm.'

That self-control, and her recognition of the power of television, were reinforced by a formidable publicity machine. In her years as Prime Minister, Whitehall's information services and the Conservatives' promotional activities were coordinated in a way which has since eluded John Major. The circumstances which allowed Lady Thatcher to enjoy what for some of her time in office was also a largely compliant news media seem unlikely to be repeated.

4

Sources Close To . . .

REPORTERS ARE proud of and highly secretive about their sources. Even between friends it is regarded as taboo for one journalist to pry too deeply into the identity and precise standing of another's contacts and informants. Journalists gain respect not simply by coming up with exclusives but also by a hard-won reputation for accuracy and reliability. Among any group of reporters who compete with each other there can be no finer tribute than a grudging recognition of the fact that one's own news stories are no longer considered as dependable as they used to be because a rival has superior sources. Nowhere does this accolade apply with greater force than in the competitive arena of political journalism, amid the swirling and often misleading sources of Whitehall and Westminster.

While political reporters, like all other journalists, want to guard and protect those from whom they obtain information, they are finding that readers, viewers and listeners have grown more demanding. The public do not appear as ready as they once were to take unattributed news stories at face value. In the lexicon of political journalism the word 'source' is the most debased term of all. It has become devalued largely because it is so over-used and abused. In an attempt to reinforce the authenticity of their everyday reporting, journalists have fallen back on an ever-lengthening list of unnamed sources, be they in Whitehall, Westminster or Downing Street, perhaps deep inside a government department or even within a faction of a party or pressure group.

The steady growth in the output of political reporting on television and radio has probably done more than anything else to undermine the credibility of many unattributed news stories. Unlike the newspaper political editors of old, who needed do no more than tell their readers that their information was based on 'informed sources', the broadcasters of today face a far more sceptical and critical audience. Increasingly viewers and listeners expect to see or hear some form of verification. If documentary evidence is not available, and the origin of the material cannot be identified, then programme editors and producers feel duty bound to insist on including interviews with supporting witnesses so as to lend weight to what is otherwise the word of just one journalist. Newspaper reporters, too, being able to write at greater length, can also skate around inconsistencies in a way which is not always possible in the all-seeing, all-hearing world of the television camera and radio microphone.

The very speed at which the electronic media have to operate imposes a discipline of its own which does not impinge in quite the same way on a newspaper delivered next morning. If television or radio journalists go too hard in playing up a political event, or try to turn outlandish claims into facts, they can be rebuked and corrected within an instant. So great is the requirement for reliability and accuracy that a news bulletin can be forced to broadcast a correction while still on air. This pressure has only added to the over-usage of 'sources'. In order to avoid being questioned or challenged, television and radio journalists often feel obliged to strengthen their reports by attributing what is probably self-evident information to a wide variety of seemingly authoritative but still undisclosed sources.

To be fair to newspaper correspondents, they too have been pushed inexorably towards pinning more of their work on to unnamed and often unspecified sources. Because of the shift away from reporting political speeches and debates, many more background and speculative stories are being written and published. In order to keep up their flow of news copy, reporters have had to make increasing use of material gathered from informants who are not prepared to be identified. Therefore press coverage of politics also tends to be peppered increasingly with references to this or that source.

The demand for greater transparency in political journalism has been mirrored by a desire for more open government. And as the machinery of public administration is exposed to higher levels of scrutiny, so too are the news media. Attempts have been made for some years to tighten up on the procedures for handling complaints about inaccurate reporting in both broadcasting and the press. Against the background of this pressure for change those who rely on the use of unidentified sources, and who wish to go on protecting them, are finding themselves increasingly on the defensive.

The system, however, will not crumble overnight: it is deeply rooted and has always been of great value to both politicians and journalists. Ministers have found that a well-placed story attributed in the loosest possible way to 'government sources' can serve a wide variety of purposes. A department can by this means float a new policy idea, test out reaction and then, if the response is unfavourable, bury the whole thing without too much trouble. When intentions are more definite a little advance publicity, inspired by a judicious leak, can sometimes do wonders in helping to defuse the shock of a forthcoming but controversial announcement. And on a more personal level, 'well-placed ministerial sources' can also do a great deal to enhance ministers' reputations.

The attractions of engaging in a touch of deft media manipulation are all too plain and for that reason remain highly addictive. James Hacker, Minister for Administrative Affairs, gave a telling illustration in the BBC comedy series *Yes Minister* of the subtleties of sourcing. In a conversation in Annie's Bar at Westminster, where MPs can drink with journalists, Hacker protests at the suggestion that a story he is leaking should be attributed to 'sources close to the minister'.

Hacker: Hey, steady on! I don't want everybody to know I told you. Can't you just say 'speculation is growing in Westminster?'
Journalist: That's a bit weak.
Hacker: Unofficial spokesman?
Journalist: I've used that twice this week already.
Hacker: Cabinet's leaking like a sieve isn't it?
Journalist: Yes. Could we attribute it to a leading member of the sieve . . . er . . . Cabinet?
Hacker: No.
Journalist: Well, how would you like to be an informed source?
Hacker: OK . . .informed source.

Most journalists will go to every conceivable length to disguise and protect their sources, so great is their gratitude for the leaks and tip-offs which might come their way. Where reporters find they come unstuck is in trying to meet the demand of their editors for a never-ending supply of exclusive stories. What might be no more than a correspondent's hunch can be given a definite touch of respectability with a liberal helping of unidentified and perhaps non-existent sources. The unsourced political 'exclusive' is becoming a daily event in tabloid journalism. Broadcasters can also end up sounding as if they are competing with each other solely on the basis of which correspondent has the most sources. At times they seem almost compelled to imply that their contacts are better than those of their colleagues or competitors. In reality they might well be giving an elevated importance to guidance which was generally available and which, if they so desired, could be sourced with greater precision.

Perhaps the greatest damage to the standing of the ubiquitous and anonymous political 'source' results from the way its use has become so institutionalised. In many cases the term is to all intents and purposes a meaningless and confusing appendage. With care it is possible to get quite close to identifying the origin of much of the information which is supplied to political correspondents, and this can be done in a way which enlightens the public. Nevertheless, however hard some reporters might try, the practice of referring to specific but unnamed informants cannot be dispensed with completely. The rules which forbid the naming of sources are still extremely tight. There has been one concerted attempt to reform the whole procedure, and some changes were indeed made; but these were largely cosmetic, and the system under which journalists accept unattributable facts and guidance from the government of the day, and also from the rest of the political establishment, remains firmly entrenched.

When the House of Commons is sitting, lobby journalists meet the Prime Minister's press secretary twice a day, at 11 a.m. in Downing Street and then again at 4 p.m., in the private lobby room in the House, which is tucked away up several flights of stairs and looks down on the Thames. The fact that meetings have been held must be kept secret and the cardinal rule of all collective lobby briefings is that the information which was divulged is unattributable. The guiding principle of the journalists who participate, as set out in the Notes on the Practice of Lobby Journalism, is a mutual obligation to 'exercise self-discipline to ensure that the system works satisfactorily for all concerned'.

In recent years the greatest defender of the status quo has been Bernard Ingham. Chief press secretary to Margaret Thatcher for all but the first few months of her eleven and a half years in office, he spent longer in the post than any of his predecessors and was sorely troubled by some members of the lobby, or to give them their full title, the parliamentary lobby journalists. At the time of Mrs Thatcher's resignation and Ingham's departure in November 1990, the political correspondents of three newspapers, the *Independent*, the *Guardian* and the *Scotsman*, were still refusing to attend his briefings. They returned shortly after John Major's newly installed press secretary Gus O'Donnell agreed to allow his guidance to be attributed to 'Downing Street sources' rather than the far vaguer 'government sources' which Ingham had always stipulated.

Ingham had to deal with what in effect was a rebellion, which he dubbed the 'Great Lobby Revolt'. It was led by Anthony Bevins, then political editor of the *Independent*. A month before its launch in October 1986, the *Independent* had announced that once its political journalists started reporting at Westminster they would be staying away from organised lobby briefings as part of the paper's attempt to force a change of practice. Political journalists on the *Guardian* gave their support and stayed away after being instructed by their editor to source the guidance they were given to 'a Downing Street spokesman' or 'Mrs Thatcher's spokesman'. Ingham refused to accept such diktats and proved a doughty champion of the lobby system, marshalling a strong case for retaining unattributable briefings. He believed they facilitated the flow of news to the media while preserving the primacy of parliament as the channel for the communication of information by government to the nation.

After a lengthy re-examination of their own rules, in 1986 lobby journalists decided by 67 votes to 55 to retain the practice of non-attribution unless informants were willing to be identified. However, it was agreed that briefings could be given on the record if this was mutually acceptable; occasionally ministers ask to meet the lobby, and have been known to allow themselves to be quoted directly. But except for this one small breach Ingham routed his opponents. He considered that in a free society journalists should use their own judgement when deciding whether to accept or reject the information imparted to them. Although there might be instances when official statements could be issued in the name of Downing Street, Ingham was adamant that he should continue to be described as a 'government source'.

In his autobiography *Kill the Messenger*, he outlined the reasons for his categoric refusal to allow the origin of his guidance to be narrowed down to a 'Downing Street source': 'That would have opened the way to direct attribution which, in turn, would have led to the broadcasters pressing, with some justice, for rights to record briefings if not to broadcast them live.' Ingham had been forced to acknowledge that the broadcasters had a case which was at least worthy of consideration. For years they had looked with envy at the access provided to journalists in the United States, where daily news briefings at the White House were not only on the record but also on camera. The President's press spokesman appeared regularly on television and radio and the American public had long regarded a free flow of information as an essential safeguard of their system.

However, there was one significant factor which was to work in Ingham's favour. By and large it is the political correspondents of the newspapers who have always been the strongest supporters of unattributable lobby briefings. Guidance which is off the record suits the press because it allows for a wider interpretation of the facts than is either possible or desirable in the tighter confines of broadcast journalism. Ingham was a newspaper journalist for almost twenty years before joining the government information service. He started as a reporter on the *Hebden Bridge Times* at the age of sixteen and worked for the *Yorkshire Post* before joining the labour staff of the *Guardian*; and despite repeated protestations of impartiality he remained a newspaper man at heart. Indeed, in *Kill the Messenger* he gave a hint of where his sympathies lay in the long-standing rivalry between press and broadcasters. He recognised that television and radio had 'a vested interest' in getting the No.10 spokesman 'on camera and on air' but was delighted by the defeat of those who had wanted to 'Americanize the lobby'.

This is not, of course, to say that his affection for his former trade blunted his opinions of some of its contemporary practitioners. Ingham's first task on arriving at Downing Street each morning was to prepare a press summary for the Prime Minister. He would work his way through the newspapers, starting, as he once told me, with: 'Why, the pops of course. They get my blood going.' He did, however, have many loyal friends in the lobby who admired his acute news sense. Gordon Leak, for thirty years a lobby journalist on the *News of the World* and then the *Sunday Express*, recalled how late one Saturday night he was desperate to get information after an attempted break-in at No. 10. 'Within half an hour of that event taking place I was able to ring Bernard at home and he had every fact. He told me precisely which drainpipe at No. 10 the intruder had tried to get in through and exactly how far he'd got along the roof in yards, feet and inches. Here was an old reporter at work, and he knew what information journalists wanted in that kind of situation.'

During the turbulent Thatcher years Ingham's great value to the lobby was his ability to reflect with such accuracy the Prime Minister's gut reaction on the big issues of the day. Even if he had not had a chance to discuss a particular development with her, he could, with considerable certainty, assess both the mood she was in and her likely response. On returning to political reporting in 1988 I soon experienced the full force of an Ingham briefing. Violent behaviour among football supporters was causing concern at the time. When asked what had transpired at a meeting with the football authorities Ingham said the Prime Minister had lost her patience with them. Therefore, he said, ministers intended to go ahead and impose a national identity scheme for spectators. This was the first that lobby journalists had heard of the decision. There was no need to check any further. Ingham could not have been more emphatic. He looked and sounded as apoplectic about the inaction of the football clubs as the Prime Minister must obviously have been herself.

Another feature of Ingham's briefings was the evident pleasure he obtained from putting journalists in their place. He relished any chance to remind the news media of their responsibilities. In March 1988, following the seizure of BBC film of two soldiers being dragged from their car at an IRA funeral, I asked Ingham if he would remind the lobby of the full extent of government legal action against journalists. He paused for effect and then said coldly that it was time that BBC reporters like myself decided whether we were 'part of society or apart from society'. When at a subsequent briefing I tried repeatedly to ask about the government's classification procedure for secret documents he displayed his aptitude for isolating maverick questioners. As I patiently rephrased my inquiry Ingham put on a show of mock surprise. At an appropriate moment he looked solemnly at the assembled journalists, saying: 'This laddie thinks he's got an exclusive.' There were cackles all round. Having diverted attention he moved swiftly to the next question.

Ingham was in his element when rubbishing exclusive news stories which he considered were inaccurate. He would happily allow Downing Street to be quoted as the source of his much-repeated, on-the-record denial of 'bunkum and balderdash'. In full flood, lambasting journalists, the press secretary was a sight to behold. As Mrs Thatcher became increasingly beset by the Conservatives' split over Europe, and her disagreements with her then Chancellor, Nigel Lawson, Ingham was easily riled, and an innocent request of mine in the summer of 1989 about how best to interpret Lawson's latest comments on the European monetary system produced a vintage performance: 'People like you will play games until the cows come home. I get fed up with it, bloody fed up. The trouble is there is too much media, too much interpretation and not enough reporting. You may continue with your seductive tones but they will get you nowhere. The trouble is you can't manipulate me and that's a problem for you.'

When Lawson resigned five months later there were reports that Mrs Thatcher had acknowledged that the next election would be her last. Ingham insisted that none of her recent remarks could possibly support any such suggestion. She was preparing to win the next election by 'popular demand'. As he had just lectured the lobby on the reasons for the government's categoric refusal to speculate about the future of the pound or interest rates I inquired rather cheekily if, as press secretary, his advice to the Prime Minister was that she should not even appear to be speculating about her own future. Ingham's admonishment was delivered with a firm wagging of his finger: 'You are into the business of trouble with a capital T. The BBC should not be in that business, if you don't mind me saying so.' My supplementary to the effect that I hoped we could still ask questions produced another equally firm riposte: 'You can ask questions but don't expect to get answers.'

This comment seemed to me to illustrate the decline into which the lobby had fallen at this period. Weakened by the absence of correspondents from the *Independent* and the *Guardian*, its collective strength seemed at an all-time low. I felt the lack of persistent questioning of Ingham meant that the lobby was failing to make any attempt to act as a check on the executive. Just as Mrs Thatcher thrived because her political opponents were divided, so her press secretary appeared to be benefiting from the disarray which existed among the political journalists. To my surprise the then deputy chief whip, David Hunt, confirmed that this was exactly the conclusion which some ministers had reached. He thought the *Independent* and the *Guardian* had played right into the government's hands. By allowing the lobby to be used simply as a channel through which Downing Street could supply information, political journalists were abandoning their opportunities, within the parliamen-

tary system, to challenge the government. Tough questioning by the
lobby could be a restraining influence.

There was another reason for the acquiescence of political journalists
from Conservative-supporting newspapers. The lobby has rarely ever
hunted as a pack and, because most correspondents are loath to let their
rivals get even a whiff of the stories they are pursuing, much of the
questioning at formal briefings has always tended to revolve around the
already declared facts. Under Ingham's no-nonsense regime those reporters who were employed by newspapers sympathetic to the government had no wish to sour relations by challenging him needlessly. They
knew they had every chance of speaking to him by phone after the
organised briefing, when they might find it easier to obtain the information they wanted.

This selectivity on the part of Downing Street press secretaries is not a
new phenomenon: several incumbents have tended to give fuller briefings to a chosen group of political editors and correspondents whom they
considered reliable. This inner circle is known traditionally as the 'white
Commonwealth.' Its origin and title go back thirty years, to the days of
tense Commonwealth conflict, when Harold Wilson as Prime Minister
built up a clique of political editors whom he trusted and whom he
invited to special briefings in Downing Street. Ingham, I knew from my
own experience, did impart more information to certain journalists than
to others, but I never felt that he made a calculated attempt to mislead
me. Indeed, he was justifiably proud of his reputation for being straight
with the facts. Journalists from Labour-supporting newspapers like the
Daily Mirror told me that in their dealings with him they found him
scrupulously impartial.

Where Ingham did seem somewhat unfair and unnecessarily belligerent was in his complaints about the conduct of broadcasters. When the
Sun broke Downing Street's embargo on the 1988 New Year's honours
list a discreet letter of apology sufficed. A year later, when Mrs Thatcher
was asked about the Lockerbie air disaster while being filmed with some
Jamaican schoolchildren, Ingham made an official complaint.
Although reporters were excluded from the photo call, they persuaded a
television cameraman to enquire if the Prime Minister had any comment. Ingham claimed this amounted to a breach of protocol which
could prejudice future relations between Downing Street and the broadcasting organisations. The television and radio correspondents whose
idea it had been felt that Ingham was being hypocritical. Mrs Thatcher
was regularly among the first public figures to visit disaster scenes. She
was always assiduous in expressing her sympathy with relatives and in
such situations responded unfailingly whenever she was approached by
reporters.

Ingham's celebrated brush with the BBC in January 1983, almost a year after the Falklands War, had clearly left its mark. On discovering that the Corporation was refusing to share with ITN its footage of Mrs Thatcher's surprise visit to Port Stanley, and her tour of the islands, Ingham, in his own words, 'detonated'. Only the BBC had film of the visit but he wanted it to be treated as a pooled facility. After making a fearsome protest, in which he threatened to stop any film leaving the Falklands that night, the BBC backed down. Ingham knew instinctively when to call the media's bluff. Equally intuitively, it seemed, he was invariably at Mrs Thatcher's side at moments of crisis when she needed to call on his skills in fending off reporters, photographers and television crews. Together they became highly proficient at handling troublesome news conferences. Ingham would usually prepare the way, deflating an awkward or provocative questioner with a well-placed aside, allowing the Prime Minister to move in instantly for the kill.

His success in shielding Mrs Thatcher from the constant demands of the news media was praised by friend and foe alike. When I compiled a radio programme entitled *The Most Important Man*, which assessed Ingham's contribution to the first ten years of the Thatcher government, there was a general recognition among the people I spoke to that the pressures Prime Minister and press secretary were under had intensified. Lord Deedes, the former editor of the *Daily Telegraph*, told me he had come to the conclusion that modern Prime Ministers needed to have a real thug at their side to give them protection against the daily assault of the media. When I recorded my interview he did not use the word 'thug' to describe the Downing Street press secretary, but said Ingham had been tenaciously loyal: 'In the circumstances in which Mrs Thatcher has had to work I think she has needed a tough beside her and even Bernard Ingham's enemies among the press, and he has quite a few, would admit that he is a tough.'

After having been intimidated by Ingham for so long, lobby correspondents were astounded when hostilities ended overnight in December 1990 with John Major's appointment of Gus O'Donnell. Political journalists felt disorientated. Habituated to expect confrontation, they suddenly found themselves having to adjust to a new press secretary in Downing Street who was no longer impugning the motives of his questioners. O'Donnell, an economist and career civil servant who had been head of information at the Treasury when Major was Chancellor, and moved with him to Downing Street, had an unassuming style which chimed in precisely with Major's own, and seemed quite at ease briefing journalists. Gone were the hectoring stricutres of his predecessor.

The new Prime Minister was immediately caught up in the unfolding drama of the Gulf War, which had the knock-on effect of putting his press secretary into a commanding position over the lobby. Journalists were eager to hear the latest from the Gulf and, as the conflict developed, the government became a prime source of news. Careful coordination between the White House and Downing Street in releasing details about American and British troop movements tended to reinforce the supremacy of the government information machine. Although O'Donnell retained the advantage in news terms he did not baulk when asked pointed questions about the continued destruction of Iraqi road and rail bridges, giving patient explanations of the military thinking behind the need to cut Saddam Hussein's supply lines to Kuwait.

O'Donnell's briefings on the work of the war Cabinet were widely praised for their thoroughness. He supplied details of the kind which were rarely offered by Ingham. On several occasions he readily corrected inaccurate information which he had given earlier. O'Donnell had clearly taken a calculated decision to ensure that the Downing Street press office did all it could to maintain a strong public consensus in Britain for the allied action. He raised no objection when television correspondents walked out of the No. 10 front door and reported live from Downing Street on information which had just been provided on an off-the-record basis at lobby briefings. When the Prime Minister was asked in the Commons by the Conservative MP Patrick Nicholls if he deplored the BBC's practice of referring to 'British' forces rather than 'our' troops, Major commended the Corporation's journalists covering the war for their 'remarkable reporting' and impartiality.

The mild-mannered approach of the new Prime Minister and his press secretary led the *Financial Times* to say that when their handling of the news media was compared with that of their two immediate predecessors it was like putting 'fluffy toys alongside Teenage Mutant Ninja Turtles'. O'Donnell was tickled pink. Subsequently, whenever he was asked a threatening question of the kind posed in Ingham's day he would crack a joke about his inability to give lobby journalists the 'Teenage Mutant' answers on which they had been reared.

Lacking as he did any journalistic experience, O'Donnell did not claim any great news sense. After the IRA mortar attack on Downing Street in February 1991 he gave an impressive but somewhat clinical account of what happened when the bomb exploded in the garden of No. 10 as the war Cabinet was meeting. He had been one of the officials sitting round the Cabinet table. Uppermost in the minds of the journalists was the need to get an idea of how close the explosion had been to Major. O'Donnell had difficulty giving an estimate. When pressed by the lobby for extra colour and an indication of how Major had reacted, he replied rather engagingly: 'I'm afraid I was not being a good journalist on that occasion. I was not convinced this was the end of the attack. I was just thinking about getting everyone away from the window and into the corridor.'

His friendly style was reinforced by a relaxation in Ingham's previous ruling that information supplied by the press secretary had to be attributed to 'government sources'. O'Donnell had no objection to journalists adopting the term 'Downing Street sources' or being even more precise if they wished by using the phrase 'Downing Street says'. Most broadcasters and newspaper reporters made the change immediately. Some started indicating that the source was 'the Prime Minister's office', which soon became another well-established formula. O'Donnell made no fuss about his initiative, nor did he try to seek any credit for what he hoped would prove a genuine improvement. While it was only a relatively superficial alteration he had opened up the prospect of further moves towards clarification by the media of the various sources of information supplied to journalists on lobby terms.

Within weeks there were signs that the *Guardian*'s political correspondents were willing to end their boycott of Downing Street briefings. They returned in July 1991, eight months after Ingham's departure. O'Donnell told me it was a vindication of the more open approach he had adopted. The following month, after President Mikhail Gorbachev was removed in a coup, Major gave a thirty-minute off-the-record briefing on ways in which the west could sustain the Soviet reform programme. Political correspondents welcomed his readiness to meet the lobby en masse. Many of the journalists who were present were hard pressed to remember the last occasion on which they had received a visit from the Prime Minister. A few weeks later correspondents from the *Independent* and the *Scotsman* also rejoined the briefings. All three newspapers welcomed the changes brought about by O'Donnell and said that the use of a clear formula for attributing Downing Street's guidance had enabled them to return to the lobby.

Information officers throughout the government were soon commenting favourably on the easy-going rapport which they were developing with the new press secretary. There was more involved than a change in atmosphere. O'Donnell's arrival heralded a loosening in the relationship between Downing Street and the press offices of each department. Ingham had always endeavoured to put his stamp on the whole of the government's publicity machine. In his final years in Downing Street, in addition to his role as chief press secretary, he took on the additional post of overall head of all government information officers, advising on senior appointments. Initially Ingham's aim was to achieve greater coordination in the presentation of government policy. On Monday evenings he was usually in the chair for the weekly meeting of the heads of information from all the Whitehall departments. Here they reviewed the effectiveness of the government's publicity of the previous week and looked ahead to forthcoming announcements and events, working out how to ensure maximum impact and avoid presentational difficulties. Ingham's powers were considerable. Among the issues discussed at these meetings were the latest bids by television and radio programmes for in-depth interviews. The press secretary was said to have firm views on those broadcasters who he thought would do a professional job and those who he considered were out to cause mischief and could not be trusted.

Ingham's many critics in the media accused him of being the consummate Machiavelli when it came to news management. In *Kill the Messenger* he takes a swipe at his tormentors: 'I plead utterly, completely and wholeheartedly guilty. Of course, I tried to manage the news. I tried – God knows, I tried – to ensure that ministers spoke with one voice . . . Dammit, that was what I was supposed to do.' He certainly proved effective over the years in tightening up Whitehall's response rate to journalists' inquiries. Press officers were urged to go on the offensive. Instead of routinely making no comment, departments were instructed to provide information and to make sure that ministers were made available for television and radio interviews so that the arguments of the government's opponents did not go unanswered. Most importantly of all, press officers were told they had to meet news deadlines: opportunities must not be missed.

Whitehall information officers at the time spoke in awe of Ingham's achievements. As his colleagues had discovered, he was a workaholic and he quickly established his authority. He was not afraid of taking a populist position and insisted that departments must be robust when challenged by the media. Their responsibility was to work out a clear line with ministers and then follow it through in their dealings with journalists. As the years went by there were few within the information service who dared challenge him. The individual heads of information had to be on their guard. As Ingham revealed in his autobiography, ministers treated him as a 'sounding board' when planning their publicity. Despite having their own departmental advisers, they would pop into his room after a meeting with the Prime Minister for 'a chat'. Ingham's role, as he described it himself, was to 'conduct the government's communications orchestra'. After being troubled to begin with by leaks from his weekly get-together he made efforts to 'trap the miscreant or miscreants'. Eventually he won through, rebuilding the trust which he said he wanted and depended on.

When Gus O'Donnell took over there was what was described as a tangible sense of relief, especially at the Monday meetings. 'It is as if peace has broken out,' was how one participant put it to me. Whitehall departments took advantage of the freer regime and the realisation that they were no longer being checked up on. As O'Donnell was not consumed by a wish to oversee all aspects of government publicity, ministers and their advisers exercised greater freedom in launching their own public relations initiatives. There was, however, an incipient danger here for the government. As a result of the very licence which would not have been tolerated previously, there was not always the synchronisation which there should have been. One departmental head of information told me that within six months of O'Donnell taking over, the close coordination on which Ingham insisted on at his weekly meetings had all but collapsed. On completing his first year as press secretary O'Donnell was quoted by David Hencke in the *Guardian* as having acknowledged publicly that 'the system has broken'. Downing Street was no longer dictating terms or even seeking to limit the flow of information from Whitehall departments and their arm's-length agencies: the aim now was to help to create open government.

As events began to rebound on Major, not least because of the conflicting and contradictory statements emerging from government departments, there were ominous mutterings within the party about the Prime Minister's failure to establish a clear command structure for promoting himself. There was evident alarm among Conservative strategists about the collapse of the tried and tested routines of the Ingham era. No longer was there the same strength and clarity to the political message emanating from Downing Street.

Despite the criticism which he had attracted over the years Ingham was in effect the linchpin of Mrs Thatcher's drive for favourable publicity, both for herself and for her government. There were clearly understood boundaries beyond which ministers and officials at Conservative headquarters strayed at their peril. Ingham effectively sat astride both government and party and, while he has since insisted with characteristic vehemence that he never broke the civil service rules forbidding his involvement in party political propaganda, there were few within the Tory hierarchy who dared question an Ingham edict or who would challenge his judgement on what was best for the Prime Minister and her administration. Ingham never made any secret of the fact that his 'thought processes were much more those of a politician than of an official' and he knew instinctively where the border lay between the work of the government, for which civil servants have responsibility, and those matters which are strictly party issues. The clarity with which he could identify the boundaries of his public duties was a help, not a hindrance, because it enabled him, through the force of his personality, to assist Mrs Thatcher in asserting a clear, uniform line which could then be communicated both by the civil servants under his control and by the publicity staff at Conservative Central Office.

Under Major, responsibility for establishing 'the line' had become diffused. In the absence of an all-powerful press adviser there seemed to be no-one who was capable of the fine tuning which was needed as the government tackled issues as diverse as the replacement of the poll tax and the introduction of controls on dangerous dogs. In addition to the perpetual Tory in-fighting over Europe, there was continuing uncertainty about the timing of a general election. The most difficult moments for the Prime Minister seemed to be at party functions, where the responsibility for briefing journalists passed either to Major's political adviser, the late Judith Chaplin, or to the Conservatives' communications director, then Shaun Woodward. Confusion in the build-up to the Conservatives' Welsh party conference in June 1991 illustrated the difficulties. Journalists started billing the Prime Minister's speech as the moment he would define 'Majorism'. There was immediate concern inside Downing Street. If this was how the speech was going to be interpreted Major might open himself up to ridicule, not least for plagiarising 'Thatcherism.'

As soon as he was aware of the speculation, on the Monday evening O'Donnell insisted there was no intention of the speech becoming the 'A to Z of Majorism'. He understood the Prime Minister wanted to set out his ideas for 'Toryism in the 1990s'. As this was a party event he told reporters they must check with Conservative Central Office. On the Friday of the conference a briefing in advance of the speech was given by Mrs Chaplin, who blamed journalists for inaccurate speculation. She said: 'Mr Major will not even mention the word Majorism. He does not think it is a very wonderful phrase anyway. No one has ever used it in No. 10.' Her briefing was the first most reporters had heard of the Prime Minister's personal dislike of the word, and some weeks later O'Donnell was still attracting criticism within the party for not having acted sooner to stamp out its use. The nub of the criticism was a belief that Ingham would have found a way of rubbishing reports which suggested an imminent definition of 'Majorism' without having been seen to interfere in party affairs.

O'Donnell was only too ready to acknowledge the difficulties which were being encountered by the Downing Street press office in liaising with party headquarters. He felt these had been heightened by uncertainty about the timing of the election and the desire of senior Conservatives for Major to deliver more of his big speeches on party platforms. If significant policy initiatives were going to be turned into party political announcements then he was stuck with his problem, however much he disliked it, of being unable to coordinate presentation as effectively as he wanted to. He had become rather irritated by the constant comparisons with his predecessor and was clearly annoyed that no mention was ever made of the fact that the strong briefing lines adopted in the Thatcher years often turned out to be the wrong ones, whereas Major's more gradual approach was allowing a consensus to develop. At no stage had the Prime Minister told his press secretary to 'rule with a rod of iron'. O'Donnell gave me the clear impression that Major was prepared to accept that under his more open style of government there might be a short-term presentational loss but the trade-off was worth it if the right policies emerged and their objectives were achieved.

Party officials and activists were divided in their opinions. Even though O'Donnell had only been doing the job for a matter of months, some of the Conservatives' advisers on publicity were already hankering for the old certainties of the Ingham era. While he accepted that on the Tory right he was probably regarded as 'just a bloody civil servant' who had not got 'a grip on things', O'Donnell was sure the left of the party appreciated the new approach. Among journalists and government press officers there was an enormous fund of goodwill for him. The lack of confrontation at lobby briefings, and his own helpfulness, were reciprocated. Political correspondents observed a mutual degree of confidentiality which had not been seen for years. Innocent mistakes by the press secretary were not leaked to non-lobby journalists or converted into snide paragraphs for newspaper diaries. Reporters who had crossed swords with Ingham over the years began writing warmly about the new press secretary. Andrew Stephen, who reported for the *Observer* on Major's visit to Kennebunkport to see President Bush, said that instead of the 'bullying, rude Bernard Ingham' accompanying the Prime Minister there was the 'benign decentness' of O'Donnell: 'A new civility, a real warmth, is suddenly in the air.' When Peter Mandelson, Labour's former communications director, met him for the first time he too joined in the praise. Writing in his weekly column in the *People*, he said it was amazing that someone as nice as O'Donnell could 'get so far in the brutal world of press communications'.

This golden glow, however, was not universal. Immediately after his appointment some old hands in the lobby predicted that the peace which had broken out in relations with Downing Street would not last. As the government's problems increased, O'Donnell was to become increasingly aware of the black arts of popular journalism. While it might not be the exact moment when the honeymoon ended, there is no doubt that the headlines which greeted Major in March 1991, on his return from talks about the Gulf War, were a severe disappointment to his press secretary. For some days the Prime Minister had been unable to shrug off an ear and throat infection. On arriving in Bermuda after an overnight flight President Bush was heard asking Major: 'Are you wiped out?' Under the headline 'Worn Out Major in Health Scare' the *Sun* reported how the Cabinet feared the Prime Minister was about to 'crack-up'. O'Donnell's disenchantment was all the greater because of the help and access to the Prime Minister which he had provided for journalists during the flight. The claim in some newspapers that Major was suffering from stress appalled him when it was obvious it had simply been a tiring visit. 'Is that journalism?' he asked me. 'Is that the media world I shall have to live through?'

Coincidentally, another tale about the in-flight entertainment which Major was allegedly providing in his RAF VC10 had gained further currency that weekend in Alastair Campbell's column in the *Sunday Mirror*. He claimed he was the original source of the observation that Major wore his shirt tucked inside his underpants. On a return flight from Washington shortly before Christmas, Major had sat with the journalists for a time. At one point when he bent over Campbell noticed that the Prime Minister had three layers of clothing – 'his trousers, followed by what looked like the elasticated top of a pair of underpants, followed by his pale blue shirt closest to his skin.' Apparently, on a subsequent flight, Campbell blurted this out. It was promptly picked up by other journalists and provided inspiration for the cartoonist Steve Bell of the *Guardian*, who took to depicting Major wearing his Y-fronts outside his trousers.

Of more immediate concern to O'Donnell was television coverage. Major had taken to watching the early evening news bulletins, so as not to miss the broadcasters' first assessment of the day's political news. He had become an inveterate channel-hopper and his recall was said to be so impressive that he could reel off his placing in each of the bulletins. Press officers were soon being instructed to make immediate complaints if he was dissatisfied. Correspondents were asked how they justified the phraseology they had used or why certain interviewees had been included and others had not. On some occasions the criticism seemed harder to pinpoint. When asked to explain Downing Street's precise concern about television coverage of the May 1991 unemployment figures, which showed that the jobless total was nearly 2.2 million, O'Donnell said the Prime Minister had not liked the 'feel' of the news reports.

Major had grown used to commanding widespread television coverage as a result of the many televised statements he made live from Downing Street during the Gulf War. As he had become so confident in front of the cameras, O'Donnell was keen for the Prime Minister to give more on-the-record news conferences. After launching the white paper on higher education and his plans for the citizen's charter in this way, Major followed up in July by giving his first televised news conference inside No. 10. The Soviet coup in August 1991 provided more useful exposure. As tanks moved in on the Russian parliament, Major seemed to be almost on the point of becoming a pundit himself, popping out of No. 10 just before the main bulletins with the latest news on the whereabouts of Mikhail Gorbachev. On a number of occasions, including when he emerged after having spoken on the phone to President Gorbachev and Boris Yeltsin, Major's impromptu news conferences were carried for several minutes, without interruption, at the top of the bulletins. Programme editors felt they were being manipulated but realised they had no choice because of the compelling news value of the material. Opinion pollsters believed that Major's active role on the international stage would create a 'halo effect' which would improve his popularity ratings. Bob Worcester, Chairman of MORI, said that when it came to voters' perceptions about the degree to which party leaders understood world problems, Major's lead over Neil Kinnock had increased markedly since he became Prime Minister.

Major was also giving many more television and radio interviews than Mrs Thatcher in her final years as Prime Minister. Nevertheless, O'Donnell was forced to acknowledge that Major could still appear unnecessarily defensive when reporters stopped him on the move and asked questions. During a visit to Ipswich in June 1991 he ended up in what looked like a rugby scrum. Reporters and television crews struggled to get in close so they could ask the Prime Minister about critical comments on the abolition of the poll tax which were being made by his predecessor. While he continued walking, extricating himself from the mêlée, he said: 'I am not despondent.' But he looked decidedly unhappy. In the inquest which followed local Conservatives were blamed for not making sure that access to Major was properly controlled, and O'Donnell had to put up with some elementary advice from his predecessor. Ingham said the incident underlined the need for Major to be warned that he must be on his guard. 'My best advice to all Prime Ministers is not to be waylaid in the first place. News is what causes trouble and the best way to control trouble is not to cause it yourself.'

Ingham's helpful hints were highlighting O'Donnell's predicament. Was it possible for a civil servant who was not a media professional to be press secretary? Had Ingham, through his long and close association with Mrs Thatcher, allowed the post to become too politicised? The incident which was to fuel these doubts struck at the very heart of the problem. In an age of instant news, twenty-four hours a day, a Prime Minister needs constant advice. There must be a clear command structure for communicating with the media. If the Downing Street spokesman loses control of what is being said it might take only a matter of hours for confidence in the government to be at risk. O'Donnell was able to ponder on these problems when he found himself sitting on the sidelines.

The close ties which Mrs Thatcher had cemented with the proprietors and editors of sympathetic newspapers provided a route through which Major could bypass his press secretary. These links were of great value during elections and at times of difficulty for the party. Editorial staff on friendly newspapers were well aware of the relationship. Their political editors often obtained information which was not made available to other news organisations whose political staff were not regarded as being sufficiently trustworthy. Major fell back on this alternative channel of communication when, after much agonising, he decided that it was finally time to put the word out officially that there would be no election in November 1991. The task was given to John Wakeham, then energy secretary, who had the additional ministerial role of coordinating the government's information services. It was agreed that he should notify the five newspapers which were considered most loyal to the Conservatives and which were therefore thought to be the most reliable – the *Times, Daily Telegraph, Daily Mail, Daily Express* and *Sun*.

Wakeham made his calls early on what was in fact the first day of the Labour conference. One political editor was notified personally at 9.30 a.m. just as he was leaving his hotel for the Brighton conference centre. An important factor which had influenced the timing had been the need to deny Neil Kinnock the chance of using his speech as party leader to accuse Major of dithering about the date of the election. Each of the five newspapers believed it had been notified exclusively, so all their political editors and correspondents were careful to avoid mentioning it to other reporters. This was more difficult than usual because of the hothouse atmosphere which develops at party conferences. The first broadcaster to get a whiff of what had happened was Elinor Goodman who broke the story that evening on Channel Four News. The back-door way in which the news was sneaked out became a bigger issue than the postponing of the election, which had been expected all along.

O'Donnell told me subsequently that he was dismayed by the way it had all backfired so badly. To begin with journalists picked up different accounts of what had happened. Some were told the press secretary was peeved at the way he had been marginalised so pointedly. The commonest explanation was that Wakeham undertook the task when O'Donnell, anxious to protect his status as a civil servant, refused point blank to do a ring-round on what was so obviously a party political issue. Once Wakeham had made his calls the Downing Street press office was told it should not contradict the story when asked for confirmation. Michael Jones, political editor of the *Sunday Times*, explained the reasoning. He said ministers had concluded there was no way O'Donnell could 'do the deed via the usual channels' because by then most of the 'nod and wink experts' in the lobby were already in Brighton at the Labour conference.

Much fun was had by political commentators when it was discovered that Wakeham, who subsequently became the Leader of the House of Lords, had been used by the Prime Minister to convey a non-attributable leak of such magnitude. Chris Patten, then party chairman, believed it would have been better if a way could have been found for O'Donnell to have made the announcement because he was well respected by the lobby and would have been believed. However, ministers were said to have acknowledged that as a civil servant the press secretary acted correctly in not getting involved. Some political correspondents nevertheless felt that O'Donnell's problem was of his own making: he had not turned out to be a tough operator, capable of masterminding the successful leaking of sensitive information.

Sir Tim Bell, who had given Mrs Thatcher so much advice and assistance when her government was in difficulty with the news media, was dismayed by the amateurish way the Wakeham operation had been conducted. He had watched with concern as the interlocking network of publicity advisers and friendly newspaper editors of which he had formed part had been allowed to wither away under Major. He considered it was particularly idiotic of Wakeham to have briefed five newspapers and then completely ignored television and radio. If the government had been anxious to get the story out and avoid leaving any fingerprints, then 'one newspaper should have been tipped off exclusively and once the story appeared it should not have been denied'.

O'Donnell's predicament was, in Bell's view, another illustration of the need for an all-party inquiry into the basis on which the No. 10 press secretary was appointed. Instead of asking a career civil servant to do the job, he wondered whether the time had come to make it a clearly signalled political appointment, as was the case with the rest of the Prime Minister's political advisers. Among those said to be sympathetic to the idea was the chief whip, Richard Ryder, who thought the day was arriving when all governments would probably have to engage more political appointees, as was already the case in the United States. When I examined this argument in 1989 for my radio profile of Ingham, I was told by the then Conservative chairman, Peter Brooke, that the party had no intention of changing the system. If the Downing Street press office was going to continue being funded by taxpayers' money then it should be headed by an official who made sure that civil service traditions of impartiality were maintained. I was also assured by the Conservative MP John Redwood, who had previously been head of Mrs Thatcher's policy unit, that the inbuilt safeguards had operated effectively in his day. He said that if there was anything overtly political to be done then Ingham always insisted on it being handled by the Prime Minister's political staff or Conservative Central Office. However, a former permanent secretary at the Ministry of Defence, Sir Frank Cooper, had concluded that the press secretary's post should be made a political appointment. During the Falklands War he found that on one occasion the Downing Street press office was claiming that a particular place had been recaptured when that was yet to happen. 'I think they wanted to influence the political scene . . . It is very much to swing and sway all the media, to provide information in a way which is calculated to do one thing, namely enhance the standing of the government of the day.'

The comparison I made for my programme was with Harold Wilson's appointment of the journalist Joe Haines as his press secretary in 1969. Haines became a civil servant and accepted civil service discipline while remaining a high-profile member of the Labour Party. 'I never disguised it,' said Haines. 'Everybody knew what my role was. My role was to serve the Prime Minister.' After the Wakeham fiasco and the consequent Conservative disarray, Neil Kinnock's staff let it be known that if he became Prime Minister he would again make the press secretary's post a political appointment. This only served to exacerbate the exposed nature of O'Donnell's position.

Within a matter of weeks Major's press secretary faced fresh turmoil when, as the *Daily Mirror* described it, he was forced to go 'scurrying around Westminster' hurriedly briefing political correspondents. O'Donnell had got drawn into the notorious quicksand of trying to answer a hypothetical question. During a Commons debate in November 1991, almost exactly a year after resigning, Mrs Thatcher reignited Tory divisions on Europe by calling for a referendum before Britain agreed to a single currency. Her demand that MPs should 'let the people speak' was a direct challenge to Major's answer the day before that he did not 'favour the idea of a referendum'. Shortly after Mrs Thatcher's speech O'Donnell walked the length of the lobby correspondents' corridor, calling in at the rooms of individual journalists, advising them that Major could not rule out a referendum because no government could bind a future parliament.

Most correspondents had expected O'Donnell to stonewall when they asked about Mrs Thatcher's call for a referendum. Instead, it appeared he had consulted Major. He was anxious to explain the constitutional position to as many correspondents as he could find. In doing so he gave some the impression that Major was seeking to appease his predecessor. Labour exploited the position within minutes, claiming the 'backseat driver had grabbed the wheel'. Downing Street was soon backpedalling furiously and, in a hastily prepared statement at the end of that evening's debate, Francis Maude, then financial secretary at the Treasury, said Major saw no need for a referendum, a point reinforced the following day by an official statement by the Prime Minister.

Next morning's newspapers were confused, with the *Sun* and *Today* still insisting that Major had in fact made a 'dramatic U-turn' by acknowledging publicly that a referendum was possible in the future. O'Donnell, although not named personally, was singled out for blame by John Deans, political correspondent of the *Daily Mail*: 'The Number 10 press department was obviously trying to dissociate itself, gently but firmly, from Mrs Thatcher's call. But in its eagerness to do this swiftly, it ended by making a serious gaffe.' Ian Aitken, writing in the *Guardian*, said the whole kerfuffle had been refreshing because for once 'a certain person with impeccable credentials actually went up and down the corridor in the press gallery with a message from You Know Who.' Aitken said this had to be a welcome change of heart from the Ingham years because the messenger could at least be identified as a 'Downing Street source'.

While political journalists appreciated O'Donnell's efforts to keep them briefed most were taken aback, never having seen him on the lobby corridor before. They could hardly believe he could have been so amateurish as to walk into their offices explaining the government's line. Journalists on the *Daily Mirror*, together with Mike Ambrose, political correspondent of the *Morning Star*, were among those given personal briefings. Once again the inevitable comparisons were made. The general view was that Ingham's tactic when he found himself in a similar pickle was to hit the phone. His aim would have been to swing the key mainstream journalists, like the political editors of *The Times*, *Daily Telegraph*, *Daily Mail*, *Daily Express* and the *Sun*. The last thing he would have done would have been to draw attention to himself or provide gratuitous amunition for papers known to be hostile to the government.

And yet, after an autumn of so much grief, O'Donnell ended the year by pulling off what was widely regarded as the Conservatives' most successful briefing since Major became Prime Minister. Morevoer, he achieved it on the back of the year's most troublesome issue, the government's negotiations with Europe. Once Britain had won its social chapter opt-out at the Maastricht summit, O'Donnell worked through the night relaying details of his own briefing, and Major's reaction, direct to his deputy Jonathan Haslam back in Downing Street. A full set of documents and briefing notes was then delivered first thing to the home of every Cabinet minister to prepare them for prearranged television and radio interviews which started with the breakfast programmes. David Hunt, then Welsh seceretary, was woken at 5 a.m. by a despatch rider with his copy of the press secretary's briefing pack. Party workers praised O'Donnell for setting up the Conservatives' best news hit of the year.

Major, who stayed up until after 3 a.m. at Maastricht giving interviews and briefing journalists, celebrated his success with the lobby the following week. Political correspondents were invited to No. 10 for a Christmas drink, hospitality which had not been offered for some years. The reception was well attended. O'Donnell skilfully worked the room, periodically lining up an assortment of correspondents, so that Major had a new group to move on to every ten minutes or so. Rapid circulation, without causing offence, requires teamwork and the Prime Minister and his press secretary were obviously at ease with each other, enjoying the occasion. They had the same sporting interests, cricket and football; they were both from south London; and, having got on well together since their days at the Treasury, they gave every indication of sharing similar political and social attitudes. Nevertheless, kindred spirits though they might be, they had certainly been through a year which would have tested any friendship.

As Major approached I overheard him chatting away like a friendly bank manager, discussing mortgages with two journalists, and teasing one about the extra tax he would have to pay under a Labour government. It reminded me of an earlier social occasion when he had extolled the advantages of opening a TESSA, the tax-free savings account which he had introduced as Chancellor. By now I was becoming rather apprehensive. On my way into the reception I had been warned by O'Donnell that the Prime Minister had a 'bone to pick with me'. I had an inkling as to what the problem might be. On *Today* that morning I had reported on the government's success the night before in gaining a majority of eighty-six votes in a debate on the Maastricht agreement. My report included interview extracts from two MPs: Norman Tebbit, who was promising to continue the campaign for a referendum, and Bill Walker, one of seven Tory rebels, who had resigned from his post as vice chairman of the Scottish Conservatives. As I feared, Major regarded this as unbalanced. He felt I should have included an interviewee supportive of the deal obtained at Maastricht. I replied rather limply that Norman Lamont (then Chancellor) had been interviewed immediately afterwards to put the government's case. Major frowned but made light of it. I was reluctant to say any more, realising it was not much of an answer. Lamont had been rather grumpy that morning; perhaps the Prime Minister had a point about the lack of balance.

Speculation about the timing of the general election dominated the first few weeks of 1992. O'Donnell laid careful plans ready for the dissolution of parliament. After the débâcle of the previous October he was determined to arrange the best possible send-off for the Prime Minister: once polling day was announced, responsibility for promoting Major would pass to Conservative Central Office.

The announcement that the election would take place on 9 April was made the day after the budget. O'Donnell's arrangements went like clockwork. In a break with previous practice he held a conference telephone call at 11 a.m. with the leading news agencies, giving them simultaneous notification that Major would be leaving shortly for Buckingham Palace. Broadcasting organisations were told to expect a statement in Downing Street two hours later. After his audience with the Queen, Major re-emerged through the No. 10 front door at precisely four minutes past one and made his formal announcement about the election live on the lunchtime news bulletins. Split-second timing had been essential. If he had walked out too early it would have clashed with the opening titles of the news bulletins; sufficient time also had to be allowed for programme presenters to hand over to the reporters in Downing Street; too late, and it would have missed the top slot. The announcement dominated the news all day, but meticulous planning had ensured maximum coverage and immaculate pictures.

If O'Donnell had been expecting Major's election victory to herald calmer days in Downing Street he had a rude awakening. Three months after the Conservatives secured a twenty-one-seat majority the Sunday newspapers broke the story of David Mellor's affair with Antonia de Sancha. 'Minister of Fun and the Actress' was the front-page headline of the *News of the World*. Major spent the summer letting it be known he would stick by his heritage secretary 'through thick and thin', but the lobby sensed that O'Donnell had his back to the wall. He looked uncomfortable when telling journalists that Major was not expecting to make 'any ministerial changes at all for a very long time'. Two days before Mellor's resignation in September the guidance was still that Major was 'fully behind' his heritage secretary. Reporters could not understand why O'Donnell was sticking to this answer so rigidly when ministers were saying privately that Mellor could not survive amid the continuing revelations, now about his acceptance of a holiday from Mona Bauwens, daughter of the finance chief of the Palestine Liberation Organisation.

Mellor's inevitable departure followed hard on the heels of Britain's exit from the European exchange rate mechanism on Black Wednesday; and both events, as it turned out, were about to be overtaken by other disasters on a helter-skelter of public relations catastrophes which would end up with the Prime Minister and his press secretary locked together trying to hold the line. The high hopes with which they set out of establishing and maintaining an open, easy-going relationship with the news media would eventually be smashed to smithereens; and in the last resort Major's political survival had to be the priority. A year later came the official confirmation of what became evident within a matter of months: O'Donnell intended to return to the Treasury. The countdown to his exit from Downing Street would be brutal and wounding.

Uproar in October 1992 over Michael Heseltine's announcement of thirty-one pit closures produced another startlingly open attempt to woo favourable coverage. Lobby journalists were invited to attend an off-the-record briefing in the Prime Minister's room in the House of Commons. We trooped in en masse. Most of us had never set foot in the room before. Major was sitting by the fireplace. Opposite him was a grandfather clock and on the walls two large mirrors. As we all poured in filling the room, he cracked a joke about having to 'get out the loaves and the fishes'. Once the briefing started he was keen to move the focus away from the coal industry. He explained how determined he had been to protect capital spending projects which provided jobs. But it was an answer about his successful negotiation at Maastricht of Britain's social chapter opt-out which caught the attention of reporters: 'People would be well advised to accept that I say what I mean on European policy. If people don't trust me, they had better find someone they do trust.'

The morning newspapers had all carried reports of an opinion survey by MORI which showed Major had become the most unpopular Prime Minister in the history of polling. Now lobby journalists saw the making of an immediate follow-up story. They could picture the headline instantly. Major's reply had only one interpretation: 'Back me or sack me.' The moment the briefing finished journalists crowded round asking the Prime Minister if they could quote him directly. He wavered for a moment but then declined. I was surprised O'Donnell had not noticed the interest and intervened immediately to stop the follow-up questions, but he had been distracted at that moment trying to clear up some confusion over statistics on coal imports. Despite months of unrelenting hostility to his government in the media, Major and his press secretary could hardly have been more helpful or accommodating.

Yet however hard he tried, the Prime Minister could not rid his government of its accident-prone image. After what it claimed was a winter of U-turns and errors of judgement, the *Economist* concluded in February 1993 that Major needed a 'wait-a-minute man' to warn him when his ministers were walking into danger. O'Donnell was singled out as one of those who should have been performing that function. The magazine wondered where he had been in the run-up to the coal fiasco. In March the *Daily Mail* claimed that the 'Tory knives' were out for the press secretary because he was seen as the 'weak link in the premier's propaganda effort'. Within days of Norman Lamont's sacking as Chancellor the build-up started to another messy ministerial resignation, this time of the Northern Ireland minister Michael Mates. Major's ill-fated attempts at damage limitation foundered as they had done so often in the past, and the loss of another minister left O'Donnell looking more exposed than ever. On the day the resignation was announced he had held the line at the morning lobby briefing, assuring reporters that Mates retained the Prime Minister's backing. Next morning the *Guardian* professed itself puzzled by the sequence of events, asking why there had been no explanation of how it was that only hours before Mates resigned 'Downing Street was still pledging him its undeflected support'.

Three days later the *Daily Mail* printed an exclusive report by its political editor Gordon Greig saying that a 'tired, bewildered and disillusioned' O'Donnell intended to leave Downing Street and resume his career as a Treasury economist. Despite an immediate and categorical denial by the Downing Street press office, Greig's report seemed well founded. He described how O'Donnell, who had a 'reputation for openness and plain dealing', had become a casualty of a wider problem in No. 10: 'the transparent lack of a rapid reaction group which could detect, then kill or deflect problems as they arose'. An alternative theory was put forward by the *Sun*'s political editor Trevor Kavanagh. He said relations between the two men had been strained since the events of Black Wednesday, when sterling was withdrawn from the exchange rate mechanism. Suggestions of a rift were refuted in a personal statement by O'Donnell, but he was not quite so categoric about his future plans. He said he expected to go on working closely with Major for 'some time to come'.

Downing Street's denials of resignations had developed a reputation for having a short shelf life. The press secretary's lasted longer than most: three months. In October, as Greig had predicted, O'Donnell announced that he would leaving at the end of the year and returning to the Treasury as the head of the monetary group, handling interest and exchange rates. 'I have had a great time at No. 10,' he said. 'Yes, it was bitter sweet, but it's time to go.'

Lobby journalists were fulsome in their tributes. But there was a widespread feeling that O'Donnell's failure to cope with the nastier side of journalism had proved a lasting handicap. In her report for Channel Four News, Elinor Goodman described how a patient O'Donnell had often looked puzzled at his own briefings, unable to understand what the journalists were up to in the questions they were asking. His mistake, she said, was to think that reporters were rational. Chris Moncrieff, political editor of the Press Association, complimented O'Donnell on his 'disarming innocence' and remarked on how he lacked 'the wiles of a press officer'. Michael White, political editor of the *Guardian*, joined in the commiseration, arguing that reporters suspected that the press secretary was often overruled by Major and 'sometimes left with impossible positions to defend'.

My view was that the course adopted by the Prime Minister and the press secretary had been flawed from the start. On the one hand they were trying to open up their relationship with the news media. More information was being supplied on the record and there was also greater access to Major. But at the same time they were expecting journalists to consider themselves honour-bound not to divulge what they discovered socially or in casual conversation. Their initial approach was both admirable and honourable, but it failed to take account of the growing intrusiveness of the media. Competition among the national newspapers had become ever more deadly and the clubby rules and regulations of the lobby could not withstand the constant pressures and insatiable appetite of television and radio.

O'Donnell might have fared better if he had gone a little further towards a totally on-the-record system of briefing political journalists and then not strayed from that privately. The realisation that his very words would be quoted directly would have forced Downing Street to have been clearer and more definite in what it wanted to say; and there would have been less danger of journalists ending up thinking they had been briefed differently. Major would also have been better advised to recognise that from the very moment he found himself in the company of newspaper reporters and broadcasters he was in effect on parade, open to scrutiny, and therefore could not expect journalists to have to decide for themselves where the dividing line lay between what he was saying publicly and what privately.

'Bastardgate', as it was described, came to epitomise the combined naivety of the Prime Minister and his press secretary. Major had to suffer the indignity of a *Daily Mirror* hotline for telephone callers replaying his off-the-cuff reference to certain Cabinet colleagues as being 'three more of the bastards'. The conversation took place immediately after the government won its vote of confidence on the Maastricht Treaty in July 1993. While gossiping away with ITN's political editor Michael Brunson during a gap between interviews, the Prime Minister failed to realise that his remarks were still being recorded by the broadcasting organisations which were hooked up to the television feed from Downing Street.

It was not the first time Major had engaged in indiscreet remarks in such circumstances. A year earlier, during the general election campaign, after completing *Election Call* on the eve of polling day he stayed to chat with the presenter, Jonathan Dimbleby. He was unconcerned about the bad opinion polls, saying he knew there were many Tory supporters who purposely refused to give pollsters a straight answer. Unknown to the Prime Minister, his remarks were still being recorded. The following year, amid the fuss over 'Bastardgate', the *Sun* managed to obtain an illicit recording of the earlier conversation. Under the front-page headline 'Major Uses The F Word' the *Sun* reprinted what it claimed was the quote in full. Major told Dimbleby: 'People are resentful of the pollsters, not only that there is a high f***-up factor among Tories.'

Many politicians are extremely wary of television and radio studios, sensing danger the moment they get within range of a camera or microphone. They are careful not to swear and tend to avoid jokes, preferring to work on the assumption that an interview has started the moment they walk through the door. Rarely have they needed reminding of the damage which can be inflicted if just one word is broadcast or printed out of context. Mrs Thatcher's reputation was legendary: the only small talk she allowed herself was about trivialities, like the origin of the water on the studio table. Her insistence on British rather than French bottled water became a favourite opening gambit in her warm-up routine. No journalist I spoke to in the wake of Bastardgate could recall ever having had an off-the-record conversation with her, when she was Prime Minister, in which she spoke so intimately and so explicitly about her Cabinet colleagues.

The *Daily Mirror*'s transcript of the tape shows the jocular tone of Major's conversation with Brunson: 'What I don't understand, Michael, is why such a complete wimp like me keeps winning everything.' Then, turning to his press secretary: 'I suppose Gus will tell me off for saying that, won't you Gus?' The transcript makes no mention of O'Donnell giving an answer but his presence is of significance. Once the conversation veered towards David Mellor's resignation, and Major's aside that he 'can't stop people sleeping with other people', the discussion had reached danger point. Either it could be left to take its course or the press secretary, donning the hat of minder, could have intervened by attracting the Prime Minister's attention or perhaps, by diverting the conversation, have cut it short.

If O'Donnell did try to curtail the discussion, his attempt was not recorded. Nevertheless, the fact that it continued for so long, and culminated in Major's reference to 'bastards', became an issue of intense interest to those government press officers who are assigned to accompany ministers. Some see their role as being partly that of guardian and protector: they do check to see if recordings are still being made when ministers start chatting to broadcasters, and they say they would definitely find a way of intervening if a minister was being tempted to make indiscreet remarks about colleagues or was on the point of swearing. However, a few of the more hard-nosed heads of information told me that O'Donnell could not possibly have interrupted Major. One chief press officer was particularly blunt in his assessment. Cabinet ministers had to know how to behave in front of journalists at what he called their 'showtime'. If their tactic was to be one of the lads and engage in loose talk with the lobby, in the hope that it might improve their image and get them a favourable mention, they could not expect senior civil servants to act as nursemaids. The last few sentences of Major's chat with Brunson were perhaps the most revealing because they do show that the Prime Minister's matiness had a purpose. After reminding Brunson that 'every one of those bloody rebels' would have accused him of 'dodging' if he had not held a vote of confidence, Major ends with a direct appeal to ITN's political editor: 'How about a little credit for that. Quite a brave judgement.'

Some months were to elapse before the final, searing act in O'Donnell's exit from Downing Street. Bastardgate was perhaps a blur, no more than an unhappy memory, as he helped draw up the guest list for the farewell dinner which the Prime Minister was to host in his honour early in January 1994. Ten journalists were invited, mainly political editors from the quality dailies as well as several broadcasters, including Brunson. Within the lobby the invitations were highly prized. By implication these were the ten whom O'Donnell considered had been the most supportive and who were perhaps regarded by Major as being the most reliable. Almost all the political editors of the tabloids, including some past chairmen of the lobby, had been excluded. Some felt aggrieved. O'Donnell had unwittingly stirred up journalistic jealousies. A number of those who had been ignored would make sure the event did not slip by unrecorded.

In his final few months as press secretary O'Donnell had taken steps to tighten up on access to the Prime Minister. Lobby correspondents who went on foreign trips had remarked for some time that on return flights Major was nowhere near as informative or free and easy as he had been initially. The need for closer supervision had been reinforced during Major's trip to Tokyo. In between interviews in the grounds of the British embassy he was heard saying that half of the Conservatives rebels were 'barmy' and that whenever mention was made of one troublesome Tory MP, Sir Richard Body, he heard the sound of 'white coats flapping'. Perhaps not surprisingly, then, there were now far fewer chances for journalists to socialise with the Prime Minister. As opportunities to hear what he might be saying in relaxed circumstances were so limited, some reporters were doubly anxious to check out whether anything of interest had taken place at the dinner.

At moments like this the lobby operates its own pairing system, which can be as catholic in its twinning of partners as that between MPs from opposing parties who sometimes absent themselves simultaneously during divisions. Journalists often find it useful to work in pairs, sharing tips-offs and quotes. They might be just good friends; or perhaps their respective newspapers or news organisations are not in direct competition and so there is no conflict of interest over news content or deadlines. These private liaisons can be particularly useful after social occasions or when entry to an event is restricted. Therefore the fact that only ten members of the lobby had been invited to O'Donnell's dinner would not necessarily restrict the flow of information if it was judged to have been newsworthy.

Next day word spread round the lobby that the *Sun* and the *Daily Mail*, neither of whose political editors was invited to the dinner, were both working on stories to the effect that the Prime Minister had made another attack on his Cabinet colleagues. I heard myself that day that ministers on the right were concerned by reports that Major was still dissatisfied with them. Even before the first editions were printed Downing Street had got wind of the story and O'Donnell started alerting journalists immediately, telling them it was inaccurate. When the two newspapers appeared, both included the same quote, alleging that Major had launched another attack on right-wing members of his Cabinet, this time for sabotaging his back-to-basics campaign: 'I'm going to f****** crucify the right for what they have done and this time I will have the party behind me.' According to the *Daily Mail*'s political editor Gordon Greig, the Prime Minister had 'lobbed a grenade at the facade of Cabinet solidarity.' Under a joint by-line in the *Sun*, the political editor Trevor Kavanagh and political correspondent Simon Walters claimed the comments were made as Major was 'having a drink with a small circle of guests' before the dinner.

Downing Street's denial next morning could not have been more categoric. The two newspapers were accused of a 'malicious fiction'. O'Donnell had spoken by phone to every guest, none of whom had heard any such remark. He had checked personally with Major, who was equally adamant he had said nothing of the kind. In a radio interview Kavanagh said the *Sun* stuck by its story: 'The source we have is absolutely reliable. He was a guest at the dinner. His account was checked and rechecked.' Several newspapers alleged that Brunson was the source. He was seen talking privately to Major after the dinner. Another factor in the identification was said to have been the close proximity of the working areas of ITN and the *Sun*, whose journalists are grouped together in the same office in the press gallery. But ITN denied their political editor was the source and Brunson said he did not know where the story originated.

O'Donnell was distraught that his farewell dinner had been abused by journalists who were not even present. But the deepening hostility towards Major which was being shown by some of the popular papers should have served as a warning. Some of those who felt they had been snubbed were on the prowl, looking for a story which would show the

Prime Minister was still at war with his right-wing colleagues. Past experience had shown that Major was always at his most vulnerable when having heart-to-heart chats with reporters. Perhaps O'Donnell would have been better advised to have no journalists at all at the dinner rather than risk causing offence by inviting only a few. There could not have been a more dismal finale to his three years as press secretary.

Among the guests had been Sir Bernard Ingham, who gave his account in the *Daily Express*. At no point during the evening, or in his conversations with Major, did he hear anything which substantiated the story. But he knew that Kavanagh and Greig hunted together as 'a very sharp team' and he believed they were 'undoubtedly told something', even though that did not mean the Prime Minister was 'lying'. Ingham drew attention to O'Donnell's 'assiduity in ringing round the guests' which some in the lobby felt had only drawn more attention to the row. In his day as press secretary, Ingham said, he would first have checked with Mrs Thatcher. If she had denied it he would have issued a statement saying the stories in the *Sun* and *Daily Mail* were 'bunkum and balderdash' and then gone to bed, because 'Prime Ministers don't lie.'

Ingham's prescription found an unexpected echo a week later when the *Guardian* unearthed a briefing paper written by the new Downing Street press secretary Christopher Meyer, whose appointment had been announced that summer. He was previously second-in-command at the British embassy in Washington, but before moving there in 1989 had spent the preceding five years as press secretary at the Foreign Office. While on a year's sabbatical at Harvard University he had drawn on his experiences to write a paper entitled 'Hacks and Pin-Striped Appeasers' which set out what he called 'The Ten Commandments of dealing with reporters'. His ninth commandment was not to 'waste time remonstrating with reporters' who failed to write as a press officer might have wished.

Meyer's checklist was a source of much amusement, especially among those correspondents who had seen him operate in a formidable but effective double-act with Ingham. They had worked closely together in the late 1980s when briefing journalists during overseas trips by Mrs Thatcher and her then Foreign Secretary, Sir Geoffrey Howe. Meyer played a straight bat when he started giving his Downing Street briefings, seemingly determined to deny the lobby the chance of ticking off the qualities which he had said a press secretary required: 'quick wits, sense of humour, histrionic skills, self-confidence and a thick skin'.

Within a few weeks he had lived up to a prediction by Philip Stephens, political editor of the *Financial Times*, that the new, self-assured press secretary looked as if he would enjoy the combat of 'selling policy to sceptical journalists'. There was an instant clarity about his briefings.

He was obviously following his own dictum that when a government could not the make the news it should deploy 'irresistible phrases' to attract attention and use the briefings to 'score points and to shape the agenda'. When the Sinn Fein president Gerry Adams received a hero's welcome from much of the American news media in February 1994, Meyer told the morning lobby that a 'smokescreen of evasion and false-hoods' would not deceive the British people. His briefing instantly made the front-page splash in the *Evening Standard* under the headline: 'Major blasts lies of Adams'.

When correspondents tackled him about the ineffectiveness of the Foreign Secretary, Douglas Hurd, in countering Adams' publicity, as he was in America at the same time, Meyer hit back: 'He worked his arse off to get on American television.' The lobby had heard nothing like it since Ingham's abrasive briefings. A suggestion next day that Adams' visit had damaged relations between Downing Street and the White House brought an equally colourful riposte: 'That is complete balls.' On being answered back in its own language the *Sun* took fright. A profile of Meyer, written by Simon Walters, claimed that Major's 'ruthless' new press secretary had set out to 'intimidate political journalists' and 'swears if they annoy him'. Meyer was to take no reprimands from the *Sun*. Six months later he was heard chiding one political editor for hav-ing asked a 'balls-aching' question.

Journalists rarely took offence on those occasions when, as the press secretary said himself, he chose to reply in undiplomatic language. As his second commandment had stipulated that the 'trick is to leave the re-porter in good humour, even if you can tell him nothing', Meyer de-veloped some colourful warm-up routines. Although he dressed quite soberly, the lobby were to be wowed by a dazzling display of accessories. The apricot braces he wore at his first lobby were replaced by a flowery pair the following week. Sometimes there was colour coordination – a blue shirt and blue braces; another day loud check socks and yellow braces. He enjoyed the repartee this provoked. 'Yes, I do change my socks every day. Do you?' was his barbed response when asked if we were getting a preview of his outfit for the Corfu summit. Once suitably softened up the lobby was less likely to be hostile.

Meyer shared Ingham's knack of hitting the odd-ball inquiry into touch. My attempt in June 1994 to tease out information about the imminent Cabinet reshuffle was parried with a theatrical flourish. 'My word, your eyes were blazing when you asked that question.' Meyer had left me feeling like the lobby's Little Red Riding Hood. Several months after that encounter I discovered that at some briefings he tried to be erudite and amusing on purpose, having decided beforehand, for tacti-cal reasons, that it was best to say nothing of consequence. Usually something of significance was planned for the next day and in order to get the lobby salivating in anticipation he tried to be as jolly as possible without saying anything to alert the journalists. Inside No. 10 these were known by his staff as Meyer's 'boring days' and they would wait to see if he had succeeded in keeping the lobby entertained but the government's plans under wraps.

Conservative MPs were in two minds about what to make of the new press secretary. After his hand was detected behind some sharp news management on the day when the Prime Minister gave short shrift to Sir George Gardiner, chairman of the pro-Thatcher 92 Group, one Major loyalist said Meyer had earned his first year's salary in his first fortnight. But George Walden, MP for Buckingham, who had worked with him at the Foreign Office, said the idea the government could outpace the media by 'snappy news management' was wrong. It was a race the government was bound to lose because mass communication techniques were predicated on the 'permanency of a bone headed public'. Matthew Parris, writing in *The Times*, also struck a note of caution, saying it was not Major's destiny to lead Britain through thrilling times, and therefore he felt the instinct of Meyer to 'touch up the greasepaint and turn up the limelight' was dangerous because it only whetted the appetite for the next fluffed line by a Prime Minister who was not a natural performer.

But Meyer was scoring points where it mattered most. He had put a firm stop to unstructured encounters between the Prime Minister and the lobby. On the plane taking Major to Moscow journalists were told they would be 'wasting their time' if they tried to ask about ministerial sex scandals back home. In his live two-way report from outside the Kremlin, Michael Brunson told *News at Ten* that Major had been very 'tough with the tabloids and given them the brush-off'. Alastair Campbell moaned about the lack of access in his column in *Today*, saying the press might as well have taken a different plane because Major had become 'the invisible man'. Less grudgingly, Major's visit a month later to see President Clinton was described by the *Sunday Telegraph*'s political correspondent Toby Helm as a 'triumph' in news management. After the Prime Minister had answered half a dozen questions at his White House press conference Meyer intervened, stopped the proceedings and whisked Major away. The aim was to make sure that the Prime Minister's exposure to the media was 'short, sharp and on the record', with none of the 'drinks parties on embassy lawns at which the Prime Minister opened his heart'.

A similarly deft touch was shown in the wake of the Conservatives' disastrous results in elections to the European Parliament. Major started off what promised to be a difficult week by holding a Monday afternoon news conference on the back lawn of No. 10. It looked for all the world like a presidential briefing in the White House rose garden and was a clever diversionary tactic which provided plenty of pictures for television and the newspapers. Major held out the prospect of a wide-ranging Cabinet reshuffle and said he hoped to hold more on-the-record news conferences. Meyer basked in the favourable publicity but was careful not to claim the credit. He told me that 'all such ideas spring from the Prime Minister.'

It was almost three months into Meyer's tenure before political journalists could claim they had caught him out. When questioned in March about arrangements for the fiftieth anniversary of VE Day, he confirmed that Germany would be playing a 'full part' in the celebrations. The tabloids were ready to pounce. 'German Army To March Through London' was the *Sun*'s headline over its claim that the Prime Minister had given the go-ahead to an event which could 'revive grim memories of goose-stepping German hordes'. Next morning correspondents were told Major would be guided by the veterans' associations. While there might be units from the modern German army, those who served in the Third Reich would not be invited, which prompted the inevitable headline next day: 'The Sun Bans The Hun'. Andrew Alexander, writing in the *Daily Mail*, said the shambles over VE Day could not be passed off by the Prime Minister's press advisers as simply 'a terrible misunderstanding'.

Inevitably as the year progressed there were other slip-ups. Some seemed self-inflicted; Meyer allowed himself to get drawn all too easily into heated and rather personal arguments with several correspondents, and while he enjoyed such spats they had a tendency to disrupt the flow of his briefings. I heard from other Downing Street staff that he realised he could 'lose sight of the ball' if provoked. But what struck me most of all was the way Meyer was observing his tenth commandment – the assumption by all press secretaries that 'everything you say will be reported.' After several months I came to the conclusion that he was in fact making a small but nonetheless noteworthy contribution towards ensuring that the lobby system does eventually become more accountable.

On busy days he went out of his way to open his briefings with what were obviously carefully scripted responses to the main news story. They were delivered in tight, punchy sentences which Meyer knew only too well would be reproduced verbatim by television, radio and the newspapers. He was in effect supplying the broadcasters with a soundbite, attributable to Downing Street, and providing a reply which could appear inside quotation marks in next day's newspapers. Perhaps the clearest example was his response in June 1994 to the television programme in which Prince Charles acknowledged publicly his adulterous affair with Camilla Parker Bowles. He said that if the Prime Minister were asked whether the Prince's admission had any constitutional implications, Major's response would be: 'Prince Charles is heir to the throne, he remains heir to the throne and when the time comes will be King.' Almost every newspaper and news bulletin carried the quote in full.

Meyer himself has refused to be drawn whenever I have asked him about the way he has approached his job, but colleagues in Downing Street, who say he has attracted praise for the firm grip he has maintained on the lobby briefings, described his technique to me. Each morning he would work out with Major a clear factual response to the most pressing issue of the day and then get sufficient background information to enable him to steer his way round difficult questions. The aim always was to make the first answer sufficiently strong so that journalists' follow-up questions remained focused firmly on the line No. 10 was taking. Meyer had a great aptitude for thinking up vibrant phrases which he knew might make headlines or soundbites and he had learned how to feed them to journalists, thus helping Major regain control over the flow of information from his government.

The importance of trying to establish a clear direction to a running story in time for the 11 a.m. lobby briefing should not be underestimated. If the press secretary can succeed in influencing the lunchtime news bulletins, then Downing Street has a much better chance of ensuring that next day's newspapers follow the same line. While his instant, first answers have been tailor-made for television, radio and the news agencies, and were being widely used, Meyer has become somewhat constrained by the knowledge that his subsequent replies, which were sometimes less precise, were also appearing as direct quotes pegged to Downing Street. Therefore, like his predecessors, he developed the habit of giving fuller briefings by phone on a selective basis, prompting talk of a new 'white Commonwealth' of political editors and correspondents whom he was prepared to trust.

After almost a year as press secretary, Meyer was in the fortunate position of being able to demonstrate to his colleagues in the higher echelons of Whitehall that it was possible for a career civil servant to bring a sense of order to the Prime Minister's media relations. He had become as aggressive as Ingham in his dealings with the lobby but had eschewed the personal publicity which Mrs Thatcher's press secretary had revelled in; and he had also proved surer-footed than Gus O'Donnell. Meyer had no hesitation in laying on Christmas drinks for the lobby and proved to be a genial host. Major and his Cabinet ministers mingled freely with the journalists invited to the reception at No. 10; there was none of the unease of the previous year and the event passed off without any snide stories in the tabloids. The first few weeks of 1995 were to provide another illustration of Meyer's steadying hand in Downing

Street and his ability to make the most of any opportunity, however short-lived, to repair Major's credibility with the electorate.

Labour were bedevilled at the turn of the year by a sucession of embarrassing policy disagreements. On top of the anxiety sparked off by Tony Blair's announcement that he wanted to abandon the party's historic Clause Four commitment to common ownership, there were conflicting statements on the approach a future Labour government might adopt towards private education and the possibility of renationalising privatised railway services. In mid-January, at the height of Labour's disarray, Major seized the initiative, holding another on-the-record, televised news conference, this time in the state dining room at Downing Street. Meyer did all he could to build up the importance of the occasion. He told the 11 a.m. lobby that the Prime Minister intended taking the afternoon briefing himself at 3.30 p.m. so that he could outline his plans for 1995 and beyond. American journalists and other members of the foreign press corps were invited. As there was insufficient space, extra seats had be provided in an overflow room next door.

Major announced that a series of meetings would be held at Chequers to look at the government's domestic and social policies for the new millennium. There could have been no clearer indication that the Prime Minister intended leading his party into the next general election. The timing could not be faulted. If the news conference had been held a month or two earlier, when the government was beset by its own problems, his plans for 'the next phase of Conservatism' might well have been met with hoots of derision from sceptical political correspondents; but because of Labour's difficulties there was a new-found respect for Major's determination to pick himself up and look ahead. He stood at a podium of the kind used at the White House and delivered a three-page statement with considerable fluency. He then answered questions. He was obviously well prepared. Before responding to several tricky questions about the Conservatives' difficulties over Europe, Major flicked over to the relevant page in his notes and then turned in some well-crafted replies.

Meyer remained at the far side of the room throughout the proceedings. He stayed well out of range of the television cameras and newspaper photographers, and at no point did he seek to intervene or draw attention to his presence. Several senior civil servants had told me of the care which he took to avoid the larger-than-life poses which Ingham had delighted in striking on such high-profile occasions. Meyer was also being praised for the contributions he was making to top-level meetings attended by ministers and their permanent secretaries: I was told by one regular participant that the press secretary frequently put forward his own ideas on future strategy.

Meyer's strategic thinking and eye for detail could be detected in the elaborate arrangements which No. 10 made towards the end of February 1995 for briefing political editors and senior correspondents about the contents of the framework document on the future of Northern Ireland. Because of a premature leak in *The Times* earlier that month about the likely proposals of the British and Irish governments, the press secretary had to proceed with great secrecy when he drew up plans for what turned out to be an unprecedented gathering of the most prominent members of the lobby.

John Major had occasionally given off-the-record briefings himself before, at other significant moments in his premiership, but his attempt to achieve a lasting political settlement in Northern Ireland had become something of a personal crusade. In order to impress on key political journalists the likely historic importance of the framework document he invited a tightly restricted group to sit with him round the Cabinet table so that he could explain what had been agreed with Dublin. For many of the journalists it was their first visit to the Cabinet room. The briefing took place at 5 p.m. on Tuesday 21 February, shortly before the Prime Minister departed for Belfast in preparation for the joint unveiling of the document next day with the Irish premier, John Bruton.

In giving press and broadcasters a detailed run-down on the eve of publication of such a controversial document Major was taking a risk, especially given the sensitivities of the Ulster Unionist MPs and the need to avoid giving any offence to the Irish government, and Meyer enforced strict conditions to ensure that secrecy was maintained. I was not one of those invited to attend the briefing. Political correspondents from three leading provincial newspapers, the *Scotsman*, *Glasgow Herald* and *Liverpool Daily Post*, protested about their failure to be invited. In piecing together what had happened I discovered that political editors from national newspapers and broadcasting organisations, together with some senior correspondents, were told to report to the Cabinet Office entrance in Whitehall which provides access to No. 10. Meyer was apparently anxious to prevent the journalists he had selected from having to walk up Downing Street where they might be filmed or photographed, thus alerting other reporters. Once they were all seated around the Cabinet table, Major surveyed what he assumed was the cream of the lobby and tried to lighten the occasion. He said he often got advice on who should make up his Cabinet, but when he looked at the assembled company he did not think it was 'much of an improvement'. Meyer's staff handed out to those present numbered copies of a summary of the framework document which had to be handed back before they left. The journalists were told they must never reveal that the briefing had taken place. As they left, Meyer slipped a note to Major and the

Prime Minister cracked another joke, saying he had been asked by his press secretary to make sure that the journalists took all their 'bugs and tape recorders' with them and didn't leave any behind. Several of the political editors had been in the Cabinet room before: Major had taken to using it, in preference to the No.10 drawing room, when giving newspaper and radio interviews, because he could lay out his papers in front of him on the Cabinet table. As at question time, when he always had with him a ring-binder file containing his briefing notes, Major appeared to be at ease and in control when he had the information he required spread out before him, at his fingertips.

Meyer deserved credit for going some way in opening up access to the Prime Minister. Major's two on-the-record briefings, in the No.10 garden and in the state dining room, were seen as welcome innovations because they were open to all lobby correspondents. Although the press secretary had won plaudits from the select band who were briefed secretly by Major in the Cabinet room, the lobby en masse were nowhere near as ecstatic in their assessment of Meyer's first year in post. When compared with the O'Donnell regime there had undoubtedly been a marked reduction in the quantity and depth of information which was being supplied about Major's thinking on the key issues of the day: if Meyer thought it inopportune to go over the background to what in fact were already well-known policy positions, he simply stonewalled.

I attempted without success to establish the basis on which Major was approaching the 1996 conference on the future of the European Union. As the Prime Minister had said repeatedly that the high-water mark of European integration had passed, I inquired if this meant that Britain believed that the tide of federalism should recede. Meyer would give no clue about Major's thinking and, as he seemed determined to brazen it out, I rather foolishly made a quip to the effect that after high water the tide usually went out. The press secretary pounced on this with glee. He started quizzing me on my nautical experience and inquired if by any chance there was an ancient mariner in the lobby that morning who could adjudicate. I realised there was no point trying again. Meyer, who was wearing bright pink socks that morning and was in a particularly bouncy mood, enjoyed his tease. I only wished it had been possible to televise our exchange. While he could get away with ridiculing a hapless BBC correspondent in the privacy of a lobby briefing, his conduct would have been extremely risky at an open news conference.

Meyer's tactic of perpetually playing down speculation about Cabinet splits on Europe usually benefited not only Major himself but also the entire Downing Street operation. Political journalists were given no opportunity to pin tales of ministerial disunity on to either the press secretary or other members of the Prime Minister's staff. In view of

Meyer's attempts to close down discussion at lobby briefings on stories about Europe, there was considerable interest when the Conservatives' communications director Tim Collins gave his own briefing early in February 1995 about the content of Major's speech to the annual dinner of Conservative Way Forward, one of the most Euro-sceptic groups in the party. Collins said Major would be setting out additional conditions which would have to be met before Britain was prepared to consider joining a European single currency. The new criteria had apparently been agreed between Major and both the Foreign Secretary, Douglas Hurd, and the Chancellor, Kenneth Clarke.

Collins' advance guidance ensured widespread news coverage, especially of Major's warning that unless the economic conditions were right, a single currency 'would tear the European Union apart'. Most attention focused on the key sentence in the speech about the new terms Major had in mind: 'By the right economic conditions, the Government does not only mean the Maastricht criteria. They are a necessary but not a sufficient condition to justify a single currency.' Next morning the story was the front-page splash in *The Times*, and the *Daily Mail* regarded Major's remarks as a clear signal that the Prime Minister had 'discounted Britain's early entry into a single currency'. The news media's interpretation of the speech as proof that Major had shifted towards a harder Euro-sceptic position alarmed pro-European ministers like Michael Heseltine, who said the government should not wrap itself 'in a national flag'. Two days later Downing Street contradicted Collins' briefing, insisting that Major had not laid down stringent new conditions and had simply drawn attention to the existing requirements in the Maastricht Treaty. However, at question time the following day Major repeated his earlier phraseology, insisting that Britain 'would require other criteria to be met' before joining a single currency.

The conflict only served to underline the wisdom of Meyer's reluctance to sum up Major's position towards Europe in a series of snapshots when it was obvious that government policy was on the move. Meyer was equally resolute in his refusal to comment on Tory party divisions over Europe. While his conduct was eminently sensible in terms of civil service proprieties, his caution and lack of clarity about the government's approach to Europe confused political journalists and reinforced the argument in favour of a publicity supremo in Downing Street who could tackle issues which affected both the government and the party.

Meyer's ability to dodge straightforward questions about Europe with impunity illustrated the one-sided nature of his briefings. Nevertheless his practice of preparing precise and succinct responses on other significant and often newsworthy issues did seem to be a worthwhile advance. Although critics of the lobby system would regard this as an

John Gummer, then agriculture minister, was awarded first prize in the *Guardian*'s contest for the most counter-productive media image of 1990 for appearing to force-feed his daughter Cordelia with a beefburger at the height of the scare about eating beef during the panic over 'mad cow' disease. His explanation for hanging on to the beefburger was that it was too hot for Cordelia to hold herself. (Anglia Press Agency)

Ron Brown's damning photo-opportunity in January 1990 was choreographed by the news media: photographers bought the bottle of champagne and handed it to him already opened. (Simon Runting/*The Sun*/Rex)

Bernard Ingham (*above*, with Margaret Thatcher and Australian premier Bob Hawke) and John Major's first press secretary Gus O'Donnell (*below*) both observing the first rule of a Downing Street media chief: don't get too close to the Prime Minister. By standing a few paces to one side they keep within earshot but do not clutter up the picture for the television cameras and newspaper photographers. (Tom Pilston/*The Independent*; Tim Bishop/Times Newspapers)

Above: Michael Heseltine with his family walking through the grounds of his country mansion at Thenford near Banbury during the 1990 Conservative leadership contest. His political opponents contrasted Heseltine's opulent surroundings with the humble origins of John Major. (Brian Harris / *The Independent*)

Below: Tony Blair had an ecstatic send-off after being elected Labour leader in July 1994, but frequently looked nervous and uneasy before finally mastering doorstep encounters with the media pack. (Graham Turner / *The Guardian*)

Spin doctors. *Above:* Peter Mandelson was advising Tony Blair long before his undercover role as 'Bobby' in the 1994 Labour leadership election. This photograph was taken at the 1990 Labour conference, Mandelson's last as the party's director of communications and Blair's first as shadow employment secretary. (John Voos/ *The Independent*) *Below:* Contact between journalists and Tony Blair was under the firm control of Alastair Campbell from the moment he became Labour's press secretary and media minder. (Don MacPhee/*The Guardian*)

Above: The photo-opportunity: how to do it. David Mellor's carefully staged family gathering in the summer of 1992, when, in an attempt to counter adverse publicity over his affair with the actress Antonia de Sancha, he called on his in-laws and his wife Joan to join in a group picture which he laid on for television crews and newspaper photographers. (Chris Bott/Express Newspapers)

Below: The photo-opportunity: how not to do it. Tim Yeo was a marked man once the *News of the World* disclosed he had a 'love child' in December 1993, and by hiding his face in his luggage on leaving the Seychelles after a family holiday he fuelled newspaper publicity, hastening his own resignation from the government. (Simon Runting/*The Sun*/Rex)

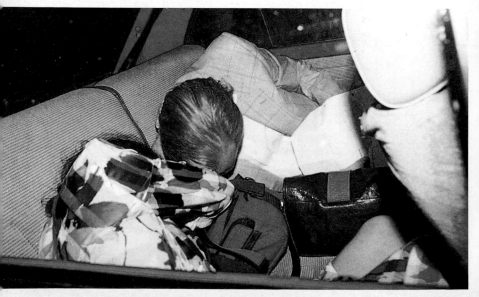

Above: Corporate affairs minister Neil Hamilton was so confident he could see off the news media during the 'cash for questions' allegations in October 1994 that he even suggested a caption when posing for photographers: 'The man who takes the biscuit!' Five days later he was forced to resign. (John Giles/PA News)
Below: BBC industrial correspondent Steve Evans waiting patiently for a soundbite from Labour's shadow chancellor Gordon Brown at the 1994 TUC Conference. (Clare Arron)

After his appointment as Chancellor of the Exchequer in May 1993 Kenneth Clarke could not resist engaging in a Morecambe and Wise double act with Chief Secretary Michael Portillo on the Treasury steps for the benefit of photographers and television crews. Afterwards he regretted being enticed into a photo-opportunity that made the two of them look like 'a couple of mafia bosses who had just taken over a night club'. (Edward Sykes / *The Independent*)

attempt to manipulate and spoon-feed political journalists, his tightly worded answers were to all intents and purposes the equivalent of on-the-record statements and could be used as a fixed point of reference when piecing together the government's response to fast-moving political events. Meyer had built successfully on Gus O'Donnell's initiative of allowing lobby correspondents to source statements directly to the Prime Minister's office. It seemed like another small, unheralded step towards the day when political journalists at Westminster, like their counterparts in Washington, might be invited to daily briefings which were on camera and could be recorded.

O'Donnell had always insisted that he was against televised briefings. He feared there was a danger the press secretary might end up becoming a personality and thus endanger the Prime Minister's standing. Meyer indicated by his demeanour that he too had no intention of attracting the attention of the news media. Labour have said consistently that they would make the post of Downing Street press secretary a party appointment. If Tony Blair became Prime Minister the job would almost certainly go to his press officer Alastair Campbell. As an experienced journalist and broadcaster, Campbell could take televised briefings in his stride if Labour were to go one step further and introduce a tightly controlled system of on-the-record briefings on camera.

One other option canvassed by Sir Bernard Ingham has been the possibility of appointing a minister with specific responsibility for explaining government policy. Ingham believed that governments had to recognise that a civil service chief press secretary could no longer perform the job which needed to be done for the party in power. His readiness to see change was welcomed by Labour's director of communications David Hill, who considered that future holders of the most politicised job in Whitehall had to be people who could 'speak about the government and about the party that government represents without fear or hindrance'. Their words only confirmed my confident belief that the whole edifice of the unattributable lobby briefing was indeed, slowly but surely, collapsing.

5

Adding the Spin

JUST AS Bernard Ingham was feared and respected within the Thatcher administration, so Peter Mandelson came to be mentioned with awe among Labour politicians. His influence has extended over a decade in which the party has been rebuilt and relaunched in the wake of successive general election defeats. Unlike a powerful press secretary in Downing Street, Mandelson had no solid base of government action or achievement around which to structure his promotional activities. In his years as Labour's publicity supremo, and more recently in his less clearcut role as unofficial media confidant to the party leadership, he could not fall back on well-ordered public events or take refuge behind unexpected international crises; all too often he was left in the unenviable position of having to put the best possible construction on unwelcome developments. He had to operate in a party hostile to change, against a background of deep public scepticism. As a result the significance of certain political events needed to be played down while others had to be hyped for all they were worth. The roles he undertook were an almost perfect job description for the work of a spin doctor, for that was what Peter Mandelson became: Labour's most celebrated media manipulator.

The names Ingham and Mandelson run like twin threads through Conservative and Labour mythology of recent years. In both parties their supposed achievements and deficiencies were seen by friend and foe alike as a yardstick against which to measure political propaganda and intrigue. Governments have far greater ability than opposition parties to control their own affairs, so Ingham could often dictate the flow of news for which he was responsible, while Mandelson was forced to respond to events: the Labour leadership had nowhere near as much say over the content and timing of the information which flowed from what was frequently a fractious party. But although he was regularly pushed on to the defensive – as, indeed, was Ingham – Mandelson had greater freedom to develop his undoubted talent as a spin doctor. His aim was to use the news stories which he supplied to journalists as a way of helping push through political change in the party. While he made enemies in the process, he demonstrated that a Labour opposition could be as successful as a Conservative government in exploiting the news media.

Any appraisal of the power which Mandelson wielded requires an understanding of the modus operandi of spin doctors and an appreciation of the complex and varied relationships which they develop with their clientele, in this case the political journalists. An essential qualification is an ability to understand and predict how reporters might think and react in any given set of circumstances. While most self-respecting publicists can dream up a story and imagine how they would like to see it presented, a far harder task is to calculate in advance what might be the worst-case scenario should the news media decide to put the least favourable interpretation on what has happened.

Political spin doctors are usually fairly open about much of their work. Their natural habitat is around Westminster and at party conferences. They give advice on the content of speeches and the likely implication of votes and decisions. Their busiest times are immediately after major political developments, when journalists are often desperate to speak to authoritative sources capable of giving them an instant interpretation of what has happened and also background guidance on the likely consequences. This can be a decisive moment, because the spin doctor is acting as a sounding board: if reporters have got the wrong impression, or their story-lines look like being damaging to the party, then considerable powers of persuasion can be called for.

The most manipulative conversations tend to take place in private. However smart or appealing a political message might appear, the opportunities for communicating it can be fluid and unpredictable. A long-planned event can easily be upstaged by another major news story. Newspapers and programmes have a nasty habit of veering off in new and unexpected directions as editorial fashions come and go. A spin doctor cannot hope to operate successfully without first having established a coterie of trusted reporters and other contacts. These journalists might move jobs and transfer between different news outlets, but relationships which have been built up over a period of years provide the surest foundation for skilful media management.

If a tricky political development is in the offing a spin doctor can start guiding and tweaking the focus of the news coverage by slipping out some well-placed leaks. If the reporters who are tipped off in advance prove reliable in what they write and broadcast, and if they also have the advantage of being respected by other journalists, then it can become clear that these initial speculative reports are not being denied and therefore should be regarded as correct, without the spin doctor having to do anything as explicit as issuing an official statement. Mission accomplished: the spin has started to work and the rest of the news media should, if all goes well, continue to follow in the right direction.

Because the whole operation can be finely balanced an accurate diagnosis is needed of the strengths and weaknesses of individual journalists. A leaked news story which backfires can cause immense damage not only to a party but also to a spin doctor's reputation. Trust is essential. As a result the usefulness of various reporters tends to be determined by the reputation which they have acquired for protecting their sources. An assessment will have to made of those journalists who should be avoided. Others might be deemed worthy of cultivation; some could appear vulnerable to discreet pressure and similarly might be useful one day.

No spin doctor can hope to prove effective without an intimate grasp of the complex and confusing hierarchies of newspaper offices and broadcasting organisations. If a complaint is to be taken notice of, or if an attempt is being made to influence news coverage, it will have to be pitched at the right point. The command structures of television and radio services can be the most baffling of all. Sometimes instant action is called for and the best course will be to rebuke the reporter concerned. If the protest is more serious an approach might be made direct to the relevant programme editor; a constructive dialogue here could help secure favourable coverage in the future.

If the spin doctor has the necessary authority, and the aim is to create maximum impact, there is always the option of going right to the top, to a senior member of the management. In this way journalists and programme staff can be put on the spot by being forced to respond unexpectedly but immediately to what has suddenly become a high-level complaint. The overall effect can be quite alarming for those concerned and the spin doctor will then have achieved the desired effect: intimidation.

Peter Mandelson was unknown and untested at Westminster when he was taken on as Labour's campaigns and communications director in 1985; but within a few years, his spin on political stories was being widely sought by many respected journalists. His appointment had the enthusiastic backing of Neil Kinnock because he brought with him what Labour badly needed: expertise in television production. He had been a producer with London Weekend for the preceding three years, first on *The London Programme* and then on the weekly political programme *Weekend World*. He has since spoken enthusiastically of how, when working with the production team, he loved 'the immersion in policy analysis' in what was a key period of the Thatcher government. Although he was a producer and not a presenter, he discovered what it felt like to be interviewed: 'Brian Walden used to practise on me on the day before his *Weekend World* showdown.'

In subsequent years Mandelson put his experience to good use in monitoring the work of television and radio journalists. If he felt a broadcaster
had let an interviewee off too lightly, or failed to ask the obvious follow-up
questions, he liked nothing more than to point this out, relishing the
chance to get embroiled in a discussion about interview techniques. My
encounters with Mandelson have been many and varied, but one of my
favourites was the set-to we had in February 1990 over his suggestion that
I had been 'too soft' when interviewing Sir Bernard Ingham about a
vitriolic attack which he had made on declining journalistic standards.
As the criticisms made by the Downing Street press secretary seemed so
outlandish, the aim of my questions was to get Ingham to substantiate
what he was saying. But Mandelson felt I should have been far more
challenging. When I bridled he became rather sniffy and pulled rank:
'Don't give me that. I know all about the come-on, come-on technique. I
used to help write the questions for Brian Walden.'

Mandelson's lasting value to the Labour leadership has been his
understanding of the factors which motivate political journalists. He
seemed to have a sixth sense: on seeing a group of them congregating in
the members' lobby, or chatting away in the press gallery, he could guess,
usually quite accurately, what the various reporters were up to and which
of the day's stories they were likely to be discussing. His knowledge of the
inner workings of television and radio newsrooms, and the background
information which he acquired about the likes and dislikes of individual
lobby correspondents, was of enormous benefit as he helped the party to
develop well-rehearsed routines for publicising policy initiatives. As the
years went by he was to become increasingly proficient at what for a spin
doctor amounted to sheer artistry: the ability to determine which journalists were likely to be of most use to him and could therefore achieve the
greatest impact in return for the information he had to offer.

Mandelson's introduction to political publicity was an opportunity to
assist Labour at the 1985 Brecon and Radnor by-election, during *Weekend
World*'s summer break. He enjoyed promoting the candidate and dealing
with journalists. Some key figures in the party were so impressed he was
encouraged to apply for the vacant post heading the department at party
headquarters which handled promotion and press liaison. His initial task
on taking up the job that October was to work out ways of improving the
party's publicity and marketing. He commissioned a report from Philip
Gould, an advertising executive, which proposed that Labour should
adopt a new corporate identity. Neil Kinnock favoured having a red rose
as the new party symbol. The designers agreed, and it duly appeared at
the 1986 party conference.

That red rose came to typify the glitzy presentation of the Kinnock era.
Mandelson was credited by most journalists as having devised and

masterminded these changes. 'Labour's red-rose guru' was a description adopted frequently by headline writers. He has always insisted to me that he had a specific role in the process. 'I delivered and negotiated the rose for Neil Kinnock...I negotiated its passage through the party.' After Labour's 1987 general election defeat he denied that the failure of their campaign was attributable to a 'triumph of style over substance'.

Mandelson's day-to-day contact with journalists, in his capacity as party spokesman, began to take up far more time than he had expected. Anti-Labour news stories were all too prevalent throughout the 1980s, putting the party leadership under constant pressure to respond. Because of his grasp of Labour's inner politics, and his ready availability, Mandelson was always in demand. His close working relationship with Kinnock made him an authoritative source; journalists would not be satisfied about the authenticity of a story or of the accuracy of the party's response until they had spoken to him personally. For the first two years he never went out on Saturday evenings as he found he was being rung up continuously by reporters busily following up the first editions of the Sunday newspapers which, he said, always had 'some appalling story' about Labour. Subsequently, looking back on his period as communications director, he said his 'worst nightmare' was the perpetual thought that the Sundays would have a damaging story which he knew nothing about. In his final years he estimated that ninety per cent of his time was being spent dealing with the news media, or what his friends and colleagues called his 'spin doctoring'.

Mandelson's aptitude for publicity, and for coordinating what had previously been the party's disparate efforts at promotion, became a key factor in the successful implementation of Labour's two-year policy review which started in 1988. By its very nature the process had to be gradual as each change provoked stiff opposition. But favourable news coverage, orchestrated by Mandelson, helped keep up the impetus towards achieving the objectives which were so dear to Kinnock's heart, like the acceptance of secret ballots before strike action and the abandoning of Labour's commitment to unilateral nuclear disarmament. Mandelson believed that it was this work which should be regarded as his main contribution. It could best be described, he said, as the 'complex political task of managing and then presenting policy change'.

Unlike the Conservative Party, which only went into top gear for general elections, Mandelson was determined Labour should aim for maximum exposure on a continuous basis. In this way he hoped the party could both get their policies across to the electorate and counter the widespread coverage which government departments could command. He never let up in his drive for publicity, proceeding at what for the opposition was an unprecedented pace. Each week the party tried to arrange a series of news conferences at Westminster in order to attack the government and promote alternative ideas. Mandelson cast his net way beyond the confines of political journalism, assigning press officers to topical subject areas so as to encourage regular contact with the widest possible range of specialist correspondents. Other press officers in his department worked closely with members of the shadow Cabinet. Once a news conference had been arranged, television and radio journalists would be alerted. Advance notification would also be issued in the press gallery. Staff would frequently phone directly to programme editors and producers, offering to fix up interviews. These approaches would then be backed up by further calls from front-benchers' research assistants, and shadow ministers would regularly ring in themselves to enquire whether they were needed. If lunchtime or afternoon programmes had not shown any interest party workers would repeat the exercise later in the day, in time for the evening bulletins.

By dint of these time-consuming procedures Mandelson forced Labour to adapt to the opportunities which had been thrown up by the growing proliferation of television and radio services. A decade earlier the Conservatives had put Labour to shame in their mastery of television deadlines. During the 1979 general election campaign Tory media strategists engineered a succession of strategically timed photo opportunities so as to ensure a constant supply of fresh pictures. Margaret Thatcher acquired a dynamic image, always on the move, ready to face fresh challenges. Labour fared no better in the 1983 election, when the party's failure to take account of the importance of presentation meant that frequently the only pictures of Michael Foot available to the television news bulletins were of the party leader walking his Tibetan terrier Dizzie on Hampstead Heath.

By the late 1980s increased competition in broadcasting had led to changing patterns in reporting. Each news programme was striving to establish a separate and distinct identity. News summaries were being revised and rewritten from one hour to the next. More often than not, the top political story of the day was also being treated differently throughout the day by the main news bulletins. This required extensive reworking and repackaging between the lunchtime, teatime and main evening news programmes. The format of rolling news, whereby stories are constantly updated, provided another ideal platform for politicians who could respond instantly. Mandelson saw the opportunities to exploit the rapid turnover which all this entailed. He knew that programme editors were insisting on fresh material, and preferably a fresh angle, for every major bulletin. Production-line journalism was open to manipulation: running stories had to be freshened-up at regular intervals whether or not there had been any significant developments. The more a political party plugged into this process, the greater were its chances of influencing the way political news was reported. The critical period was immediately before the editorial decisions were taken on how each story would be updated: this was the moment to offer an alternative interview or suggest a fresh news line.

Labour became adept at maximising their chances. Staff tracked the progress of the principal political stories as they moved through each day's bulletins and programmes. The party was then in a position to respond the moment an opportunity arose. Whenever possible Mandelson monitored the output himself. If he thought Labour's views had been ignored or misrepresented he would telephone the reporter, producer or editor, depending on the strength of the point he wanted to make. During parliamentary recesses Labour attempted to maintain media interest by continuing to hold frequent news conferences and photo opportunities. Staff would seek out the names of the correspondents allocated to particular stories or assigned to weekend duty so they could make instant contact should the need arise. Another precaution was to obtain the phone numbers of temporary newsrooms established during party conferences. Mandelson's strategy was clear: if the opposition were to stand any chance of beating the inbuilt advantages of the party in power they had to initiate stories and establish superior lines of communication. His effectiveness was one of the factors which forced Ingham to step up his efforts to strengthen the coordination of government publicity.

The more Mandelson opened up Labour's access to television and radio, the greater became his authority in advising on and then deciding how the party should capitalise on this extra exposure. Rather than ring round the whole of the shadow Cabinet, programme editors and producers started to deal directly with Mandelson when making their bids to interview front-bench spokesmen. Ultimately he was to insist that all such requests should be channelled through his office. Some shadow ministers grew suspicious, claiming they were not being allocated interviews because Mandelson considered they were too left-wing or not sufficiently telegenic for Labour's new image. Michael Meacher was one of the first to complain. He was switched in November 1989 from employment to social security after a disagreement with Kinnock over trade union rights. He became convinced Mandelson had worked to remove him from the political front line. I was told at the time by Mandelson that the reason for the *frisson* which had arisen with Kinnock was that Meacher was allowing an impression to be created that Labour might put the clock back to before 1979 on employment law. After he lost the trade and industry brief, Bryan Gould became equally critical of what he suspected was the involvement of the party's publicity director. John Prescott, who also complained that he was being kept off the television screens, caused much amusement at the Red Revue at the 1989 party conference by performing a sketch in which he accused Mandelson of trying to impose a thirty-year secrecy rule on the information which he was 'feeding to journalists'.

While some Labour politicians felt excluded from the Mandelson publicity machine there were others who benefited, most notably the newly appointed trade and industry spokesman Gordon Brown and the new shadow employment secretary Tony Blair – indeed, the publicising of these two 'rising stars' by Mandelson was described by the *Financial Times* in December 1989 as having caused irritation throughout the shadow Cabinet. Another beneficiary was Mo Mowlam, who had joined the front bench as city affairs specialist. Mandelson advised her to insist on being addressed as 'Dr Marjorie Mowlam' because, as the *Independent on Sunday* put it, Labour's spin doctor considered 'Mo' was 'too fluffy and lightweight a moniker' for a rising politician. Unlike some of those who had been taken under Mandelson's wing, Ms Mowlam went her own way and remained Mo. She was often quite risqué when talking about him and, in acknowledging that 'Dr Marjorie' was probably more authoritative, she said she knew she should have followed his advice because: 'Peter is usually right.' We were chatting away while waiting for a television crew to arrive so that she could react to a report on insider trading. I had expected to interview the trade and industry spokesman Gordon Brown but Ms Mowlam turned up instead. She seemed quite flattered: 'I really am pleased to be doing this for the BBC. Usually Peter only lets me do Sky.'

Mandelson's influence and patronage became a considerable talking point among political journalists. Broadcasters and news agency reporters, who had begun to resent being badgered and bullied by him, started to take notice of the way they would be told, especially at weekends, to pay special attention to the stories of certain newspaper reporters. I was sometimes directed, as were my colleagues, to the work of Andrew Grice, political correspondent of the *Sunday Times*, who had built up a remarkable reputation for the accuracy of his stories on the Labour Party. Six months before Michael Meacher was moved to social security, Grice had predicted exclusively, in a front-page splash, that Kinnock would sack his employment spokesman because of 'a row over union policy'.

Sunday newspapers have always been regarded by politicians as a valuable platform for their views and a useful means of floating controversial proposals. Because they have to look for material which is different from that which has appeared during the week, and as they tend to have more editorial space than the daily newspapers, the Sundays are always on the hunt for exclusive stories. Their journalists will willingly cooperate, either individually or in groups, with organisations which are prepared to provide them with information which has not been supplied to the daily press or to television and radio. Most ministers and opposition MPs are happy to talk to them on an unattributable basis. Sunday newspapers have to be taken notice of: they sell more copies each weekend than the combined weekday sale of all the national dailies and also claim a wider readership, because Sunday editions are more likely to be shared between members of the same household and looked at again later in the week.

Downing Street press secretaries recognise the importance of weekend news coverage, putting on a weekly lobby briefing each Friday at which attendance is restricted solely to political correspondents representing Sunday newspapers. Mandelson and his deputy Colin Byrne also went to considerable lengths to brief the same correspondents. They were anxious to do all they could to make sure that stories about Labour's activities were correct because of the heavy concentration of political news and analysis in the Sunday press. Reporters working for television and radio, and also for the Press Association news agency, would frequently have to spend much of the weekend checking out Sunday newspaper exclusives. Mandelson, or Byrne when he was deputising, would readily give advice on which stories they thought were correct and worth pursuing. At a farewell dinner after the 1990 party conference in Blackpool, the last for Mandelson as communications director, Andrew Grice was one of the journalists whose work he praised. In later years Grice told me that reporting Labour's affairs could be tiresome because there was so much conflicting information.

Mandelson was anxious to ensure that the *Sunday Times'* coverage of Labour's affairs was reliable because he considered it was one of the newspapers which played a key role in setting the political agenda for journalists in television and radio. When asked by Emma Freud on Channel Four's *Media Show* to look back on his work for the party he said that while television provided the bulk of the information on which people formed a political judgement, the role of newspapers in influencing broadcasters could not be overlooked. Therefore as publicity director he had to be the main point of contact between Labour and the press. Trevor Kavanagh, the *Sun's* political editor, who appeared on the same programme, complimented Mandelson for monitoring the BBC, ITN and the Press Association so closely and for being 'so quick to correct their mistakes'.

Most television and radio journalists were highly amused at seeing the *Sun* join Labour in reprimanding the broadcasting organisations for allegedly having a reputation for inaccuracy. Indeed, the *Media Show* rounded off what had already been a highly entertaining conference week in Blackpool. It had opened with a memorable display of the petulant behaviour for which Mandelson had become renowned. After my own brushes with Labour's communications director I naturally took a passing interest in the experiences of my colleagues. When ITN's political correspondent Mark Webster stood his ground in one disagreement which I witnessed Mandelson was decidedly provocative, saying: 'We all know about ITN's reputation for fairness.' I had experienced the same technique: the aim was to put Webster on the defensive.

Labour's publicity staff would sometimes stand around open-mouthed, hardly believing that their director could ridicule reporters so publicly and still get away with it. Gez Sagar, a former chief press officer for the party, told me at the time how he and his colleagues would watch Mandelson with awe when he picked up the phone in his office to complain to a journalist. At no point did he get cross or bang the table but instead made a succession of withering remarks. His show of total disdain tended to destabilise the journalists at the other end of the phone. The moment they started to bluster, or say something which was innaccurate or offensive, Mandelson would hit back and ram home his complaint.

His ability to wind up political correspondents was displayed publicly on the Sunday before the 1990 conference. For their first report ITN had filmed workmen adding the final touches to the platform inside the Winter Gardens at Blackpool. The conference set featured Labour's new campaign slogan, 'Looking to the Future'. Mandelson was furious. He claimed that neither ITN nor the BBC had the right to take pictures without permission. ITN's political editor Michael Brunson was in no mood to be lectured by Mandelson. He said that if Labour wanted to impose conditions for media acccess to the Winter Gardens they should set them down in writing beforehand:

Brunson: You are trying to dictate the pictures we use. There are no rules at all. All you want is adulatory pictures. But if Labour want to stage manage the conference so be it.
Mandelson: That is a very interesting point, Michael. The only adulatory pictures I have seen from you are all your flag-waving stuff from the Thatcher tour of Czechoslovakia and Hungary.
Brunson: Don't you impugn my integrity.

At this point ITN's political editor grabbed Mandelson's lapels. Brunson acknowledged afterwards that he lost his cool, but felt he had been unfairly provoked. He regarded Mandelson as a sharp operator who 'never let go' once he started making a complaint.

The significance of these outbursts should not underestimated. In view of his strong belief that it was television and radio which turned people's votes, Mandelson's priority always was to stop the peak-time news bulletins repeating mistakes which he might have seen or heard in earlier programmes. Newspaper reporters often pick up information from television and radio, so there was the added danger that incorrect or damaging information might be printed in next day's papers. He once described to me how keeping an eye open for potentially troublesome stories was rather like watching a radar screen for dangerous blips: evasive action had to be taken quickly. He knew he could strike fear into the hearts of lowly producers and reporters; he also knew that it was important never to retreat or 'bottle out', and he had developed 'nerves of steel' when making complaints at whatever level.

A profile written by Neil Lyndon for the *Evening Standard* in 1991 gave an account of just such an occasion. Mandelson was apparently watching television news in the company of a journalist he knew well. Although conceding that the main political item in the bulletin was 'half true anyway', the communications director immediately picked up the phone and called the reporter concerned. 'When he finally got through, he went into an extraordinary performance... "I've never seen such crap in all my life... That story was crap and you know it...It was like the *Daily Express* on television!" Then he thumped down the phone, smiled at me and said: "They're all my friends, really." '

Possibly his very assiduity in complaining could be counterproductive. When the BBC's then director of news and current affairs Ian Hargreaves was asked by *Breakfast News* in June 1990 about the likely impact of Mandelson's complaints, he denied that the Corporation's journalists had been forced to change the way they reported stories because of Labour's protests. Hargreaves said he did not think the BBC had been intimidated by Mandelson: 'You learn to ignore the dog which barks too often.' Even so, many political journalists were reluctant to disagree or argue with Mandelson, let alone ignore him, because his guidance was invaluable. For a time his working relationship with Neil Kinnock appeared to be almost as close as the Ingham–Thatcher partnership. In the same way that Ingham briefed the lobby without needing to check everything beforehand with the Prime Minister, so Mandelson could speak authoritatively on behalf of the Labour leader.

Having benefited so much from the rebuilding of the party's publicity machine and the tight control which was being exercised over the supply of information, Kinnock was naturally upset and disappointed when, in the autumn of 1989, his communications director applied to become the candidate in the safe Labour seat of Hartlepool. Mandelson was criticised for seeking the nomination while still serving as a senior party official. I was sent to investigate the row for *The World at One* but had to concede in my report that 'wherever I went in Hartlepool I found that Mandelson had got there before me.' He had taken the precaution of ensuring that none of his backers spoke to the news media in case they broke the rules which forbid attempts to canvas for support. My lack of success in Hartlepool amused Alastair Campbell, then political editor of the *Daily Mirror*, who claimed the BBC had been 'conned' into paying so much attention to the story because it was obvious Mandelson had 'stoked up all the media interest himself in the first place'. He trounced his opponents, winning the nomination with 63.3 per cent of the vote.

His final few months controlling party publicity, in the lead-up to the 1990 conference, were obviously a strain. Colin Byrne, his deputy, had told me of the pressure his boss was under. Mandelson's last big event was the unveiling that May of the policy document *Looking to the Future*. I saw him afterwards and he appeared exhausted. He told journalists he could hardly face organising another news conference. Because of his impending departure his relationship with Kinnock was nowhere near as close it had been, but his planning for the policy launch had been meticulous. His operational note setting out the arrangements went into great detail, even listing the roses which would be needed: 'two bowls of fifty each for the platform and 20 buttonholes, all to be available at 10 am.' When Kinnock, together with his front-bench team, walked on to the platform at the International Press Centre, Mandelson was standing with the photographers and television crews. He choreographed the occasion precisely. At the appropriate moment he shouted out: 'Eyes here and some smiles please.'

The platform seating plan was an illustration of the shifting fortunes in the shadow Cabinet. Tony Blair and Gordon Brown were both on the front row. John Prescott had been put behind Blair and Bryan Gould was placed behind Brown. In the months that followed, when Mandelson found himself outside the inner circle, he maintained close contact with Brown and Blair, advising them both on publicity. Journalists also noted the keenness with which the two front-bench spokesmen would seek his advice and discuss with him possible lines of reply when they were faced with difficult television or radio interviews.

One notable absentee from the platform was Michael Meacher. A year later when the left-wing magazine *Labour Briefing* nominated Mandelson as 'class traitor of the month' it claimed the communications director had spent days looking for a formula to exclude Meacher from the launch because he was 'one of his pet hates'. *Labour Briefing* described Mandelson's approach to the politically unreliable soft left as a mixture of carrot and stick: only if they did as they were told would they be 'rewarded with a positive place in Labour's media profile'. Mandelson told me such reports were untrue and malicious. His job was to promote Labour's policies; he could not be held responsible for internal rivalries and jealousies. Nevertheless in June 1990, when John Underwood, another television producer, was chosen to succeed Mandelson, one reason given for his appointment, which was made against the wish of Kinnock, was a strong feeling by a majority on the ruling national executive committee that they wanted to avoid further complaints of favouritism. Underwood was seen as having no prior allegiances within the shadow Cabinet and he had promised to be even-handed when it came to television interviews and participation in high-profile events. His appointment was welcomed by most Labour MPs.

Underwood was a former ITN home affairs correspondent and had also been a producer on programmes such as *A Week in Politics*. The party leadership hoped his experience would be of value as Labour prepared for the next election. Broadcasters were also encouraged on hearing that the party's new director had an extensive background in television production, hoping this boded well for a positive relationship. Underwood himself was excited by the opportunities and told me he considered the parties were witnessing a further shift in the way voters received political information. He believed it was television and radio, rather than the press, which were tending increasingly to set the agenda for the news media.

By contrast, some newspaper lobby correspondents were not enamoured of the appointment. Although he was well liked, a number said they found that the new director did not seem especially concerned about the press, nor was he particularly authoritative on party affairs: journalists who needed updating frequently, when covering meetings of the parliamentary party or the national executive, began to discover that information was not as easy to come by as it had been. But day-to-day relations were much friendlier under the new regime. One improvement appreciated by television and radio newsrooms, and also by staff of the Press Association news agency, was that they were no longer being constantly badgered by Mandelson.

A personal complication for Underwood was that he found it difficult to work with the party's chief press officer Colin Byrne, who had been disappointed by his failure to win promotion. Byrne remained a close friend of Mandelson, who had backed him for the director's job, having told journalists of his 'great faith' in his deputy. Relations were not improved when Mandelson was recalled unexpectedly in May 1991 to help out in the Monmouth by-election. Labour won the seat after a skilful campaign which played on fears that the local hospital might opt out of the health service, a claim which the Conservatives described as a 'lie' and said was black propaganda.

A month after Labour's victory in Monmouth, Underwood resigned. He claimed he had been put in an 'untenable position'. He had informed Kinnock of his 'reservations' about working with Byrne but was told his deputy would not be moved to another job. He found that unacceptable and said afterwards he considered he was not given a fair chance. The Labour MP Clare Short, who had supported Underwood when the appointment was made by the national executive, said she considered the director's authority had been undermined. She said she shared what she believed was Underwood's suspicion that Mandelson had continued to be an influence behind the scenes. The former director denied any involvement. In a weekly column which he was writing for the *People*, Mandelson said these reports owed more to 'wild imagination than to fact'.

However, the week before Underwood resigned a graphic account of the 'civil war' going on inside the communications department was given by Patrick Wintour, the *Guardian*'s political correspondent. Wintour, like Andrew Grice of the *Sunday Times*, was highly respected by other journalists for the accuracy of his reports about Labour's internal affairs. His article was regarded as something of a catalyst in the final break-up because it forced the feud into the open. Wintour wrote of there being 'well-founded reports' that Mandelson was going to be 'invited back' by Kinnock to help Labour get ready for the general election and would be assigned to special duties. Wintour's report described the centralised publicity regime which Mandelson had operated, built around the party leader, using the 'most appropriate' front-bench spokesmen to put Labour's case. As it turned out, although Mandelson was anxious to get involved in the campaign, as the *Guardian* had been informed, he was in fact excluded. His former deputy Colin Byrne also missed the final preparations for the election: he resigned four months after Underwood quit.

Labour's fourth election defeat in April 1992, after their high hopes of beating John Major, led to another agonising inquest into the failure of their campaign tactics. Mandelson, as the newly elected MP for Hartlepool, was one of the first to highlight what he thought were the mistakes. He said Kinnock was wrong to have promised a cross-party examination of the possibility of changing the electoral system by the introduction of proportional representation. This was not a 'strong suit' for the party because it led to speculation about a hung parliament and a Lib–Lab pact, which only detracted from Labour's campaign. Mandelson was also critical of what he considered was 'panic' in the campaign team over the row about Labour's 'Jennifer's ear' election broadcast. This featured a young girl with excruciating earache who waited nine months for an operation. Much of the initial impact was lost amid allegations that the Conservatives had leaked the girl's name. Mandelson considered the broadcast had been 'bungled', both by party officials and by members of the shadow Cabinet who had then retreated unnecessarily. He acknowledged that when a news story went wrong, spinning out of control, party workers probably did feel as if they were in the path of a 'runaway train' and only wanted to get out of the way. But if they had kept their cool it might have worked out differently.

Mandelson's unease about the conduct of the campaign was a theme to which he returned quite regularly. In an interview in November 1992 for *The House Magazine* he described how he had found waiting around for the election a 'most difficult period'. He had hoped to use his experience helping the party nationally and was 'sorry' he was not asked. He had concluded that Labour lost because the party had 'not changed enough'. A year later, writing in *Fabian Conference News*, he said that despite having all the information which was necessary to understand voters' misgivings about a false perception of Labour being reckless on taxation, the party had buried the issue, allowing the Tories to concentrate their fire on where Labour's defences were weakest.

The task of pulling together Labour's 1992 campaign was entrusted in the end to David Hill, who had been an unsuccessful candidate when Underwood was appointed. He was an old hand at briefing journalists, having spent almost twenty years as a political adviser and press spokesman for Roy Hattersley, who was then the party's deputy leader. Unlike the rest of the staff in the communications department Hill had experienced a taste of power when Labour were last in office. His long years of service included a period in the late 1970s assisting Hattersley when he was Secretary of State for Prices and Consumer Protection.

After the bitter infighting which had surrounded his ill-fated predecessor, the new communications director was welcomed effusively by political journalists. Chris Moncrieff, political editor of the Press Association, was sure Labour had made the right choice. He said that although Hill looked and sounded like a 'ferocious Mexican bandit, mustachioed and rackety', he knew exactly what journalists wanted. He did not deal in 'nuances, subtleties and ironies' and had a 'tough-talking, no-nonsense approach'. Patrick Wintour of the *Guardian* added his endorsement and said the new director had the 'guile to throw an over-inquisitive reporter off the scent'.

Hill had nine months to prepare for the election. Like the rest of the campaign team he was buoyed up initially by Labour's favourable showing in the opinion polls. He was dismayed when the journalistic frenzy over the 'Jennifer's ear' broadcast made it difficult for the party to keep the news media's attention focused on hospital waiting lists; but he insisted the case they chose was representative of what was happening in the health service. Hill was also a firm defender of the tactic of reminding voters that Labour had an open mind on electoral reform. He told me it was a 'sensible piece of news management' to emphasise the party's consensual approach towards constitutional issues.

In the ensuing debate about Labour's fourth successive defeat Hill put much of the blame on the heavy concentration of anti-Labour bias in the tabloid newspapers. One example he quoted was the eight-page spread in the *Sun* entitled 'Nightmare on Kinnock Street'. The Conservatives claimed it was a 'brilliant example of popular journalism', but Hill was convinced the 'desperate smear tactics of the Tory press' had influenced floating voters and that this helped explain why Labour failed to capture all the marginal seats they had targeted. Some party strategists doubted the significance of the anti-Kinnock coverage, but Hill was still asserting a year later that the popular press had 'played a more influential part' in their defeat than was 'healthy for a pluralistic democracy'. Writing in the *Independent* in April 1993 he acknowledged that in the year which had elapsed since the Conservatives were returned all the national titles owned by Rupert Murdoch had been highly critical of John Major's government; but he felt they would revert to type when faced with another election and the reality of a change of government. 'I am under no illusion about the future. As always it will be the broadcasters upon whom we will have to rely for fair and objective coverage as the next election approaches.'

Hill had not always had such a regard for the reliability of the broadcast media. On taking up the job which he had coveted for so long, like his two immediate predecessors he concentrated much of his fire on the broadcasters. He monitored news bulletins and jumped on television and radio journalists the moment he detected inaccuracies or felt Labour's case had been ignored. Mandelson spoke warmly of Hill's ability as a firefighter when instant action was required – and Hill's rapid-fire response could just as readily be aimed at the press. Two months before the election he showed his mettle when Labour heard that the *Sunday Times* was about to publish potentially damaging allegations about the contact which had taken place over the years between Labour MPs and the Soviet embassy in London. As part of a deliberate spoiler, aimed at rubbishing the story, Hill tipped off six of the national dailies. He told their political correspondents that an attempt was about to be made to smear Neil Kinnock. He knew it was a dangerous ploy but, by implying that the Conservatives might be involved in a coordinated move to destabilise Labour, he hoped to persuade the rest of the news media to question the motives of the *Sunday Times*.

Most of the newspapers that Saturday morning followed Hill's line, concentrating on the smear allegations. But, whether he liked it or not, he had provided a stunning front-page splash. Some of the stories were far more lurid than he hoped. Under the headline 'Kinnock And Moscow Files', the *Daily Express* referred to the Labour leader's 'astonishing links' with the Kremlin at the height of the cold war. The television and radio news bulletins reacted as Hill expected: their reports led off on protests by Labour and Liberal Democrat MPs warning of what they feared was a calculated attempt to influence the outcome of the general election.

When the *Sunday Times* finally appeared it devoted almost four pages to its account of Labour's 'dialogue with the Kremlin'. It gave details of embassy telegrams discovered in Moscow which revealed the private views of Labour leaders. But the smear story was running hard elsewhere and dominated the follow-up coverage. Andrew Neil, then the *Sunday Times* editor, had been caught off guard by the activities of his own promotion department. He was forced to disown billboards outside newsagents which advertised his paper under the slogan: 'Official: Kinnock's Kremlin Connection'. Neil admitted the words were inaccurate and that the billboards had 'over-hyped the story'. His admission provided the *Daily Mail* with a fitting headline: 'Editor Climbs Down on Kinnock Kremlin Link.'

Newspaper columnists were divided about Hill's tactics. Hugo Young, writing in the *Guardian*, said that while Labour did not have clean hands themselves, and were quite capable of countering deception with their own misinformation, they were right to have protested about a 'fabrication that didn't survive half a day's scrutiny'. An editorial in the *Sunday Times* the following week claimed that by shrieking 'smear' even before publication Labour had engaged in the 'most wide-ranging attempt to intimidate the press in recent times'. Backing up the leader column was an article by Robert Harris which congratulated Hill for having guaranteed maximum coverage for the story.

Hill met with some criticism within the party for having helped publicise the allegations, but his fellow press officers believed he had been highly effective. By going on the offensive well before publiciation he succeeded in persuading most journalists to raise doubts about the status of the *Sunday Times* story. Broadcasters had also accepted without further question his assurances that the embassy had merely collated details of what was normal contact between diplomats and politicians. Gez Sagar, who had taken over as chief press officer, said Labour's success owed much to the intense circulation war. Most newspapers were anxious to denigrate their rivals' stories, and on getting wind of what was happening they were only too keen to pre-empt an exclusive in the *Sunday Times*. John Underwood also complimented his successor. He told me that Hill had carried off a textbook example of how a spin doctor could 'take the sting out of a smear story'. Labour had faced the choice of either doing nothing or hitting as hard as they could. They had chosen the latter and their tactic had worked, turning an attack on Kinnock into a 'story about newspaper dirty tricks'.

Hill was all the more gratified by his success because the previous month Labour had been highly embarrassed when Kinnock's pre-election attempt to make the acquaintance of some of the newer political correspondents backfired spectacularly. Having cancelled his weekly lobby briefings, the Labour leader relied on occasional social events as a way of meeting journalists. Six were invited to join him at a private dinner which he hosted at Luigi's restaurant in Covent Garden. He was accompanied by his wife Glenys, his personal press officer Julie Hall and parliamentary private secretary Adam Ingram. Hill was not present. Unexpectedly, during the meal Kinnock went out of his way to emphasise that the party's policy documents had made it clear all along that the higher national insurance contributions which Labour were proposing would be phased in gradually. As the election was only weeks away, Labour's tax plans were coming under increasing attack from the Conservatives. Several of the journalists felt they detected a shift in the party's position. Alison Smith got the front-page splash in the *Financial Times* for her story suggesting the Labour leadership were ready to 'scale back' plans for sharp increases in national insurance. She waited until the day after the dinner to file her report. As the evening deadlines got closer other political correspondents heard that the *Financial Times* intended leading on Labour's tax plans.

I spoke to Hill myself at 9.30 that evening. He said he was telling all reporters that there was nothing new in the story. Labour had always made it clear that any tax changes would be phased in. When I rang back half an hour later to tell him the story was the front-page lead in the *Financial Times* he came back immediately with a categorical denial that Kinnock had indicated a shift in policy; but his attempts to play down the story were ineffectual and too late. By then Tim Collins, the Conservatives' director of communications, and Patrick Rock, special adviser to the Tory chairman Chris Patten, were touring the press gallery, briefing journalists. They were handing out a press statement in which Patten claimed Kinnock's reported statement on phasing-in showed that Labour's tax plans were in a shambles and 'not worth the paper they're written on'.

Kinnock, like so many politicians before him, had paid a heavy price for thinking he could improve his image with some discreet and selective hospitality. In addition to Ms Smith the five other journalists at the dinner were from the *The Times*, the *Guardian*, the *Daily Mirror*, BBC and ITN. To reporters on the Tory tabloids, who had all been excluded, the guest list was tantamount to provocation. The action, the reaction and the consequences presaged the fate of Gus O'Donnell's farewell dinner. Once news of the event trickled out, as it invariably tended to, the spurned tabloids set to work with a vengeance. Long-serving correspondents joined in the fun. Anthony Bevins, political editor of the *Independent*, said the six who were chosen were all from the lobby's younger generation and 'had not yet put themselves in Kinnock's abundant bad books'. Bevins reminded his readers of another of the Labour leader's unhappy meals when, at lunch with the *Independent*'s political staff, he revealed 'the first moves away from nuclear unilateralism'.

A detailed reconstruction of the dinner was written for the *Sunday Times* by Andrew Grice. He described how the journalists, all from 'the more respectable end of the media market', were apparently 'gobsmacked' on hearing Kinnock's revelation. They were not aware of Labour's 'get-out clause' on national insurance and knew 'the tabloids would go bonkers' on hearing of Labour's U-turn. Grice hit on the reason why Kinnock had been so unwise to talk about a complicated tax issue while having a meal with journalists: 'As it had been a private dinner and he could not be quoted directly, he was apparently unaware of the impact his words would have.' Ms Smith attributed her story to 'senior party figures'.

Private lunches and dinners with ministers and MPs are a prime source of material for political correspondents. Some journalists like to work on their own and prefer to dine with only one guest at a time. They have complete trust in their own ability to winkle out useful information. Other reporters hunt in pairs, believing that two, working together, can follow up each other's leads and questions and thus keep the conversation turning on the issues which they think are most fruitful. Group meals of the kind hosted by Kinnock do however present something of a problem. Six journalists at a dinner are unlikely to have all heard the same set of answers and will probably have formed different impressions of what was said. If the reporters are friendly with one another they will invariably pool their recollections afterwards, perhaps in the taxi back to the House of the Commons. In this way, with the reporters each chipping in what they have remembered, it is possible to construct a seemingly authoritative account of what took place. And, because all the reporters agree to use identical facts and the same quotes, any subsequent denials by a press officer are unlikely to be believed.

Kinnock's unguarded comments were all the more surprising in view of his previous indiscretions on policy issues. His personal press officer Julie Hall, a former ITN political correspondent, was intensely loyal and extremely attentive when Kinnock was being interviewed by television and radio, but many journalists felt she was out her depth when dealing with the tabloid press. Her decision to leave ITN to work for him was a matter of great personal pride for the Labour leader; I had heard frequent accounts from within the party of how pleased he was to introduce Ms Hall as an example of the good which could come out of the unprincipled world of journalism. Her conduct during the dinner provoked discussion among other political press officers. They wondered whether she heard what Kinnock had said on national insurance, whether she realised the significance of it, and, if she had, whether she took any evasive action.

Peter Mandelson told me that all press officers are in a quandary when a party leader wants to loosen up and talk frankly to journalists. If he had been at Luigi's that night, and if Kinnock had in fact started to rewrite Labour's tax plans, then he was sure he would have been alert enough to have diverted the journalists' attention and to have tried to change the course of the conversation. Olly Grender, the Liberal Democrats' director of communications, sympathised with Ms Hall. The start of their 1991 party conference in Bournemouth had been overshadowed by remarks attributed to Paddy Ashdown during a private pre-conference dinner with journalists at which he was reported to have said he had been conducting 'war games' with colleagues over the prospects for a hung parliament. Ms Grender felt many politicians had a tendency, when dining with journalists, to start chatting away about the very last thing they had been discussing with their advisers. 'It is a worry when a party leader dines with journalists. It can be very hard to stop them talking once they are in full flow. Naturally they like to defend themselves and they can easily trickle out the party's latest line of defence without realising they might be making a tactical mistake.'

The election of the late John Smith to succeed Kinnock as party leader in July 1992 heralded a period of calm consolidation, not least in Labour's communications department. Smith had little time for personal publicity. Within a few months of taking over he told colleagues he had decided against having his own press officer. Instead he asked David Hill to take on the responsibility of being chief spokesman for the leader's office as well as the party. Hill had told me on previous occasions of his fear that he might perhaps have been held back by his urbanity and lack of theatricals, but obviously his temperament suited Smith.

Derek Foster, Labour's chief whip, said most MPs welcomed Smith's relaxed approach. The parliamentary party had grown weary of Kinnock's constant battles with the news media. 'John Smith is just like Margaret Thatcher really. He doesn't give a monkey about the media and just gets bored by it all. They say it was just the same with Clem Attlee. He wasn't worried by what the journalists were saying about him. All he used to read the newspapers for was the cricket scores.' Foster's assessment was endorsed by Graham Allen, then a spokesman on home affairs. He thought Labour had benefited straight away by having a more measured relationship with the media. 'We felt Neil Kinnock was always in a permanent dialogue with the press. It was as though he was always saying to journalists: "Ask me another." We don't want John Smith to do that.'

BBC journalists in Scotland, who met the family regularly, said Smith's wife Elizabeth and his three daughters often remarked on the patient way he dealt with photographers when they kept asking him to pose for pictures. 'Having three daughters must be what keeps him down to earth,' said one reporter. 'Whenever we arrive with a television crew he never seems fazed. He certainly isn't preoccupied by his appearance or fretting about how he looks.' When Smith recorded his first broadcast as party leader, responding to the November 1992 budget, a BBC producer found he was so friendly and approachable during the rehearsal that, thinking his Scottish accent made it difficult to understand what he was saying, she queried his pronunciation at one point. 'He just smiled back at me and said: "You let me say it as I like, wee lassie." He couldn't have been nicer really.'

Smith's reasons for dispensing with a personal press secretary became clearer as the year progressed. As his advisers suspected, he had come to the conclusion that it was often far more trouble than it was worth getting too deeply involved with journalists. He also feared that that if he established his own team of publicity advisers then it might become somewhat separated from the promotional activities of the party. Mandelson had his reservations about this strategy. While a low-key response might be suitable for the first half of a parliament, he felt that closer to an election Smith would need a high-profile spokesman of his own. 'He will require someone to look ahead, give a strategic overview, assess the impact he has made and also be alert enough to know what political journalists are thinking. A party leader needs presenting and promoting as an individual. You can't do that just through policy issues. Publicity for the leader has to connect with the overall promotion of the party.' Alastair Campbell, then with the *Daily Mirror*, told me he also thought that once an election got nearer Smith would need more support so as to improve his personal projection and publicity.

Disquiet about the direction of the media strategy being pursued by the party began surfacing publicly in 1993. Alan Leaman, press officer and adviser to Paddy Ashdown, said the Liberal Democrats were mystified by Labour's failure to promote Smith. 'He hardly seems to be doing anything at all, and when he does do something he comes over as boring and unimaginative.' Smith's easy-going attitude was being compared increasingly with that of the highly active Ashdown, whose position had been strengthened immeasurably by his party's by-election successes. Mandelson acquired first-hand experience of the Liberal Democrats' effectiveness during the Newbury by-election where, in addition to his duties as an MP, he acted as press officer for the campaign. He explained away his party's lost deposit by claiming that Labour had helped ensure the Conservatives' massive defeat. Olly Grender said the Liberal Democrats were highly amused by Mandelson's attempt to associate Labour with their trouncing of the Tories; but she acknowledged his tactical skill in joining in the attempts to ridicule the Conservatives' young and rather plump candidate, Julian Davidson, for being a Mr Blobby look-alike. 'Mandelson knew all about how to paint unfavourable images of a political opponent and then get them to stick in the media.'

After Labour lost another deposit in the Christchurch by-election, Mandelson voiced his concern about Labour's failure to counter the growing upsurge in Liberal Democrat support in southern England. Writing in the *Independent* in August 1993, he said the party had to develop a higher level of year-round campaigning in key seats, and called for 'more concerted national communications by the party, to lay the foundations for further policy detail nearer the election.' Mandelson alerted the *Independent*'s political staff to what he had written in case they thought it was worth a separate news story. His doubts over the potency of Labour's publicity appeared in print after a particularly unsuccessful weekend for David Hill. Even before he read the *Independent* that Tuesday morning, Labour's communications director had been angered by his repeated failure to persuade television and radio programmes to make use of Labour's spokesmen. Stung perhaps by Mandelson's implied rebuke, that afternoon he wrote a letter of complaint to the BBC's director general, John Birt.

The nub of Hill's criticism was that the BBC (and also ITN, with whom he registered a similar protest) were not offering 'balanced coverage' as often as Labour felt appropriate. He supplied a long list of occasions during the preceding four days when BBC news bulletins and programmes had transmitted interviews with a succession of ministers but had pointedly failed either to request or to use a Labour voice. The tenor of his letter, his citation of chapter and verse to each rebuff, revealed the depth of his exasperation: 'Today the struggle has continued . . . I do not see how there can be any excuse for this omission . . . I am writing this during the afternoon and, at the moment, no request has come in for a balancing interview.' By abandoning all attempts to 'reflect balance between the parties' the BBC was allowing viewers and listeners to 'conclude that the Labour Party has disengaged itself during the summer'. Hill said a further consequence would be that political commentators would speculate on the reasons for the absence of Labour politicians and then criticise the party for being inactive.

In order to strengthen his complaint Hill issued his letter as a press release. He handed a copy of it personally to the Press Association's political editor Chris Moncrieff, who was amused by the fuss Labour were making in what after all was the holiday month of August. Political correspondents get used to fending off politicians who feel they are not being reported adequately. Hill's long catalogue of complaints, which ran to two closely typed pages, was regarded in the lobby as a real 'green-ink job' – one of those tiresome letters journalists attract, full of incomprehensible criticism, usually hand-written and underlined in a variety of coloured inks. If Hill, as a communications director, had penned such a convoluted letter of complaint and issued it as a press release, he could hardly expect journalists to take it seriously.

Two days later Hill expressed further annoyance when the BBC failed both to broadcast a radio interview given by Labour's defence spokesman, Dr David Clark, and to offer him a televised appearance. Dr Clark had gone to the BBC's studios in Newcastle to provide a prerecorded response for *The World at One* on the latest NATO decision affecting Bosnia. Hill notified the Press Association that the interview was about to be broadcast in case Dr Clark's reaction merited a news story. Sian Clare, one of the political correspondents, was assigned to listen to the lunchtime programme; Hill had to ring her later to apologise when he found the interview had been dropped.

In claiming there could be no excuse for the refusal of BBC television news even to seek an interview with Dr Clark, Hill had failed to acknowledge basic news values. Both the defence secretary Malcolm Rifkind and the Liberal Democrat leader Paddy Ashdown were in Bosnia at the time, visiting troops. They were interviewed at length because they were regarded as having first-hand experience of a changing situation. Hill's complaint mystified *The Times*, which advised Labour to 'beware of drawing attention to its own limitations'. Before complaining about being 'cold-shouldered' by the BBC, Hill should have considered whether the party had a 'heavyweight' spokesman who could be placed alongside Rifkind or Ashdown and who was capable of answering questions about Bosnia. In an attempt to cheer him up, *The Times* reminded Hill that he need not fear Labour's affairs would be underreported for ever, because in a few weeks it would be time for Labour's annual conference in Brighton, when the party would doubtless get hours of air time and 'then complain about too much coverage, not too little'.

The cautionary words of *The Times'* leader writer were prophetic: the 1993 party conference developed into a cliff-hanger for John Smith. While Hill was trying to ensure that the party's voice was heard on Bosnia, some of the biggest trade unions were stepping up their campaign against the introduction of one member one vote in the procedure for selecting Labour's parliamentary candidates. Smith's determination during the spring and summer of that year to press ahead with reform of the party's constitution, and the abolition at the constituency level of all block votes, had set him on a collision course with several powerful union leaders. As a result, Hill and the party's communications staff found themselves in conflict with some of the union movement's most effective publicity advisers.

After suffering so many reverses during the Thatcher years the largest unions had all gone to considerable lengths to improve their image. Most had established highly professional departments to handle their campaigns and communications. As the use of strike action declined, so the unions became more sophisticated in their attempts to exploit the news media in order to put over their case against the employers and promote the need for improved workers' rights. During general election campaigns many of these trade union press officers were seconded to help bolster Labour's publicity machine. Their detailed knowledge and experience in making the best out of what were often negative news stories was found to be invaluable. Years of hostility from much of the tabloid press had left them extremely adept at handling sensitive issues. However, if those same union press officers were to be asked to turn their campaigning skills against the party leadership they would be a force to be reckoned with. They certainly knew how to whet the media's appetite when it came to provoking potentially embarrassing stories about Labour's link with the unions.

The introduction of one member one vote was finally approved at Brighton, but only by the narrow margin of 0.2 per cent of the total conference vote. Fearing defeat, Smith had turned in his hour of need to John Prescott to make one last appeal for support. It was his impassioned plea which was seen as having been decisive in influencing undecided delegates. David Hill ran an impressive publicity operation, but was handicapped from the start because the Labour leadership were having to struggle to claw back lost ground: when they arrived at the conference many of the largest union delegations were already mandated to oppose any move which might weaken their relationship with the party. On the eve of the vote Hill admitted that it still looked as if the leadership would lose. But he was encouraged by the way reporters had approached him saying they personally backed the stand which Smith was making. Having attended party conferences for twenty-five years Hill could not remember an occasion when political journalists had been so supportive or supplied him with so many useful titbits of information which he could use against the opponents of reform.

John Edmonds, general secretary of the General, Municipal and Boilermakers' Union, was at the forefront of those arguing against a reduction in union influence in the choice of Labour's candidates. His union's communications department, headed by a former *Newsnight* producer, Phil Woollas, had been extremely active. Their campaign had generated considerable concern about the possibility of there being a hidden agenda to cut the ties between the unions and the party. A MORI opinion poll, commissioned in May 1993 by the four biggest unions, including the GMB, had shown that three-quarters of their membership wanted to keep the existing link with Labour.

Woollas subsequently acknowledged that there was unease within the Labour leadership about the activities of union press officers. He realised that he and his colleagues might sometimes be seen as posing a threat to the party because of their ability to generate potentially unfavourable publicity. He also recognised that the success of unions like the GMB in publicising the looming split over the union link had made Smith's task as leader more difficult and might perhaps have reduced the chances of a last-minute compromise. But the unions were attracting far more public sympathy than in previous years and Woollas said that, like the party, they too had developed close links with many journalists. If the unions considered their interests were at stake then obviously they would do all they could to take advantage of the access and opportunities which the news media afforded them. He felt the Brighton conference was a salutary reminder to the party leadership of the need to look for agreement with the unions rather than risk confrontation.

The effectiveness of the unions in stirring up hostility to the changes in the party had alarmed Tony Blair and Peter Mandelson. In the months preceding the conference they feared that Smith would be forced to give ground to the unions and might fail to get approval for one member one vote. After having spent so long in the background giving others advice on how to respond to the media, Mandelson had at last found an issue on which he could speak out with authority both as an MP and as an advocate of reform. Because of his close association with those who were seen as the leading modernisers in the party he was regarded as an ideal interviewee for television and radio. As Woollas had said himself, the unions were running an emotive campaign: their aim was to put the party hierarchy on the defensive. Mandelson was soon in the thick of it.

The most damaging charge being made against the Labour modernisers was that they were intent on severing the unions' links with the party. Clare Short, whose position as a member of the national executive committee gave her a privileged vantage point, had become alarmed by the infighting. She accepted the need for reform but felt the party would be destroyed if it kicked out the unions. Five months before the conference she gave an interview to *The World this Weekend* in which she claimed that some prominent modernisers were engaged in 'a poisonous whispering campaign' which was designed to persuade the news media to think that Smith's real intention was to ditch the unions. She accused Mandelson of being one of the 'whisperers' who were putting it around that the leadership were preparing for 'a big war at the conference'. Responding on the same programme on behalf of the reformers, Mandelson said they had no wish to break the link. Their aim was to ensure that union members were recruited en masse into their local constituency parties so that they could participate fully in the decision-making which would flow from the introduction of one member one vote.

Mandelson was rather disappointed with himself afterwards for not having been more forceful in denying the claims being made by Ms Short. He told me that he had been asked by Smith to speak out publicly in support of the reforms. The previous evening, when interviewed on *A Week in Politics*, he had described the abolition of union block votes in the selection of parliamentary candidates as 'an important litmus test' of the party's ability to make Labour electable at the next election. He was anxious to do all he could to help the leadership, but he agreed that it might be rather difficult for him because he was regarded as something of a whipping boy by those MPs and trade unionists who were resisting change.

In addition to acting as a propagandist for Smith's reforms, and helping out at the Newbury by-election, Mandelson always seemed to be only too ready to assist his fellow MPs when they needed instant advice on how best to respond when challenged by reporters. His long experience in thinking on his feet when faced by unexpected questions from journalists made him an ideal person with whom to discuss possible answers. Although he had only the status of a backbench MP, his opinions were still widely sought by some leading members of the shadow Cabinet. On one occasion, during a break in the committee stage of the Finance Bill in May 1993, I approached Harriet Harman, who was then number two in Labour's Treasury team, to request an interview. We were standing together in the long committee corridor. I explained to Ms Harman that I was seeking reaction to a new warning on possible public expenditure cuts which had been made by the Treasury chief secretary, Michael Portillo. Mandelson, who was also serving on the committee, was standing nearby. I was somewhat taken aback when he walked over and mocked my presence, almost as if to suggest my request should be treated with caution; immediately Ms Harman turned to ask him whether he thought it would be wise for her to answer my questions. As Ms Harman was shadowing Portillo I considered my approach had been entirely legitimate. After a short conversation with Mandelson she agreed to respond, but I was only able to record one short answer because at that precise moment the committee stage resumed and she had to leave. Luckily I noticed that Offa, David Blunkett's guide dog, was poking its head out of the door to the committee corridor lift. As Blunkett was then Labour's health spokesman I realised he was ideally placed to respond. He agreed without hesitation to give his reaction to Portillo's warning on spending cuts.

I was not entirely surprised when Ms Harman asked Mandelson for his opinion about recording an interview as I knew she thought highly of his advice. The regard was mutual: when writing his weekly diary for the *People* during the 1992 general election he had tipped Ms Harman as 'a star in the making' on Labour's front bench. Mandelson had also named Tony Blair as another star of Labour's election campaign, and had said that Blair was 'the first politician to have emerged entirely unscathed from the BBC's notoriously tricky *Election Call*'.

Mandelson believed the assistance which he was giving shadow Cabinet members was being widely misunderstood within the party. His critics regarded him as the ultimate spin doctor and puppet master, capable of pulling the strings which controlled the lips of those politicians he deigned to favour. He considered such talk far-fetched nonsense; the expertise which he offered was geared far more towards assessing how the news media might react to a given set of answers. His judgement was certainly greatly appreciated, especially when party spokesmen were having to tread a careful path through complex policy disputes. As I knew from personal experience, he had a gift for sensing which out of several responses was most likely to be the one which would be chosen as the soundbite for television and radio news bulletins. He would happily hazard a guess and give his opinion if journalists were in any doubt as to which was the most significant answer or the main point of a speech. His knack of being able to think on the same wavelength as the broadcasters meant he could give advice beforehand on where the greatest emphasis should be placed.

The criticism which Mandelson resented most of all was the accusation that he was being manipulative. He assured me that he had never told Gordon Brown or Tony Blair what to say and he regarded such suggestions as an insult. Again, I knew from my own observations that in the tense moments before an interview most politicians are grateful for a receptive but confidential ear; they like nothing more than an opportunity to talk through the probable line of questioning they will face and a chance to try out their most suitable responses. While I have always accepted that some of the powers attributed to Mandelson were wildly exaggerated, I was still intrigued by the influence he might be having on Brown and Blair, because striking differences were emerging in the way the shadow Chancellor and the shadow Home Secretary were responding to the news media.

In contrast to the news-related approach of Brown, who commented on almost every economic statistic released, Blair was becoming less reactive. Instead of churning out endless soundbites, he was using his home affairs brief to develop longer-term strategies. Because he was not popping up so frequently on news bulletins, programme producers tended to think there was a rarity value about Blair, and accordingly when he did appear on television or radio he seemed to get more air time than Brown, who had become overexposed. When I asked Mandelson about Blair's preference for longer, more considered interviews he agreed that the shadow Home Secretary had been wise to adopt a thoughtful stance. He said that much of the pressure on Brown to respond so frequently came from journalists who were seeking his reaction to the regular flow of economic statistics. But Blair, while anxious to challenge the government on law and order, was also keen to develop his own ideas on ideological issues and party matters, and that meant he had to be more reflective.

Phil Woollas of the GMB union took a close interest in the way the two men were relating to the media. He regarded Brown as a positionist who was doing all he possibly could to exploit the news of the day, whereas Blair, instead of just reacting to what had happened, was trying to set the agenda. He recognised that the contrast had a great deal to do with the respective positions the two men held. All Labour shadow Chancellors tended to face the same dilemma: because the Conservatives could seize on any remarks they made about taxation or spending they had to be circumspect about Labour's likely economic policies. However, home affairs was an issue which lent itself to long-term thinking. 'Blair realises that he can't keep going on television all the time and then just stick the boot in about the government's handling of law and order. What he is trying to do is be proactive and look ahead to what a Labour government might accomplish. Unfortunately for Brown the demand for instant reaction about the economy is so great that shadow Chancellors can easily begin to sound like a rent-a-quote and, because there are so many constraints on what they can say, they can't talk as confidently about the future direction of Labour's economic plans.'

These two contrasting media profiles, and Mandelson's relationship with the men behind them, were to be suddenly thrown into focus by an event which none of the three had anticipated, and which jolted Labour's evolving relationship with the news media into an entirely new phase.

6

Staying in Control

$\mathcal{J}$OHN SMITH's death in May 1994 was a doubly traumatic blow for Messrs Brown, Blair and Mandelson. Not only had they lost a senior figure whom they all respected, but they also faced several weeks of anguished discussion as the party prepared for the ensuing leadership contest. Long-standing friendships were about to be strained as never before. Brown and Blair had both been talked of frequently as possible future leaders and, because of his close working relationship with them, Mandelson was immediately portrayed by the news media as someone who might be in a pivotal position. He faced a dilemma which was all the greater because of his efforts over the years to assist and promote both of his friends.

Although the shadow Chancellor had always considered himself to be the senior and more influential half of the Brown–Blair partnership, the shadow Home Secretary had gradually been acquiring the mantle of heir apparent. Most newspapers were convinced Blair was the automatic front-runner – on the day of Smith's death Alastair Campbell told fellow journalists that he thought Blair was the obvious successor – and once the first opinion polls were taken he emerged as the clear favourite. For many in the party establishment the only outstanding question seemed to be whether Brown would challenge Blair or instead stand aside so as to give his colleague a clear a run against any candidates from the left.

There was an agonising period as Brown struggled to decide what to do. MPs who were close to the shadow Chancellor told me that he had been taken aback by Blair's determination to run for the leadership, come what may. They had been saddened to discover there was no suggestion at any point by Blair that he might stand aside and make way for Brown. However, in a front-page splash in the *Sunday Times* three days after Smith's death, Andrew Grice reported that the two men had reached a 'secret pact' not to stand against each other. Initially they would allow both their names to be discussed as leadership contenders. Once campaigning was over for the European Parliament elections the following month they would allow their colleagues to 'weigh up which of them has the strongest support'; the other would then 'stand aside and throw his weight behind the chosen candidate'.

When Mandelson was questioned that Sunday morning on *Breakfast with Frost* about the existence of this 'secret pact' he confirmed that the two men would decide between themselves who should stand. He said the agreement they had reached to sort it out together was in the best interests of the party. After the programme Mandelson told me that he understood that the *Sunday Times* story was correct. An unpleasant decision would have to be made at some point in the future, but the two men were close friends. He said that Blair was 'completely unmoved and unswayed' by all the media hype which he was attracting and would not be commenting about his future while the party was still in mourning.

Although Blair had distanced himself from the speculation, one of his supporters, the Labour MP Tony Wright, told *The World this Weekend* that he thought the party would be 'forever grateful' if Brown stood aside. Mandelson said he thought Wright's appeal was 'nicely done' but insisted he would not be seeking to influence Brown one way or the other. 'I will support Gordon whatever he decides. I am his friend.' But a Brown supporter, the Scottish MP Nigel Griffiths, accused Mandelson of campaigning for Blair in breach of the understanding. Griffiths withdrew his criticism almost immediately and the incident was soon smoothed over, but it was the first public indication of shifting loyalties. Mandelson was about to embark on his most delicate assignment. He would eventually be revealed as a key adviser in the Blair campaign and one of those who helped to mastermind his runaway victory.

Private discussions, including a dinner together, continued for a fortnight as the two principal challengers talked over their options. Finally, the week before the European elections, Brown announced his decision to stand aside for Blair. His announcement caused disquiet within the party because all the likely contenders had given an undertaking that they would stay their hand until after the European elections. According to the *Guardian*'s political correspondent, Patrick Wintour, the news started to leak out after Brown informed his own campaign lieutenants. The shadow Chancellor was then forced to seek the consent of party officials to make a formal announcement.

News of his withdrawal emerged much earlier in the day than Brown expected. The shadow Chancellor's press officer Charlie Whelan said he received a call that morning from Mandelson, who informed him that he had already rung 'Robin, Mike, Adam and Elinor' and given them 'operational warning of Gordon's decision'. The four names mentioned by Mandelson were the television political editors: Robin Oakley (BBC), Michael Brunson (ITN), Adam Boulton (Sky) and Elinor Goodman (Channel Four). Advance warning can be of critical importance on significant stories because it allows broadcasting organisations sufficient time to put in interviews bids, allocate film crews and line up production facilities. Whelan was nevertheless surprised by what had happened. It had been his intention to release the news later in the day, and he was rather annoyed that Mandelson had got in first by alerting the political editors even before the lunchtime television news bulletins.

Mandelson slipped into his new role with ease but also with caution. Once the leadership campaign got under way he went to extraordinary lengths to avoid being revealed as Blair's spin doctor. Because his methods were misunderstood, even reviled by some sections of the party, he was determined to remain in the background, fearing that if he was associated publicly with the campaign it might damage Blair's chances. He was therefore anxious to work as an undercover adviser. The need for secrecy intensified as the election approached because a number of the favourite's supporters indicated they would withdraw their backing for Blair if they found that Mandelson was part of the campaign team. Once the contest was over Austin Mitchell claimed that several Labour MPs, including two members of the shadow Cabinet, were given personal assurances that the party's former publicity director had no authority to speak for Blair.

Mandelson's most significant contribution was to give advice on how best to pitch the presentation of Blair's keynote speeches and then to follow that through by briefing journalists. When advance texts were supplied to reporters, the front page of each news release carried the main points in headline form. The theme would then be reproduced in a condensed version, with vital phrases highlighted so as to guide reporters to the message which Blair was seeking to convey. Alerting journalists to the line which Blair intended to take was a discreet yet complex task. Broadcasters were the first priority. Mandelson would ask or arrange for them to be bleeped on their pagers. They would be told to ring him so that he could brief them on the likely content. Advance warning about the significance of that day's speech allowed correspondents to plan their coverage. As Blair was often speaking on joint platforms with the two other declared candidates for the leadership, John Prescott and Margaret Beckett, Mandelson was anxious to ensure that significant speeches were not overlooked.

The two other challengers also had well-organised campaign teams, having drafted in former party press officers to handle their promotion. Gez Sagar ran the media side of Prescott's campaign; Mrs Beckett was being advised by John Underwood. All three candidates appeared together at hustings meetings around the country and they attracted considerable news coverage. When their speeches were reported on television and radio they tended to get equal time. Although the campaign produced no unexpected fireworks Mandelson was constantly on his guard against news stories which he thought might cause trouble. Mandelson has always placed great emphasis on team management and strong staff discipline during election campaigns. Now he took immediate steps to ensure that he was alerted immediately if there were any problems involving journalists. Three members of Blair's staff who handled media enquiries, Tim Allan, Peter Hyman and Tom Restrick, were told by him they must always refer up if they found themselves facing difficult decisions. He monitored the output of BBC and ITN and was regularly on the phone to reporters, producers and editors offering briefings, correcting mistakes and seeking information about future story-lines.

Soon after nominations closed in mid-June I found myself in the Mandelson firing line during a day which provided one more illustration of his tenacity and persistence. Blair had a commanding lead from the start and his victory was never in doubt; but there was still concern among his supporters over who might win the separate election for deputy leader, which had become a straight run-off between Prescott and Beckett. Because some leading Blair supporters were nominating Mrs Beckett for deputy I suggested in my report for the *One o'Clock News* that a Blair–Beckett ticket seemed to be a possibility. Mandelson complained. He insisted that Blair intended to remain neutral. There was no evidence of any coordinated move by his supporters in favour of either candidate. To show that he was being scrupulous in his neutrality Blair would not be casting a vote in the contest for deputy. Mandelson accused me of allowing myself to be manipulated by the Beckett camp. They had 'obviously launched a dawn operation' aimed at giving the impression she had the backing of the modernisers. In my report for the *Six o'Clock News* I tried to be more precise, explaining how Mrs Beckett's bid to be deputy had gained the support of some of Blair's most prominent backers, including Gordon Brown, Nigel Griffiths and Margaret Hodge. But again I was reprimanded for having omitted to mention Blair's outright refusal to express a preference and also for failing to make it clear that while some of his supporters were opting for Mrs Beckett, others were going for Prescott. In my final report of the day, for the *Nine o'Clock News*, I took care to stress Blair's neutrality.

All told, I was bleeped to ring Mandelson five times that day. In the event he proved to be entirely correct in his prediction: a significant shift towards Mrs Beckett did not materialise among Blair's supporters. As Mandelson had been so upfront in seeking to influence my reporting, and, his critics would say, in attempting to manipulate me, I tried to cross-question him about his precise status in the campaign team. He brushed my enquiries aside: 'I have no formal or official role in this. You know the relationship I have. I do talk to Tony. I do speak to him before interviews. Our relationship is governed by our friendship. I only exist to serve.'

I was intrigued by the care with which Mandelson sought to define his role. I knew only too well that he was working for Blair behind the scenes and that other television and radio journalists were getting the same extensive briefings; in fact, BBC and ITN political correspondents were enjoying themselves privately by checking up with each other to see who had received the most bleeps to ring him in any one day. Reporters were told by Mandelson that their conversations with him had 'not taken place' and did 'not exist'. The fact that they had been briefed by him could not be disclosed to journalistic colleagues or to anyone else in the party. I had no wish to break Mandelson's cover while the leadership election was taking place, and I took great care not to mention his name in any of my broadcasts. Journalists depend on information which is imparted to them on an operational basis and which is not for immediate use. The insight which I had gained into the inner workings of the three campaign teams had to be respected while the election was in progress. I felt that until the outcome was known it would have been entirely wrong to have made use of inside information, gained through the privileged access which was allowed to broadcasters, in a way which might have disadvantaged one or other of the candidates.

Newspaper reporters, too, were fascinated by Mandelson's shadowy role and by the secret contact which he was having with television and radio journalists. Andy McSmith of the *Observer* was one of the first political correspondents to reveal that Mandelson was 'back in action, doing what he does best, talking privately to selected journalists'. McSmith described how BBC and ITN correspondents were all given identical advance warning of a speech by Blair to GMB union delegates in Blackpool in which he intended to go 'beyond slogans' and 'broaden the agenda.' McSmith was left in no doubt that Mandelson was extremely perturbed on hearing that the *Observer* intended to expose his role in promoting Blair.

Several days later Mandelson was quoted by name, and at length, in a news story by Chris Moncrieff, the Press Association's political editor, who described him as a member of 'Blair's campaign team' and quoted him as promising that the launch of Blair's campaign statement would give the clearest vision so far of what Britain would be like under 'a Blair-led government'. Moncrieff said Mandelson complained to him afterwards and insisted that all their future conversations must be regarded as being 'strictly off the record'. When I checked with Mandelson myself, and asked rather mischievously if Moncrieff's story might perhaps be an indication that he intended going public about his work for Blair, he gave me a frosty reply: 'It was an error and it won't be repeated again, either by you or by anyone else.'

Mandelson was especially vigilant in maintaining contact with those correspondents who were assigned to cover hustings meetings attended by trade union members, as it was thought their vote might favour Prescott or Beckett. While waiting in Scarborough for the start of a weekend conference arranged by the big public service union Unison, I spoke to him on the phone several times. He said Blair intended to stress his hope that the unions would play a vital part in the nation's life, so long as it was within a firm and settled legislative framework. During a break in the proceedings Blair took me aside. He seemed rather nervous and was clearly anxious to obtain some feedback from the conference. I sensed that he found his speeches on union platforms the toughest part of the campaign.

In my main report for radio news that afternoon I used a recording of Blair's pledge to provide a worthwhile role for the unions. However, after a later speech by Prescott, who promised he would abolish hospital trusts, I switched subjects for the late evening television news bulletin and concentrated on Labour's plans for the health service. Blair had been nowhere near as categoric as Prescott and had spoken only of the need to put hospital trusts under 'democratic control'. On meeting Blair some days later we discussed the Unison conference. I referred light-heartedly to the way I had probably been more helpful to him in my radio report than on television. He just shrugged his shoulders and smiled, but he acknowledged that my comments accorded precisely with the assessment he had been given by Mandelson.

Our conversation reinforced my conclusion that television and radio reports about the election campaign were still being monitored extremely closely. But Blair impressed me, as he had done on previous occasions, by his easy-going attitude when talking to reporters and his ability to discuss our work in a detached way. He seemed to be genuinely immune to the impact of the widespread news coverage which he was attracting. When asked on *Breakfast with Frost* if he was ever upset by what the newspapers were saying about him, Blair insisted that he acted out of conviction. 'When you do that, you worry less about what the newspapers are saying... So I say don't worry about the newspapers; act with conviction.'

While Mandelson could be extremely critical of my reporting, I cannot recall ever being reproached by Blair. Having said that, however, he rarely volunteered information or gave anything away about his intentions or reactions – a disciplined approach he maintained when being interviewed on television and radio. Hugo Young, writing in the *Guardian*, was struck by the fact that Blair invariably kept control of the agenda in his interviews and said no more than he wanted to. 'It may be perverse to say that evasion was a sign of serious leadership but this added to his weight. It showed who was boss.' Blair's confident appearances drew praise from the author and Labour fund-raiser, Ken Follett. In an interview for *The Times* he said Blair's idealism and pragmatism seemed to come across well on television. Henry Porter, writing in the *Daily Telegraph*, said that neither of his two rivals displayed quite the same attentiveness which Blair did when he was in front of the camera. 'He listens, then says what people want to hear, and even when delivering unpleasantness allows a smile to play at the corner of his mouth.'

Profiles of the three candidates prepared by Michael Brunson for *News at Ten* further illustrated Blair's superiority as a communicator. The film of Blair was full of subliminal messages. It showed him playing football with his children. He spoke of the importance of spending time with them even 'if only for an hour in the evening'. Brunson's report then cut to a shot of Blair with his wife Cherie, sitting together on a garden wall. Blair mentioned the care with which he and Cherie had discussed the possible loss of family time should he win the party leadership: 'We weighed this up very carefully when we decided to go for it.' Viewers could not but have been impressed by the depth and strength of Blair's relationship with his wife and family.

As the campaign progressed Blair seemed to make a point of looking more relaxed when being filmed on the move. On arriving at the GMB conference in Blackpool he walked nonchalantly through the Norbreck Castle Hotel. It was a sweltering day in mid-June and Blair had his thumb hooked through the top of his jacket, which was slung casually over his shoulder. He waved with his other hand at the union members who were sitting around in the reception area. For another set-up shot I had filmed John Prescott, hard at work finishing off his speech. He looked hot and sweaty. He was in his shirt sleeves, without a tie, sitting crouched over papers and documents which were strewn all over the bed in his hotel room. When David Hill saw my television news report that evening he said the contrast could not have been greater. 'There was Blair looking for all the world like President Kennedy, giving a wave to everyone, just as if he was in Camelot. But Prescott, by letting you film him in his bedroom, writing his speech at the last minute, did not appear as if he was in control.'

In fact I disagreed with Hill's assessment of the Prescott pictures. I felt it was his readiness to allow himself to be seen like that, warts and all, which made him so endearing and so popular with Labour's rank and file. My opinion was shared by other members of Prescott's campaign team; but Prescott himself was filled with self-doubt. Later he told me that he had received a lot of stick for letting my television crew film inside his room. 'They all said those pictures made me look like a last-minute man.' He paused for a moment and then laughed. 'But I suppose that's what I really am sometimes.' I still do not think my film did Prescott a disservice. Five months later, in December 1994, when he signed up Labour's 300,000th member in a recruitment drive for the party, he told *On the Record* that his exposure on television had been of great help when he toured the constituencies. 'Party workers and supporters have an idea of what my personality is like because they have seen me on television . . . I want to use that to help the party.'

Criticism of Prescott's image during the contest was as nothing when set alongside the abuse heaped on the head of Robin Cook, who had become the butt of newspaper columnists for 'looking like a garden gnome'. Although fed up with having been written off as untelegenic, Cook told me he did not care what the commentators thought about his appearance; when considering whether to stand for the leadership he had been guided throughout by the likely level of support which he might attract. Letters appeared in newspapers and magazines saying he should ignore the claptrap about being 'too ugly' and allow his name to go forward. Peter Tory in the *Daily Express* was an unexpected fan: 'Cook is the only chap I ever listen to. Maybe he's the man.' Mark Lawson, writing in the *Independent*, deplored the way the election had been turned into a beauty contest. The suggestion that the commanding lead of the front-runner could be attributed to 'some kind of mass hormonal hysteria is patronising to the public and insulting to Blair'.

Nevertheless, whenever newspapers reported rank-and-file opinions there was frequent mention of Blair's televisual appeal, and this was given as one reason why it was felt he would make an effective leader. Encouraging feedback spurred on Blair's advisers to think through his television appearances with even greater care, not least because the candidates' television images were of unprecedented importance in this campaign. The introduction of one member one vote had taken power away from the trade unions and from those constituency parties which were controlled by the left. Instead of voting as a block, individual party members and trade unionists would be deciding for themselves how to vote, and, just as in a general election, those members would be influenced by what they saw and heard on television and radio. And the parallels with a general election, of course, went further. Andrew Marr, writing in the *Independent*, said that politicians who performed badly on television had to recognise that they could be a liability to their parties because they might end up jeopardising the support of millions of potential voters. Failure to communicate effectively through television was not 'an endearing personal flaw but an act of lethal political incompetence'. Marr welcomed the fact that so many Labour members would be making their decision on the basis of what they had seen on television. 'They will be judging in a way not so dissimilar to the way millions of uncommitted voters will judge that same person in a general election.'

However, commentators and spin doctors were confused about the effectiveness of *Panorama*'s televised debate between the three candidates. Nick Robinson, the programme's deputy editor, claimed their 'made-for-TV event' was a first, because until then neither Labour nor Conservative leadership contenders had ever agreed to debate with each other on television. David Hill felt the programme demonstrated the strength of the underlying unity in the party; the only differences which emerged were over style, not policies. He intended to write to *Panorama*'s editor Glenwyn Benson to thank her for a 'marvellous party political broadcast for Labour'. But Peter Mandelson had doubts about the programme's impact and considered it was a 'very tacky production'. Alastair Campbell was equally dismissive in his column in *Today*, where he described *Panorama* as a 'dog's dinner' and said that in her role as one of the questioners, Ann Leslie of the *Daily Mail* was the 'clear winner in the silliest questions of our time contest'. If television was going to be the decisive battleground for the contest, Campbell thought, *Panorama* should have done better than this. Christopher Bell, the *Daily Mail*'s political reporter, put the blame on the candidates. Their failure to leave viewers any the wiser about what they stood for had only reinforced the impression that the contest would be 'settled on image alone'.

The election itself proved to be the foregone conclusion which so many in the party predicted. Blair scored a resounding victory with 57 per cent of the total vote, well ahead of Prescott on 24.1 per cent and Mrs Beckett on 18.9 per cent. Prescott's winning margin over Mrs Beckett in the contest for deputy leader was equally clear-cut: 56.5 per cent to 43.5 per cent. All told, nearly a million votes were cast in a postal ballot. Participation by trade unionists was lower than expected: only 20 per cent of the four million who were eligible used their votes. But the level of interest was far higher in the constituencies, with almost 70 per cent of party members returning their ballot forms.

In his acceptance speech at a rally in London, Blair said the contest had been fought 'without bitterness and with dignity'. Labour should be proud of 'the largest exercise in party democracy' the country had ever seen. He promised to build a new 'left-of-centre agenda' which would offer 'the genuine hope of a new politics to take us into a new millennium'. Prescott turned in another vintage performance and got roars of laughter when he added an unscripted pay-off to his speech. He praised Blair's commanding 'moral authority and political respect' and continued: 'This man, our new leader, has got what it takes...He scares the life out of the Tories...and me!'

Prescott had succeeded at his third attempt to become deputy leader. At his celebration party on board the *Tattershall Castle*, moored near Westminster pier, he told me that the turning point had been when he began to demonstrate that his campaign theme of full employment was backed up by the firm policy proposals which he had been promoting for the previous decade. 'I came across as a conviction politician, not just a careerist.' He took considerable care with his acceptance speech. 'I made sure I only wrote enough for five minutes. I didn't want to race my words and it came in at around ten minutes, just as I had hoped.'

In contrast to the open-house razzmatazz of Prescott's get-together, Blair celebrated privately with his campaign team. In thanking them for their work he singled out 'Bobby' for special tribute. Some of Gordon Brown's aides, who had been invited to the party, were mystified; on inquiring, they were told that 'Bobby' was the codename which Blair's staff had used when referring to Peter Mandelson. As soon as journalists picked up news of this coded reference to Labour's most famous spin doctor there was renewed interest in the extent of his involvement. Speculation about his activities had subsided after what had looked like an authoritative story in the Labour weekly *Tribune*, which stated categorically that it was 'quite clear that the Blair camp have distanced themselves from Hartlepool's Machiavelli' for the 'good reason' that Blair had recognised that any close association with Mandelson 'wouldn't do his chances within the Parliamentary Labour Party much good'.

The first public mention of 'Bobby' appeared in the *Daily Telegraph*'s Peterborough diary column, which said that, although he was acting unofficially, Mandelson had been working 'furiously for Blair'. A few days later Peterborough revealed that the codename had been chosen 'in tribute to the late Bobby Kennedy, who handled much of his brother Jack's tricky business'. Blair's thank-you to 'Bobby' provided a timely headline for my own assessment of Mandelson's contribution to the leadership campaign which was published in the *Guardian*'s media section. My conclusion was that his 'professional guidance was invaluable' and that he should take much of the credit for an election campaign which, in publicity terms, was 'remarkably trouble-free'. I even went so far as to suggest that if Labour won the next election Blair should appoint Mandelson as his minister without portfolio with a specific brief to 'coordinate the government's media presentation and to watch out for the banana skins on which John Major has so frequently come a cropper'.

I spoke to Mandelson in the final week of the contest and told him of my plans for the *Guardian* article. He said he hoped my account of what had happened would be accurate. 'I don't like exaggeration or the suggestion that what I do is sinister or manipulative, that I somehow manipulate the media against the other candidates. I am not out to destroy Beckett or hinder Prescott. The idea that I am a puppet master is simply not true. Yes, I have worked for Blair throughout the campaign, for his interests, his policies and his strategies. That is what I have been looking after in every respect. I am out to protect the interests of my friends. That is what has been important.'

Some of the criticism directed at Mandelson seemed to be rooted in envy. Many senior Labour politicians were jealous of his status. In their eyes he was still a newly elected backbench MP for the unprepossessing constituency of Hartlepool. They were infuriated by his self-importance and air of superiority. They could not understand why he was so respected by editors, producers and reporters. The reason was simple: he spoke with Blair's authority. As the Labour MP Austin Mitchell observed, Mandelson was able to exercise real power over the broadcasting organisations because he had the ability during the campaign to 'deliver the candidate, the photo opportunities and the interviews'. Mandelson's influence was detected again a few hours after the leadership result was announced. There was a disagreement over whether Blair was going to be interviewed by the BBC's political editor Robin Oakley or by *Newsnight*'s Jeremy Paxman. Although Oakley was apparently favoured by Blair's campaign team, *Newsnight* stood its ground and Paxman did the interview. Negotiations of this kind, behind the scenes, were commonplace; but it was only after Mandelson's intervention that this particular dispute was resolved.

Needless to say, my action in revealing in the *Guardian* details of the methods used to promote Blair's candidacy provoked a highly critical response from the Labour leader's entourage. Mandelson left me in no doubt that he felt I had driven 'a coach and horses through normal lobby conventions'. As time went by I could see that he was exasperated at the way my disclosures had been picked up by his critics in the parliamentary party. Mandelson told me subsequently that because of my 'devilment' in writing about the mechanics of his work I had provided his opponents with fresh ammunition with which to 'demonise' his activities. 'You have used your privileged access as a broadcaster to write about me and then allowed others to apply the demonology. I am tired of it.' Mandelson considered I had done both him and Blair a disservice. Some months later, while I was standing on my own in the committee corridor, awaiting the conclusion of the weekly meeting of the Conservatives' 1922 committee of backbenchers, Blair walked by on his way to attend that evening's meeting of the Parliamentary Labour Party. He paused momentarily and looked at me rather sternly, enquiring: 'What mischief are you causing today?' Despite the harshness of his question, I could see a hint of a smile at the corner of his mouth and we were soon chatting away. I was convinced that whatever might be said within the party about the activities of his spin doctor, Blair had great faith in Mandelson's judgement, and the two of them were more than capable of withstanding any criticism.

Nonetheless, there was never any doubt in my mind that once he was elected party leader Blair would want his own upfront media minder. Most political correspondents assumed that the job would go automatically to Alastair Campbell, who had been a long-standing friend of both Blair and Mandelson. Campbell had worked closely with the party leadership for some years and had been tipped as a likely Downing Street press secretary should Neil Kinnock have won the 1992 general election. Once the summer holidays were over the speculation increased as the autumn conferences approached. In addition to Campbell several other names were being mentioned as possible candidates, including Colin Byrne, the party's former chief press officer, Phil Woollas of the GMB and Philip Bassett, industrial editor of *The Times*. Again the favourite won: Campbell's appointment was announced while Blair was attending the TUC conference in Blackpool, where his media relations were being handled jointly by David Hill and the TUC's communications director John Healey.

Campbell could not have been more forthright over the years in parading his support for Labour. As a columnist for *Today*, and before that as political editor of the *Daily Mirror*, he had shown himself to be a doughty campaigner for the party. He enjoyed rebuking other journalists whom he thought lacked conviction. I was teased quite regularly for sitting on the fence when reporting on the government's difficulties. Campbell would huff and puff whenever I reminded him that broadcasters were not supposed to be propagandists. Eventually he would relent and he usually marched off muttering something to the effect that he was about to get back to the 'red meat of political propaganda'. In an interview with Valerie Grove of *The Times* he said he did not think it would be difficult to be a 'poacher turned gamekeeper' once he began working for Blair because had never projected himself as being independent. 'I have much more time for frankly biased journalism than for people who just pretend they are reporting objectively.' Some of his colleagues in the press gallery had predicted that Campbell would be unwilling to take a salary cut or give up his freelance earnings to work for Blair, but they misjudged him.

Not only was Campbell a highly effective operator in the competitive area of reporting politics for the popular press, he had also established a not inconsiderable reputation as a broadcaster. He was a regular presenter of *The Week in Westminster* and frequently gave the morning newspaper review on *Breakfast News*. His knowledge of the inner workings of television and radio was an added qualification. He had made the acquaintance of a vast array of editors and producers and it was obvious that he would be entirely at home in the private arm-twisting which takes place when programmes make their bids for live interviews. I suggested in a profile of Campbell for the *Guardian* that the timing of his appointment, in the middle of the TUC conference, was symbolic: Blair was indicating in effect that Labour's future dealings with the news media were going to be as tough and as ruthless as the party's relationship with the trade unions.

Not only could Blair's new press secretary easily replicate many of Mandelson's undoubted skills in media management, he could do so without being hampered by the antagonism between Mandelson and some sections of the party that had built up over the years. Campbell was widely respected among Labour MPs as a diligent, campaigning journalist. Although forthright in his opinions about the party's internal affairs, he had not got drawn into the personality clashes in which Mandelson became embroiled through having to allocate high-profile media exposure among members of the shadow Cabinet.

Campbell went out of his way to give his public backing to the Blair–Prescott partnership. In his column in *Tribune*, the week after the leadership contest, he complimented Prescott on his election campaign. He said Mrs Beckett's mistake was to think she could be the honoured candidate of the left, defending CND and secondary picketing, while also suggesting she was the legitimate inheritor of John Smith's political legacy. It was not just Prescott's 'fine television performances, his energy and his wit' which built up his support among right-wingers and left-wingers alike, but the fact that he 'talked straight, had a simple coherent message and he hammered it unrelentingly'.

In what clearly had all the makings of a hazardous debut, Campbell arrived at the party's 1994 annual conference in Blackpool in the dual capacity of press secretary to the Labour leader and political columnist for *Today*. He had complained bitterly about being dropped by *Breakfast News* and other BBC programmes once his appointment was announced, though as he had crossed the dividing line between journalism and public relations he could hardly have expected anything else. Nevertheless, I detected signs of withdrawal symptons in Campbell's behaviour. Over the years he had become something of a personality and was obviously missing the pleasure and notoriety of being called on by television and radio programmes to give his expert opinion. Although he intended leaving *Today* the following week, at the end of the Conservative conference, he wanted to carry on writing newspaper articles and columns. I thought he might find it difficult to combine the job of press secretary with that of columnist and personality. Once he was working full time for Blair, I felt, he would have to lower his own profile. When I suggested this on *Conference Live*, which was providing televised coverage of the proceedings, Campbell remonstrated with me afterwards. He thought my comments were singularly misplaced.

Most press secretaries assigned to party leaders and ministers try to avoid personal publicity. They realise that if they were ever considered celebrities in their own right they might easily get distracted or become preoccupied about their own appearance, rather than remaining vigilant on behalf of their charge. In some situations this could endanger the politicians they were employed to promote. In the 1992 general election Campbell's predecessor, Julie Hall, embarrassed Neil Kinnock with an emotional outburst during a chaotic news conference about the 'Jennifer's ear' political broadcast. Because Ms Hall was upset Kinnock forgot himself and ended up being abusive about a *Sunday Express* reporter, Bruce Anderson. Correspondents could not recall an occasion when a party leader was upstaged so comprehensively by a press officer or when the sight of Kinnock losing his cool had been immortalised so clearly on television.

Campbell had himself acquired a reputation for volatile behaviour after getting involved in a celebrated punch-up in the press gallery. He was working for the *Daily Mirror* at the time. During an argument about Robert Maxwell's death he lashed out at the *Guardian*'s political editor Michael White and punched him on the jaw. Campbell thought he had been taunted unfairly but White retaliated, hitting his assailant even harder. On the basis of this well-documented encounter I finished off my profile of Campbell for the *Guardian* by suggesting, rather tongue in cheek, that Blair might be 'upstaged too one day if his press officer is sufficiently provoked'. I had no idea when writing that a fortnight before the Labour conference that I would end up becoming the first political correspondent to feel the lash of Campbell's tongue in a public dressing down which transfixed fellow journalists in the press room. Within a few minutes of another of my appearances on *Conference Live* the air was blue as Campbell belaboured me with accusations of 'mischievous and unprofessional conduct'.

Reporters covering the conference had been well and truly ambushed by Blair's surprise announcement that he wanted to rewrite Clause Four of Labour's constitution. Campbell had been in on the secret from the start; Blair had discussed it with him when their families met up during their summer holidays in France. Rarely had the party's publicity staff managed to pull off a coup of such magnitude. Labour were notorious for unauthorised disclosures about policy changes, and Campbell was widely praised for the part he had played in a stunningly successful operation. Not a word had leaked out about Blair's wish to abandon Labour's historic commitment to the 'common ownership of the means of production, distribution and exchange'.

Next day, as union leaders and delegates on the left began adjusting to what they considered was Blair's audacity in seeking to tamper with a sacred text, journalists started digging around to see whether there had been any prior consultation within the party. I made a point of checking out John Prescott's involvement after watching untransmitted footage of a BBC interview in which he spoke rather cryptically about Clause Four. In order to ensure secrecy and maintain an element of surprise while Blair was speaking, the last three pages of his text were not handed out to reporters in advance. That evening, when Prescott was interviewed for *Breakfast News*, he could be seen on film chatting away to Alastair Campbell. He asked if it was correct that the speech was issued to journalists with the final pages removed. Campbell confirmed this, saying the section on Clause Four was not given out until the end. Prescott then said that he had been given a full copy of the speech personally by Blair. 'I told him to sign it: The day we went down the swanny.' At this point Campbell leant across and said that none of Prescott's remarks could be broadcast.

MPs and union leaders who were close to the deputy leader told me they knew he had some serious misgivings about the wisdom of abandoning Clause Four. From what I could gather he had only been won over in the final week before the conference. All Prescott would say himself was that he had known of the announcement for 'a little while'. When asked on *Conference Live* for an update about what had gone on behind the scenes, I gave this resumé: 'Yes, there is a lot of speculation. It seems some of those closest to Tony Blair knew a fortnight ago but John Prescott was only on board a week ago and did advise against it.' I then recounted how in an off-camera remark Prescott had joked with Blair about this being the day Labour went 'down the swanny'.

Although he was spending much of his time with Blair, Campbell tended to operate out of the press centre when the conference was in session. He was writing a daily commentary for *Today* and, like the other newspaper journalists, could often be seen working at a computer terminal or discussing the day's news with colleagues. Apparently one or two reporters who heard my broadcast approached Campbell for more details. Phil Woollas of the GMB inquired if the new press secretary had a strategy for handling questions about Prescott. Campbell asked to see me. When I walked into the press centre I could see he was furious. He told me I had acted unprofessionally. He said that if I had asked people who knew what was happening I would have discovered that Prescott had been aware of the Clause Four decision for several weeks and had been 'fully on board every step of the way'. Not only had it been cleared by Prescott but he had 'helped in every possible way' in preparing for Blair's announcement. I said that if Campbell was giving me that information on the record, and if it could be attributed to the party, I would make sure that it was broadcast as quickly as possible.

At the next available break in the speeches, when I was interviewed again by *Conference Live*, I explained that since my earlier broadcast the BBC had been given a full statement detailing Prescott's involvement which made it abundantly clear that the deputy leader was in total support of the constitutional changes which Blair was seeking. However, when I checked back with the union leaders and MPs with whom I had discussed Prescott's position, they assured me that my original version was correct. They reiterated that he did have reservations and was only won round in the final week. Other BBC correspondents reported that Prescott had personally warned Blair that there could be trouble if he went ahead with his announcement. Apparently he feared that delegates might 'tear up their membership cards' in protest. Prescott's support was critical to Blair's strategy because it would reassure conference delegates. Several newspaper journalists recalled that immediately after Blair's speech Campbell went on a 'snow job' round the press room saying that Prescott had been a key player all along in wanting to abandon Clause Four. Prescott himself smiled enigmatically when I asked him again what prior contact there had been. He was more interested in cross-questioning me about the motives for my broadcast and in finding out whom I had spoken to.

Next morning I asked Campbell if he actually saw my broadcast before he made his protest because it seemed to me that my remarks were very similar to what other BBC journalists were saying. Campbell brushed aside my offer of a transcript. He insisted that Prescott had been involved in all the pre-conference discussions. They had debated what to do if Blair's announcement led to protests on the conference floor. Campbell said that he was the person who had mentioned the possibility of membership cards being torn up, not Prescott.

As Campbell seemed satisfied with my second broadcast, and the unambiguous clarification which I had given, I thought the matter was closed. However, I foolishly overlooked the fact that Blair's new spin doctor had sized me up as suitable guinea pig on which to practise. He seemed determined to teach me a lesson I would not forget. When he first tackled me I realised other journalists were looking on in amazement. Michael Brunson of ITN was highly amused. He was delighted to see me being reprimanded by Blair's 'friendly new press officer' who, as he said, just happened to be accredited to the conference as a *Today* journalist. Another onlooker was Mark Lawson of the *Independent*.

In a profile he wrote some weeks later entitled 'Blair Presumptive', Lawson said the new Labour leader should avoid surrounding himself with 'too many zealous non-elected lieutenants' as it might repeat the alienation of the Kinnock years. 'Blair's boys, in particular his excitable press secretary, Alastair Campbell, and his aide Tim Allan, have already created similar resentments among press and backbenchers.' My confrontation with Campbell must also have been witnessed by the *Independent*'s political editor, Donald Macintyre, because he led off his report next day with a graphic description. He said Campbell had given 'a loud and public dressing-down to a BBC reporter who dared to suggest that John Prescott had been told only a few days before the party conference, as a fait accompli, that Blair would be seeking the replacement of Clause Four. We all make mistakes, and the row is a sign of the highly pro-active briefing style of the new Blair office.'

I thought Macintyre had been rather economical with the facts and had probably not heard precisely what I said on *Conference Live*. His story was followed up by Joanna Coles, who was in Blackpool filming a report on the new press secretary for *The Late Show*. She said they had already interviewed Campbell who had told them that he had forced the BBC to broadcast a 'correction'. She wanted my reaction. I told her that *Conference Live* had responded immediately when challenged by Campbell. I had clarified my original story as quickly as possible and we had broadcast Labour's on-the-record statement in full. At no point had I retracted my original version or admitted having made a 'mistake'. However, I could see that I was at a serious disadvantage: if the spin on a story is to be effective it always helps to get in first and persuade journalists and presenters to take the press officer's version of the 'facts'. Campbell had demonstrated with considerable aplomb that he was going to be a dab hand as a spin doctor. When he was interviewed again, and at length, *The Late Show* appeared to make no attempt to question his version of events. Campbell pulled no punches: 'Why should he [Jones] be allowed to put out a complete load of nonsense and not be forced to correct it? That story was nonsense and if similar stories are put out I shall make sure the public know that.'

The complaint about my *Conference Live* broadcast was soon overtaken by other more substantive criticisms of the BBC's coverage. Two days after Blair's speech, delegates rejected his call to abandon Clause Four, voting narrowly, by 50.9 per cent to 49.1 per cent, in favour of a motion which urged the retention of the commitment to public ownership. Immediately after the leadership's defeat Campbell escorted Blair to the BBC's conference studio so that he could be interviewed for *The World at One*. When the presenter Nick Clarke reached the tiny studio, which contained just one small table, he found that Campbell was already inside, sitting next to Blair. Press officers are usually required to wait outside in the control cubicle so that presenters can feel at ease with their guests. Gareth Butler, the producer, asked Campbell to leave the studio. He refused. The previous morning Jim Naughtie, who was presenting *Today* from Blackpool, was surprised when Campbell insisted on sitting next to Blair in their mobile studio. Naughtie said he did not like having a politician's minder looking at him over the microphone. In the comparable circumstances of a live television interview the studio director would have insisted that Campbell move out of the away, otherwise he would have appeared in the shot. In reply to Nick Clarke's first question Blair accused *The World at One* of getting into a 'pathetic kerfuffle' and said he was not worried by the Clause Four defeat. I was surprised to hear Blair launch into an immediate criticism of the programme. He had always impressed me by what I took to be a calculated decision on his part to avoid knee-jerk abuse of the media. I could only conclude that Campbell's agitation about the BBC had somehow had an effect on Blair's response. Mark Lawson seemed to share my assessment of Campbell's influence because he wrote later in the *Independent* of how 'rather worryingly' Blair was being encouraged by his press secretary to 'become a whinger' and complain about the conduct of television and radio interviewers.

As the week progressed Campbell had become increasingly irritated by what he considered the unacceptable behaviour of BBC producers. He claimed they had inundated him with interview requests. Using the privileged position of his *Today* column he set out to lambast the BBC. In one commentary he condemned what he said had been the Corporation's 'near hysterical response' to the Clause Four vote; a few days later he widened his attack to take in *Newsnight*, the *One o'Clock News* and indeed almost the entire conference production team. He said it was time the BBC understood that Blair intended to take a new approach to the media: 'It means that if we say Blair is not doing *Newsnight* tonight, but he might do it tomorrow, that is it. It is not an invitation for armies of researchers to spin different lines to different Blair aides, or for presenter Peter Snow to seek to stop Blair and plead with him direct as the Labour leader is rushing to (yet another) BBC interview.'

Campbell contrasted the BBC's conduct with that of the *Sun*, which had splashed on an exclusive report about a topless 'girlie magazine cover star', Carole Caplin, who was staying at the main conference hotel and acting as 'girl Friday' for Cherie Blair. In marked contrast to the BBC, the *Sun* had kept Blair's office 'fully informed' about its story on 'Cherie's topless friend'. When the *Sun* asked for an end-of-conference session with Blair, Campbell said it was easy to decide what do do: 'They got one. *Newsnight* didn't.'

BBC journalists were puzzled by Campbell's attitude and his suggestion that they should model their behaviour on that of the *Sun*. Part of the problem for the producers was their impression that he was treating interview bids on an hour-by-hour basis, as dictated by events at the conference. This meant producers had to keep checking with him, because if there was any doubt about Blair's availability programmes were left with no alternative but to line up standby guests. Broadcasting staff were also totally confused about the delegation of responsibility within the party. They assumed that, as in previous years, all interview bids relating to the conference should be channelled through Labour's communications director, David Hill, and his team of press officers. However, Campbell and his aides were also fielding enquiries and sometimes the two teams made conflicting decisions. Labour's broadcasting officer Mish Tullar said a BBC television crew could film Blair at a party disco. Shortly before his arrival the cameraman was asked to leave: Hilary Coffman, one of Campbell's aides, said Blair's office had decided that no pictures could be taken. The lack of a clear command structure made life even more difficult for the journalists who were providing news stories on a twenty-four-hour basis for television, radio and the news agencies. On some occasions they found they were having to deal with three spin doctors: Campbell, Hill and Mandelson.

Confusion surrounded the advance briefings on Blair's speech. Campbell gave most of the press a run-down on the likely content the evening before. However, several newspaper reporters complained afterwards that they had not been briefed as extensively as others were. They claimed this was because they were not on Campbell's 'white Commonwealth' list of approved journalists. Hill told broadcasters that he could supply them with only the briefest outline of the speech and they must speak to Campbell; but he proved difficult to track down and correspondents spoke instead to his assistant Tim Allan.

Late that evening tempers became a little frayed. James Hardy, political editor of the Press Assocation, told me he considered it was inexcusable of Campbell to have excluded the country's biggest news agency from his press briefing on the speech. Hardy said he met Mandelson at 2 a.m. and told him it was time Labour stopped 'playing silly games'. He thought the party should have briefed all journalists together, at the same time, as happened at Conservative and Liberal Democrat conferences. When *Breakfast News* reported later that morning that some journalists had been left to fill in the holes themselves as to what Blair was likely to say, Hill was furious. He told me that the party's publicity department had not been given that task. 'I am going to draw a line from now on... I am not responsible for giving briefings on Blair's speech.' Broadcasters were not given any inkling of what Blair intended to say about Clause Four; but party sources supplied the London *Evening Standard* with a run-down in time for its last edition.

Although I had not been involved in previewing Blair's speech I had found it difficult to work out which spin doctor was in charge. On the eve of the conference, when some of the biggest unions announced that their delegations would be voting collectively and not individually, I was asked by Mandelson to quote him verbatim remarks by the GMB leader John Edmonds. Mandelson was standing at the time in the foyer of the Imperial Hotel, holding a mobile phone, and he relayed what I said to the Labour leader's office upstairs. I realised that Blair must have been in the process of being briefed about what Edmonds had said, because within a few minutes he made a statement deploring the apparent refusal of some union leaders to allow their delegates to participate in the conference on the basis of one member one vote.

The day after Blair's speech Mandelson gave a prerecorded interview for *The World at One* in which he suggested that if a consensus developed behind the move to rewrite Labour's constitution then the issue should be resolved quickly so that the debate over Clause Four did not dominate the 1995 autumn conference. On hearing him confirm publicly what was being said privately I ended my own report for the *One o'Clock News* by saying that some of Blair's 'closest advisers' hoped the issue could be settled at a special conference early in 1995, as they believed this would prevent Labour spending the whole year 'bogged down in a messy internal debate'. Prescott immediately rejected this suggestion on *Conference Live*: a special conference, he said, would not be necessary. Hill complained about my story, saying it was incorrect and he wanted the idea 'killed off once and for all'. Clause Four was a constitutional issue which, Hill said, would have to go to the annual conference. Yet two months later, at its December meeting, Labour's national executive committee followed Blair's advice and agreed to hold a special conference in April 1995 to seek approval for a new version of the party's constitution.

The spectacle of Labour's spin doctors competing for attention became a news event in itself. Their self-indulgence hardly mattered because the party was basking in the favourable publicity which Blair's speech had generated. A few unfavourable stories about disarray among Labour's communications staff were as nothing when set against the Conservatives' split over Europe and the disenchantment of many Tory MPs with John Major. Nevertheless Campbell was obviously aware there might be a problem in the future. Immediately before the conference he told his readers in *Today* that he had been given some 'blood-curdling' tips by Sir Bernard Ingham when the two men had met to review the Sunday papers together on *Breakfast with Frost*. While not supplying any details, Campbell had said in his column next day that he intended to take some of Ingham's 'wise advice'. A diary item in the *Daily Telegraph* revealed that after the programme, when they sat down to breakfast, Ingham asked Campbell what he intended to do about the reports that Mandelson was apparently determined to go on offering journalists rival briefings on Blair's behalf. Ingham offered Campbell his own solution: 'The answer is simple. Slit his throat!' Ingham kept the story going in his own column in the *Daily Express*. While he deplored the fact that his 'sound advice, however metaphorically expressed' had been leaked to 'yobbish broadsheet gossips' he said experience had taught him that 'Campbell must be master in his own house. Oppositions, like governments, should speak with one voice.'

When journalists asked Mandelson whether he was still acting as a spokesman for Blair, he made light of it. He told the *Daily Mail* that Campbell was only a 'trainee spin doctor'. Campbell got his own back in *Today*. He described Mandelson as the 'spin doctor's spin doctor' of whom John Smith had 'once memorably said that he was so devious he would one day disappear up his own something or other'. Campbell took another swipe at a suggestion by *The Times* that Mandelson had helped write Blair's speech. He knew from Mandelson's days as a columnist for the *People* that 'writing was never his strong point, and that he had to look to his friends to help him out. Know what I mean?'

Campbell had taken something of a risk in sending up Mandelson during the conference week, because his column in *Today* provided a free hit for the other tabloids. That morning the *Sun*'s political correspondent, Simon Walters, was standing at the reception desk in the Pembroke Hotel when he saw Mandelson approaching. He beckoned him over and asked if he had seen what Campbell had written about him in the 'gutter press'. Walters said Mandelson looked none too pleased. Although the *Sun* was praised publicly by Blair's press secretary for the way it dealt with its exclusive about the 'former topless raunchy dancer' who was in Blackpool helping out the Labour leader's wife, Walters said that in fact Campbell had 'moaned' to him about it and had complained of his distaste in having to deal with the *Sun* over what he described as the first 'really nasty' story about the Blair family. Walters told Campbell that if he felt like that he should 'go and lie down' to recover.

Jokes about Labour's warring spin doctors dominated the closing session of the conference. In giving the vote of thanks on behalf of the press, Kevin Maguire, labour editor of the *Daily Mirror*, said it had been like 'popping into Spinulike' for a snack all week: if political journalists did not like the spin which was on that day's menu, they just changed doctors. Maguire complimented Campbell for the expeditious way he had ejected the *Sun*'s newspaper seller from the foyer of the Imperial

Hotel. He thought this was quite a feat because Blair's press secretary was still on Rupert Murdoch's payroll as a *Today* journalist and might have been expected to show more respect for a fellow employee. Unexpectedly, Labour's outgoing general secretary Larry Whitty took the side of the media, commiserating with the reporters. He recalled his surprise before the 1992 election when Mandelson chose to become a parliamentary candidate at the very moment he had lobby journalists 'eating out of his hand'. Whitty said he had not realised that Mandelson could do more than one job at once and would carry on as a spin doctor once he became Hartlepool's MP. However, as other 'pale imitation Mandelsons' had gone round the conference briefing the press, Whitty said he understood why the journalists had complained all week of 'repetitive spin injury'.

Most political correspondents agreed with the *Daily Mail*'s verdict that the inexperience of Blair's new team was the most likely reason why Labour's spin doctors had had such a 'funny turn' at the conference. Campbell had always been extremely popular in the lobby and despite the confusion over the briefings on Blair's speech, and the hiatus surrounding the leadership's subsequent defeat in the Clause Four vote, there was a genuine wish to see him succeed.

What struck me about the way Campbell handled his first big assignment as press secretary was that he seemed far more at ease with reporters from the popular papers than with television or radio correspondents. Despite his experience as a presenter he did not appear to have the depth of Mandelson's understanding of the mechanics of broadcasting or any real appreciation of the tensions which develop during hour upon hour of live programming. I also noticed that Campbell seemed to be more involved in thinking about the content of tabloid newspapers than in worrying about the overall impression which Blair might be creating on television and radio.

In his interview with *The Late Show*'s Joanna Coles Campbell confirmed what I had suspected. He said that while television and radio were 'extremely important' it was the press which set the political agenda. Unlike Mandelson, who had spent so much time briefing the heavyweight daily and Sunday newspapers because of their influence on the broadcasters, Campbell believed Labour should be far less hung up about what the *Guardian* and the *Independent* were saying and more concerned with what was being reported by the *Sun*, *Daily Star*, *Daily Mirror*, *Daily Mail* and *Daily Express*, because they were the papers which reached the 'big numbers'. The day after Campbell's appearance, Blair repeated his point in his first speech as leader to the Parliamentary Labour Party. He told Labour MPs that they all had to work harder at getting 'more positive coverage' in the mass-circulation tabloids.

Campbell had been developing this theme for some months. In *Tribune*, the previous year, he had outlined the new opportunities with which he thought Labour had been presented. He said the Tory press had 'deserted, or at least distanced itself' from the Major government, for both political and commercial reasons. 'The hostility to Major gives Labour a chance to cultivate the press in a way that would have been futile in the run-up to the last election, to cultivate journalists on a personal level, unpleasant though that can sometimes be, and to cultivate the press as an issue.' Campbell's assessment appeared to be vindicated three weeks after Blair's election when, in an interview for the German magazine *Der Spiegel*, Rupert Murdoch indicated that his staunchly Tory newspapers, *The Times*, the *Sunday Times*, the *Sun* and the *News of the World*, might support the new Labour leader. Murdoch had been challenged over the backing his organisation gave to Conservative politicians in his three main areas of operation, Britain, the United States and Australia. In defending his company Murdoch said his newspapers had assisted the last Labour Prime Minister, Harold Wilson; and: 'Only last year we helped the Labor government in Canberra. I could even imagine myself supporting the British Labour leader, Tony Blair.'

Murdoch gave his interview to *Der Spiegel* in early August. A fortnight later, as the main holiday month was drawing to a close, the *News of the World* devoted half a page to news and comment under Blair's by-line. It was a well-presented selection of short, topical news stories and bore all the hallmarks of Campbell's handiwork. The lead item was a punchily written commentary in which the Labour leader wished the best of luck to people who worked hard and became wealthy. He had 'no intention of punishing middle-income families with ever higher taxes as the Tories have done'. Blair's 'bloke-next-door' performance, reassuring voters that he would not penalise success, was described by the *Independent* as a carefully crafted package aimed at soft spots in the electorate which were usually supplied with a diet of anti-Labour writing from the pen of the *News of the World*'s regular columnist Woodrow Wyatt.

But there were those who saw a poisoned chalice being proffered. Michael Leapman, the *Independent*'s media commentator, urged Blair to beware of this tentative signal of support. Flirting with Labour had harsh economic logic for Murdoch. He was obviously hoping to persuade Blair to put Labour's plans for curbing media monopolies like News International on to the 'back burner' in exchange for editorial support. Alex Mitchell, London correspondent of the *Sydney Sun-Herald*, was sure that Murdoch was guided solely by self-interest. Writing in the *Evening Standard*, Mitchell had no doubts about his advice to Blair: 'Don't let Rupert come the raw prawn on you. Surely you should be able to win the election on your own merits; you'll feel a whole lot cleaner if you do.'

Bernard Ingham took an equally jaundiced view of Murdoch's motives. The trade-off was straightforward: support for Blair in return for Labour's refusal to interfere in Murdoch's 'cross-media ownership and buccaneering price-cutting ways'. Ingham went further, casting doubt on Campbell's theory that Labour might be able to make an impression on the Tory tabloids. He thought John Major would still go into the next election with the 'lion's share of the national press more or less behind him'. Ingham doubted whether there would be any fundamental change in the stance of United Newspapers, publishers of the *Daily Express*, *Daily Star* and *Sunday Express*; of Associated Newspapers, publishers of the *Daily Mail*, *Mail on Sunday* and *Evening Standard*; or of the *Daily Telegraph* or *Sunday Telegraph*. He also believed that all Murdoch's titles, except the Labour-supporting *Today*, would remain 'more or less on board' behind Major.

I shared Ingham's assessment of the long-term inclinations of the newspaper proprietors. I also doubted whether an occasional half page of Blair's opinions, tucked deep inside the *News of the World*, would do much to redress years of biased political reporting. Murdoch had used the same tactic while supporting the Thatcher government in demolishing the power of the trade unions in the early 1980s, when as a sop to public opinion his papers occasionally made over the odd comment column to a union leader: these were token gestures and made no difference to the commercial strategy of News International or to Murdoch's determination to smash the restrictive practices of the print workers. In fact, for a time, he lulled the print union leaders into thinking that he would not carry out his threat to switch production of his papers to a new plant at Wapping.

Nevertheless, as the weeks went by Campbell's strategy of wooing the tabloid papers, and especially the Murdoch titles, started to prove increasingly effective. Immediately after the Conservatives' annual conference in October, a full-page article by Blair was published by the *News of the World* under the heading: 'Major is a failure and he knows it.' After the government's defeat in December over doubling VAT on domestic fuel, the Labour leader provided an article for the *Sun*. Then at the end of the month the *Independent* revealed that in September, shortly before Labour's annual conference, Murdoch and his wife Anna had hosted a private dinner for Blair and his wife Cherie at a London restaurant. Gus Fischer, the chief executive of News International, and his wife Gillian were also present. The dinner was described as a 'getting-to-know-you session' at which politics provided the main talking point. Both News International and Blair's office said Labour's likely policy towards Murdoch's media interests was not discussed.

Having suggested in August that Labour should be wary of Murdoch because of his inclination to 'snuggle up to people who have power or look like gaining it', Michael Leapman reinforced his warning on hearing of the dinner. In another colourful exposé in the *Independent* he recalled how Murdoch had switched sides strategically so as to protect his media interests in Australia, where at one time or other over recent years he had supported three of the country's Labor Prime Ministers. Leapman concluded that in making approaches to Blair, Murdoch was acting true to form. 'Even if he does not believe that Labour will win the election, the move is a useful signal to John Major's government that his support cannot be taken for granted next time.'

Campbell was quoted by the *Independent* as saying that it would be absurd if Labour did not do all it could to get a fair hearing from Murdoch's newspapers, and he made no apology for seeking to get the party's message across to 'millions of people'. Speculation that the tactics being adopted by Blair and Campbell could produce spectacular results was heightened by a prediction from Andrew Neil, former editor of the *Sunday Times*, that another of Murdoch's national newspapers, in addition to *Today*, would end up supporting Blair at the next election. Publicity about the contacts between Murdoch and Blair certainly caused no apparent difficulty to either side: in January 1995 the *News of the World* devoted its leader page to another article by the Labour leader. If Campbell could continue achieving a hit rate like that for Blair's comment columns then he would be achieving the kind of turnaround in the tabloids' treatment of Labour that many in the party thought was impossible.

However, Campbell himself was careful not to overstate the possibilities of winning support from previously hostile newspapers like the *Sun* and *The Times*, and indeed his first few weeks as press secretary provided a salutary reminder of the underlying strength of the anti-Labour sentiments of other newspapers like the *Daily Mail* and *Daily Express*. Any hope of establishing a new rapport with them seemed as remote as ever after a succession of potentially damaging stories. Jack Straw, the shadow Home Secretary, provoked a rash of hostile coverage when he predicted in a *Panorama* interview that the party's plans for constitutional reform would 'hasten the process towards a more Scandinavian monarchy'. Labour were immediately put on the defensive. Under the banner headline 'Don't Destroy Our Monarchy' the *Daily Express* claimed that Labour were 'trying to tear Britain's heart out' by stripping the Queen of most of her powers. Campbell spent a busy morning telling broadcasters that the suggested reduction in the size of the royal family was Straw's idea and not official party policy.

For its part, the *Daily Mail* produced a front-page splash on Tony and Cherie Blair's decision to send their son Euan to the grant-maintained

London Oratory School, eight miles from their home in Islington. Choosing a school which had opted out of local authority control, the paper said, made a 'mockery' of Labour's education policy. The *Mail* then went on to take Blair to task in an inconclusive 'exposé' over whether or not he had spent £60 on a haircut. The article was entitled 'The Hair Apparent' and suggested that the Labour leader was having his 'tresses tended at home by a royal crimper'. When Blair's office denied that his trim cost anything like £60, the editor, Paul Dacre, insisted their investigation was 'meant to be humorous'. Campbell complained to the paper's political staff, and also took the precaution of reminding television and radio journalists that he did not want Blair to be asked about his haircut during interviews; but his protests only drew attention to a story which Labour might have been well advised to have ignored altogether.

The tabloid stories were not all hostile, however. The discovery of three intruders inside Blair's private office at the House of Commons provided Campbell with some sensational material with which to brief his former colleagues in the popular press. 'Blairgate' was the banner headline across the *Daily Star*'s front page. One of those detained in the office by Blair's administrative officer Sue Jackson was Andrew Hull, a research assistant to the Conservative MP David Atkinson. Campbell said it was significant that Ms Jackson believed the intruders had been in Blair's office for around ten minutes. Peter Mandelson also briefed journalists: he said there were signs that papers had been 'rifled through' and that the door to Blair's inner sanctum had been opened. After inquiries by the House authorities, the Speaker, Betty Boothroyd, assured MPs there was no malice whatsoever in what had been a 'mischievous walkabout' by two research assistants and a guest after an excess of seasonal spirit.

In any case, Labour's runaway victory in the Dudley West by-election in mid December put paid to any real worries about the continued sniping of the Tory press. The swing was 29 per cent – the biggest in Labour's favour for sixty years. Blair, whose popularity was mentioned quite frequently when voters were interviewed in the constituency, gained considerable television exposure during the campaign. Campbell had begun taking great care over the way the party leader was being framed for set-up shots and the positions in which he was being filmed when answering questions. Producers had detected a change in the press secretary's attitude. These days he seemed far more receptive when asked about picture opportunities or interviews and he went out of his way to remind television correspondents of topical footage which had been taken on previous occasions. When Blair finished giving a BBC interview on the morning after Labour's by-election triumph he made a point of staying put until Campbell had checked out the next location: he had grown wise to the dangers of being caught off-guard. If producers or television crews tried to start filming Blair in the press secretary's absence they were told to wait until his return.

One consequence of Campbell's attentiveness was that whenever the Labour leader was being filmed or photographed during constituency visits or at party meetings there was every chance the press secretary might end up in the picture as well; and indeed Campbell could usually be seen either walking alongside Blair or following behind him, or perhaps standing or sitting close by. Except when they are conducting news conferences, most press officers try to avoid getting into the same shot as ministers or leading politicians. They have no wish to attract attention to themselves, believing they can be more effective out of the glare of publicity. Press officers also realise that if they get in the way continuously they can annoy television crews and photographers, who do not always want a crowded shot. Often valuable footage is discarded during editing of film because party officials or minders get too close: if there are people in the shot other than the main subject who have to be identified unnecessarily, this can make the script confusing. Sometimes there is no alternative but to use pictures which are second-best, but uncluttered; on other occasions shots which do contain extraneous people have to be used because there are no others available. When press officers see themselves on television getting in the way, cluttering up the picture, they realise why it is so important to stand back. The rule about keeping out of camera range, and well clear of doorways during arrivals and departures, is applied quite strictly in Downing Street and outside government offices.

As December 1994 wore on, another sensational news story seemed to be in the making when Labour obtained what they thought was the first page of John Major's private speech to the annual Christmas party at Conservative Central Office. Charles Reiss, political editor of the *Evening Standard*, reported how Labour had 'gleefully circulated' the leaked text. It was followed up by ITN's political editor Michael Brunson. Major was reported to have said the Conservatives were at 'a low ebb' and had to pick themselves up 'off the floor'. Jeremy Hanley, the Tory chairman, said Major had not spoken from a text or notes and did not use the words attributed to him: it was 'pathetic politics' to suggest a scrappy piece of paper had any importance and it showed that Blair's 'new' Labour Party contained 'just the same old dirty tricks'. Campbell denied Labour had ever suggested it was Major's notes: the text had been found by a photocopier and passed on to journalists so that they could check it out.

There was much amusement in Downing Street and Central Office at Labour's hurried retreat. The general verdict among Conservative media advisers was that they had Campbell 'banged to rights', and they could not believe their good fortune that when the tide of publicity was running so strongly against Major, Blair had a press secretary who was happily conceding own goals. In fact, some of the Tory strategists I spoke to thought Campbell might prove to be a weak link in Blair's private office. In his years as a journalist on Labour-supporting tabloids he had heaped vitriolic abuse on Major and his ministers, and party researchers intended trawling through Campbell's many columns in *Today* and the *Daily Mirror* for ammunition which they might be able to use against him should his conduct become a source of controversy. One article which was drawn to my attention was from *Tribune* in July 1994 when Campbell supported the action of a reporter from the *Sunday Times* who, posing as a businessman, offered £1,000 to two Tory MPs, Graham Riddick and David Tredinnick, in return for asking parliamentary questions, and then secretly recorded their answers. Campbell described it as 'a legitimate enough trap to lay'. I was told Campbell's endorsement of the *Sunday Times'* sting was one of the quotes which would be stored away against any future attempt by Blair or his press officer to castigate newspapers which used underhand methods to expose potentially dubious activities by Labour MPs.

New Year's Eve produced more problems for Labour's publicity staff. Copies of the front pages of the *Sunday Times* and the *Mail on Sunday*, which were faxed to television and radio newsrooms the evening before publication, revealed that Labour were considering the possibility of imposing VAT on fees paid for pupils at private schools. Both newspapers quoted Labour's education spokesman David Blunkett. I tried without success to contact him. Later that evening I spoke to David Hill, who had just arrived home from the airport after an eight-day holiday in Leningrad. He knew nothing about the possibility of VAT on school fees, but confirmed Labour were thinking of ending the charitable status of private schools. At 10.30 the next morning I managed to get through to Blunkett on the telephone and I recorded an interview. He confirmed that Labour wanted to look at both the removal of charitable status and the possibility of putting VAT on fees to see which would be the fairest way of tackling the issue of privileged education. Shortly after 12 noon, as I was preparing my television and radio reports for the lunchtime bulletins on New Year's Day, I received an urgent telephone call from David Hill giving me a categorical statement that Labour would definitely not be imposing VAT on private school fees. Within the hour Blunkett appeared live on *The World this Weekend* to confirm that the idea had been ruled out completely. He said that since recording the earlier interview he had received fresh information. 'Both the shadow Chancellor and the leader of the party think it is helpful to rule out this possibility in order to avoid confusion. I'm very happy to accept that.'

There could hardly have been a clearer example of the difficulties which the party still faced in coordinating the presentation of their policies to the news media. Blunkett had spoken to two newspapers and recorded a BBC interview without knowing that the shadow Chancellor Gordon Brown had apparently ruled out the option of VAT on school fees some weeks before; Labour's communications director did not know of the story on New Year's Eve. Once it had appeared, Blair and his advisers took immediate evasive action and were obviously determined to stop any further speculation because it so clearly contradicted the Labour leader's own promise that the party had 'no intention of punishing middle-income families'; but it was not until 12 noon on New Year's Day that any moves were made to kill the story, and by then I had recorded my interview with Blunkett. If Labour's spin doctors had been alert they would have got to the party's education spokesman before I did and sorted out an agreed line. It would then have been easier for them to have played down the significance of the reports in the *Sunday Times* and the *Mail on Sunday*, a tactic ruled out by my having recorded Blunkett's initial answer. Blunkett's forced climbdown attracted considerable publicity. According to the *New Statesman* it amounted to the 'ruthless humiliation' of the shadow education secretary. There was an immediate and sharp reminder at the next shadow Cabinet meeting that Blair expected all policy statements to be checked first with his office before being released to the news media.

Hill's subsequent suggestion that the Treasury team had already considered and rejected the VAT option led to further confusion. The shadow Chancellor's press officer, Charlie Whelan, said Brown had never even considered putting VAT on private school fees, so he could hardly have ruled it out. Later, in an even more perplexing twist, it emerged that Blunkett's immediate predecessor, Ann Taylor, had examined the possibility when she was shadow education secretary, but found that the imposition of VAT on school fees was not permitted under a European Union directive. However, this rather conclusive piece of information seemed to have escaped the combined notice of Blair, Brown, Blunkett and Labour's communications department.

A fortnight later Alastair Campbell became enmeshed in an equally tortuous sequence of events as Labour tried to define their response to railway privatisation. Instead of working behind the scenes, briefing journalists and helping to coordinate the policy pronouncements of Labour's front-bench team, the press secretary decided to try his hand as a high-profile public spokesman. He ended up getting a name-check from the Prime Minister and being praised by the *Daily Mail*. Ever since he had rebuked me at the party conference for daring to suggest on *Conference Live* that there were dangers in trying to combine the role of press secretary with that of media personality, Campbell seemed to have gone out of his way to prove that he could master both roles simultaneously. He clearly believed he had nothing to fear from the lure of publicity.

A weekend of wall-to-wall coverage began on Friday evening with his appearance as a panellist on the Radio 4 programme *Any Questions*. Next day he became embroiled with the *Sunday Times* in their preparation of a report about an opinion poll of seventy-five Labour MPs which showed them evenly split in their support for the abolition of Clause Four in the party's constitution. The story was printed on the front page of the first edition but was not considered strong enough to make the lead. However, when the Press Association filed a story quoting an unnamed Labour source as claiming the poll was part of 'a conspiracy involving the *Sunday Times*, Conservative Central Office and the hard-left Campaign Group of Labour MPs' the matter was immediately seen as having far greater significance and it was made the front-page splash in later editions. Through his own incautious comments, Campbell had effectively hyped up a story which he should have played down. Next morning he appeared on *Breakfast with Frost* reviewing the Sunday newspapers. According to the *Sunday Times*' own account of what happened, when Campbell was quizzed by Sir David Frost, he admitted he 'had gone over the top' in suggesting to the Press Association that there was a conspiracy involving the newspaper. All he had meant to say was that there was 'a shared interest' among those seeking to publicise backbench opposition to Clause Four.

Despite having lectured Tory politicians, including the Conservative chairman Jeremy Hanley, on the dangers of giving off-the-cuff answers on early-morning television programmes, Campbell then threw caution to the wind when he was then asked by Frost if he could clear up the confusion over Labour's precise plans for returning the railways to public ownership. He announced that Labour had in fact set up a working group before Christmas to see how a future Labour government could reintroduce a publicly owned and publicly accountable railway system. On seeing Campbell's announcement on *Breakfast with Frost*, the BBC's television and radio newsrooms both used recordings of his reply in their next news bulletins at 9 a.m. His answer appeared to indicate a much firmer position than had previously been revealed publicly. Earlier in the week Tony Blair had seemed to indicate that the party leadership had no specific proposals in mind. He told a news conference that he was 'not about to start spraying around commitments' over what Labour's approach would be to rail privatisation.

In choosing to upstage the deputy Labour leader John Prescott, who seemed to be caught off guard when he was interviewed later in the day about rail privatisation, and in pre-empting any statement by the party's transport spokesman Michael Meacher, Campbell provided the Conservatives with just the opening they were looking for. Dr Brian Mawhinney, the transport secretary, poured scorn on Labour's confusion, claiming that Campbell's announcement was at odds with what Blair had said the previous Monday. The *Daily Mail* leader column congratulated Campbell for putting Labour's entire front-bench team in the shade. While 'inhibited shadow ministers enter TV studios in trepidation lest they prematurely give precision to a vague commitment,' Blair's press secretary 'boldly' exploited *Breakfast with Frost* by straightening out Labour's contorted stance on renationalising the railways. It was a 'fascinating' episode which revealed 'how and through whom' Blair wielded power. At question time in the Commons next day John Major poked fun at inconsistencies in Labour's position which he said had persisted through Friday, Saturday, Sunday and Monday, despite the best efforts of Blair's 'own spokesmen on the front bench, past and present, and his press spokesman'. The following weekend the *Sunday Times* joined in the fun with an array of unsourced quotes from shadow ministers and Labour MPs who were allegedly appalled by the way Campbell was trying to turn himself into a household name. They said that when he was appointed as Blair's spin doctor 'showing off' was not meant to have been part of the bargain. What was the point, they asked, in getting elected as an MP and serving on the shadow Cabinet, if Campbell was going to be allowed to speak for the party on television and radio?

In selecting a top political journalist as his press secretary Blair was seen from the start as having opted to live dangerously in his relationship with television, radio and the newspapers. Media strategists working in both party politics and government consider that there are some drawbacks in putting journalists in charge of a publicity department. They say ex-reporters can be too energetic and have a tendency to see every development, however small, as a potential story, forgetting there can be times when it might be advisable to lower the political tempo or keep out of the news altogether. Many of the government's leading press officers are career civil servants, and they recognise the need, and also the value, of quiet periods when their departments rarely get mentioned. The Conservatives tend to recruit many of their publicity experts from the advertising and public relations industry, where again staff have experience of occasions when there might be good commercial reasons for avoiding public exposure at all costs. An unnamed Tory media minder quoted by the *Sunday Times* was said to have been 'gobsmacked' at the way Campbell appeared on both *Any Questions* and *Breakfast with Frost* 'selling himself as well as his boss'.

Alan Duncan was one Conservative MP who followed the activities of Blair's press secretary with great interest. He told me that he thought

Campbell's yearning for self-promotion made him especially vulnerable. At a time when Labour's position in the opinion polls meant that Blair could be 'cool with power', his press secretary was sowing seeds of doubt. 'Campbell has always been a kicker. He has always been kicking other people politically in his newspaper columns and on television and radio. Inevitably if he goes on raising his own public profile the ride will get rougher. From what we have seen so far Blair and Campbell don't like it when the going gets tough and that means they are easily rattled and likely to trip themselves up.'

However, not withstanding any such lurking pitfalls, Campbell's talent for tabloid journalism, and his diligence in placing newspaper articles under Tony Blair's by-line, continued to prove surprisingly effective. Blair's columns always had a populist streak. One theme was an interest in football which the Labour leader shared with his press secretary. Campbell had always been an avid Burnley fan and had once said that the greatest day of his life was when Burnley beat Liverpool in the League Cup. By far the most topical of Blair's comment columns was his contribution to the leader page of the *Sun* on the morning after the riot by English fans during a friendly international match at Dublin in February 1995. The first seven pages were devoted to a graphic account of what the *Sun* had headlined England's 'Night Of Shame'. In a prominent place on page six was Blair's tightly written column expressing his concern at the way a game 'we love is once more condemned by a group of idiots who shame our country'.

Blair's interest in soccer had already secured him considerable exposure in the tabloid press. The week before the Dublin riot, the *Daily Star* had reported on what it said was Blair's 'blueprint for shaking up the game'. Blair, a Newcastle fan 'since a lad', was said to want a pact with the football authorities. Labour planned to tighten up on 'rocketing' transfer fees; demand that turnstile prices were cut so that low-paid people could attend; and persuade the clubs to stop 'ripping off' youngsters. The *Daily Star* was in fact following up a well-reported speech the month before in which Blair had warned that football could be set for 'sporting and social decline' because of 'the extent to which money is so often its motivation'. This speech, at a dinner given by the Football Writers' Assocation in honour of the eightieth birthday of Sir Stanley Matthews, had been well trailed that morning in the *Mail on Sunday* in another of the Labour leader's newspaper columns. He wrote of how the transfer of Newcastle United's striker Andy Cole to Manchester United for £7 million had caused 'grieving in the Blair household'. Newcastle was the closest Premier League club to Blair's Sedgefield constituency and he shared the dismay of local fans at the loss of a key player. Blair was uneasy at the way clubs like Manchester United were having to finance 'lottery-type money' for transfer fees through 'exclusive TV deals, merchandising and expensive seats'. At the Stanley Matthews dinner he reinforced his warning that football might be losing touch with its roots, claiming that Manchester United's policy of selling rapidly changing replica football strips to young fans trod a 'fine line between marketing and exploitation'.

Blair's remarks provided one of the principal talking points next morning on *Breakfast News* and other television and radio programmes. Politicians have a tendency to come across as rather patronising when trying to communicate with sporting audiences, but Blair seemed to have pitched his intervention at just the right level. Both he and Campbell had young sons who were also avid football fans and their anxieties about the future direction of soccer reflected a widespread wish to keep it as a game which families could attend and enjoy.

Blair's success in obtaining a platform in newspapers like the *Sun* and the *News of World* aroused some concern within the party once details emerged of his private dinner with Rupert Murdoch. In mid-February the former Labour leader Michael Foot urged Blair 'not to submit to the pressures of the Murdoch newspaper monopolists, as both the Thatcherites and the Majorites have so sychophantly agreed'. Writing in the *Guardian*, Foot said that if Blair had 'played with that fire' then he should be ultra-careful in future, even if 'his close adviser Peter Mandelson recommends a few such long-spooned suppers'.

Foot had been alarmed by the publicity which Cherie Blair attracted when the *Independent on Sunday* revealed that in her work as a barrister she had pursued poll-tax defaulters. The paper claimed that in one case she had asked a High Court judge to 'return a bailed poll-tax defaulter to jail, even though she knew he was penniless'. Fellow lawyers rallied to her support. They said that under the 'cab-rank rule' barristers were obliged to take any case which they were offered within their competence, and that the cases involved defendants who had been found guilty of wilful non-payment of their poll tax. A few days later the *Sun* claimed that the right-wing Freedom Association had reported Mrs Blair, who used her maiden name of Booth when appearing as a barrister, to the Bar Council for bringing the legal profession into disrepute. The Association accused Ms Booth of breaking the rules by giving a job to the son of Barry Cox, the former London Weekend Television director, who had contributed to Blair's leadership campaign. Labour denied that any rules had been broken because Cox's son had not been employed by Ms Booth's chambers but was working with her, without pay, as part of his training as a law student. The party said there were signs of a concerted vendetta against the Labour leader's wife. Foot feared the consequences of the 'evil pressures of modern publicity' which were being directed against Mrs Blair. He was comforted by the fact that she had 'a Liverpool socialist upbringing' which was 'pure working class', and hoped she would have the courage to withstand the 'shameful' pressures such as those which had been exerted on Hillary Clinton and which obviously had 'a deep and sinister political purpose'.

Foot's appeal to Blair to reject any overtures from the Murdoch newspapers with his 'customary candour' could hardly have been more timely. Within days of his article appearing in the *Guardian*, Foot was accused by the *Sunday Times* of having been 'an agent of influence' for the KGB. The story was based on interviews with former Soviet spies, but within hours the editor John Witherow admitted that he personally did not think the accusation was correct, maintaining however that it was important for contemporary history to explain that this was what the KGB believed. Labour accused the paper of a deliberate distortion aimed at smearing Foot, which the party considered all the more unforgivable because of the paper's unfounded allegations in 1992 that Neil Kinnock also had a 'Kremlin connection'. Foot said the paper had been fooled by the Soviet secret police. To the best of his knowledge he had never met the KGB, nor had he ever received any money from the KGB, either for himself or for the Labour newspaper *Tribune*. He regarded the attack as another example of the way Murdoch-owned newspapers were reviving a 'McCarthy-style witch-hunt against people who were unable to face and cross-examine their unidentified accusers'. Later that week Foot announced that he intended to start libel proceedings against Murdoch and the *Sunday Times*. According to his solicitor David Price, the former Labour leader held Murdoch 'personally responsible' and wanted him brought before a jury because of the 'gravity of these lies'.

If Labour's rival spin doctors had by any chance made a combined New Year resolution for 1995 to avoid competing with each other, as happened with dire effects at the 1994 party conference, their good intentions were short-lived. Their renewed jockeying for the ear of the news media was perhaps one of the reasons for Campbell's increasingly erratic behaviour. Peter Mandelson had become a valuable alternative source of information about Blair's position on key issues affecting the redrafting of the party's constitution. As feedback from the constituencies and trade unions showed increasing resistance to abandoning Clause Four, Mandelson's private briefings were in great demand. David Hill was also vying for attention, having been placed in an invidious position because of an imminent shake-up at party headquarters. The national executive committee decided in January to appoint a single all-powerful director who would be responsible for the party's media and elections strategy. Advertisements began appearing in February and invited applications for 'a dynamic, skilled media and elections strategist to manage Labour's overall campaigning'. The new director would require 'a proven record of successfully leading campaigns and elections, and dealing with all aspects of the media'. Hill told me he would not be applying for the job but intended to remain Labour's chief spokesman on party and policy issues. The new director would be responsible for election strategy, and although that would require an input into media relations Hill expected that he would still be speaking for the party and taking late-night and weekend calls from television, radio and the newspapers.

Several days before the interviews were to be conducted for the new post of campaigns director it emerged that Joy Johnson, the BBC's political news editor at Westminster, had obtained Tony Blair's backing and was certain to get the job. After twenty years in television news and production, first with ATV, then with ITN and latterly with the BBC, her move surprised her colleagues, but it was neither entirely unexpected nor out of character, for she was a committed Labour Party supporter and had made no secret of her often forthright left-wing views. She had been head-hunted by the party, but before finally being told the job was hers she was subjected to what was described as a thorough grilling by Blair as he checked out the depth of her commitment to the party; the strength of her determination to see Labour win the next election; and whether she could remain resolute and ruthless under fire.

Ms Johnson had the strong support of Gordon Brown and several other members of the shadow Cabinet, with whom she had established a close working relationship during her stint as political news editor for the BBC. Her flair when editing *Conference Live* the previous autumn had also made a big impression among Blair's advisers. Effusive praise in the *Guardian* for her 'imagination and energy' in transforming the BBC's live coverage of the political conferences provided a timely testimonial. In his weekly commentary, Martin Kettle described Ms Johnson as the 'Madam Speaker' of these seaside rituals, the 'Lion Queen of the party-conference jungle'. Kettle said she had proved to be a 'true moderniser' of British politics because she had turned the conferences into a democratic forum in which politicians and delegates were constantly interviewed and re-interviewed about developments inside and outside the hall. By adapting for television 'the writing press's ancient freedom' to move around the conference bars and corridors, *Conference Live*'s interviewers had become 'key players in the chemistry of breaking news'. As a result party managers had to pay almost as much attention to the live coverage as they did to the conference itself.

I knew from personal experience that Ms Johnson could be a hard task-mistress. She could be unforgiving if she felt that an interviewer or correspondent had failed to ask the right question or had not spotted the latest twist to a news story; and she could be equally tough with a producer who had failed to track down a politician or a cameraman who had missed a vital shot. Her appointment was seen as quite a coup by the party because her intimate knowledge of the inner workings of the BBC and ITN complemented Alastair Campbell's wide experience in the tabloid press. Nevertheless, some words of caution were uttered. Some Labour MPs felt the party had become top-heavy with spin doctors and publicists. Among newspaper political editors the appointment confirmed suspicions that Blair and his closest advisers were mesmerised by television. Ms Johnson's duties were to include that of being the party's 'elections strategist to manage Labour's overall campaigning', a role which looked like testing her capabilities to the full: indeed, some surprise was expressed by Conservative publicity specialists that a television news editor had been selected to undertake the critical task of helping plan Labour's strategy for the next election.

In the week when it became clear that Ms Johnson had got the job, Blair gave the *Evening Standard* an indication of his plans. In an interview with the paper's political editor Charles Reiss, he said it would be a mistake for Labour to enter the general election campaign with 'a manifesto stuffed with detailed policies'. Blair considered that Labour had 'suffered far too much from writing such documents' and he thought it more important to get the principles right rather than publish '300-page screeds on health, education and the rest'. It also emerged that Ms Johnson had plans to improve the presentation of Labour's news conferences, many of which she hoped Gordon Brown would chair once an election campaign got under way.

The prospect of such a major realignment in the party's publicity hierarchy only served to heighten the unease among Labour staff over how best to handle dissension over Clause Four, and the unresolved fault lines within Labour's procedures for briefing the media were easily exploited by political journalists. On an issue as contentious as Clause Four there were considerable advantages in being able to pick and choose between Campbell, Mandelson and Hill when seeking information, and their parallel presence opened up the chance of teasing out comments from one spin doctor without the knowledge, or perhaps the approval, of the other two.

The consequences of Blair's failure to impose a clear command structure became all too apparent when BBC news bulletins quoted 'close supporters of Tony Blair' as having accused Bill Morris, general secretary of the Transport and General Workers Union, of being 'confused, muddled and pusillanimous' in seeking to retain Clause Four. As the union would be wielding a block vote of 825,000 at the special conference in April 1995 to approve a new version of Labour's constitution, an attack of that nature would have to have been sanctioned at the highest level. The quote was used extensively on television and radio news bulletins.

When Morris appeared next morning on *Breakfast with Frost* he was asked for his reaction. He was clearly deeply offended and had apparently accepted that the BBC would have been unlikely to have used the attack so prominently unless it had come from an authoritative source. Morris said he regretted that a 'creeping intolerance' seemed to be getting into the Clause Four debate. 'I expected men in white coats to come along and say I was muddled and confused and take me off to Siberia.'

As I was the BBC's duty political correspondent that Sunday morning I immediately asked Blair's staff for a response and for some guidance as to whether it was correct to go on attributing the 'pusillanimous' quote to 'close supporters of Tony Blair'. A few minutes later one of the Labour leader's press officers, Tim Allan, rang me back with an on-the-record statement that the words being used by the BBC had not been 'said by Blair himself, any of his press officers or any member of his staff'. The one likely source which did not appear to have been covered by this blanket denial was Peter Mandelson, whose position was that of a 'close supporter'. On hearing the quote the previous day my first thought was that it was exactly the kind of phraseology which I had heard Mandelson use so frequently on previous occasions when he had spoken critically of union leaders. My own enquiries confirmed my original suspicion. Although the union was not seeking to name Mandelson publicly, I was told by the Transport and General that Morris was certain that Mandelson was the source.

Political journalists were intrigued by what had happened. Despite Mandelson's categorical denials that he was the person responsible for the quote, three newspapers named him as the source. According to the *Guardian* 'there was no doubt that Mandelson was the culprit' and the *Sun* was equally categoric, claiming that Mandelson's identity had been confirmed by 'senior Labour and BBC insiders'. The *Daily Express* was less certain, but suggested that Mandelson had to be a suspect because he specialised in 'unattributable briefings'.

Alastair Campbell's apparent inability to exercise control over what was being said on Blair's behalf elicited plenty of helpful suggestions from political commentators. In his weekly column in *Tribune*, Hugh Macpherson said Campbell could not have it both ways. If he wanted to be taken seriously as the leader's press secretary he had to take responsibility for the utterances being made in Blair's name and he should insist on statements being made on the record. 'Either he is responsible for the stream of unattributable, arrogant statements made from Tony Blair's largely unelected entourage or he must deny them and deny them swiftly to minimise their effect.' In his own column in *Tribune*, Campbell wrote rather plaintively that he did not know who was responsible for describing Morris as 'puzzled, confused and pusillanimous' but 'it wasn't me, guv. They are not my kind of words'. Ian Aitken, writing in the *New Statesman*, said the attack on Morris was as counterproductive as the suggestion by another unnamed 'Blair aide' that thirty Labour Members of the European Parliament, who had denounced the abandoning of Clause Four, were 'infantile nonentities'. As Campbell had a 'belligerent personality and a vocabulary to match it' he suggested that Blair should invite his press secretary to Sunday lunch. Blair could then explain 'over the Yorkshire pudding' that while he found Campbell's loyalty heartwarming, it would be helpful if he tried in future to express it 'less brutally'. Aitken had one final tip for Blair's next Sunday lunch: 'Better still, he could invite Peter Mandelson as well.'

The ability to wound a political opponent is one of the great tests of an effective spin doctor because the timing and placing of an unattributable attack are as important as the choice of the words which are used. Union leaders have been a regular target of these unofficial rebukes because of the influence they exercise at party conferences. Although Mandelson had become more open in his criticism of what he thought were the abuses of union power since becoming an MP, his jibes were rather tame when compared with the invective of long-standing union-baiters like the former Tory minister, Norman Tebbit. During my years as a labour correspondent I was always impressed by Tebbit's grasp of the intricacies of union rule-books and his ability to poke fun at union leaders. During the 1983 water workers' dispute, when he was employment secretary, he accused the then GMB general secretary, the late David Basnett, of lacking a mandate for the strike. When I arrived to interview Tebbit he had with him his own copy of the GMB rule-book flagged with markers, and he gave me chapter and verse as to why the union had no authority for the stoppage. Government press officers had told me how effective Tebbit could be in attacking his opponents in the labour movement. If he had to prepare answers to awkward questions from Labour MPs, or perhaps think up a way of rebuking a union leader, he would ask his head of information if the department happened to have anything on the files of a damaging nature about the person concerned. Apparently Tebbit enjoyed watching the reaction of senior civil servants. When they demurred, saying this was hardly an appropriate request, Tebbit would smile and pull open the drawer of his desk to reveal a collection of press clippings and other material which he had accumulated as potential ammunition and which usually contained what he was looking for.

Tebbit, a great admirer of Labour's eminent spin doctor, obviously regarded Mandelson as a kindred spirit. In the 1987 general election campaign Mandelson was pitted against Tebbit, who was then Conservative party chairman. At the end of the 1990 Labour conference, Mandelson's last as communications director, he was interviewed jointly by

Tebbit and Austin Mitchell, who were joint presenters of Sky TV's weekly political programme *Target*. Tebbit was fulsome in his praise of Mandelson, complimenting him not only on the way in which he had improved the party's presentation but also for having helped change and modernise Labour's policies. Tebbit paid him the ultimate accolade: 'Oh yes, I respect his professionalism. I think the Labour Party owes Peter Mandelson a very great debt. I would have employed him at the drop of a hat if he had come over to our side.' As in Mandelson's case, judgement on a political propagandist's proficiency is usually reserved until a spin doctor has been blooded in a general election. If John Major does delay polling day until 1997, Alastair Campbell will get an extended honeymoon before his political opponents are prepared to be categoric in their assessment of Tony Blair's press secretary.

7

Casualties and Survivors

*T*HE BREAKDOWN in traditional Tory discipline which became so marked during John Major's second term as Prime Minister contributed to an equally serious erosion in the Conservatives' ability to deliver effective party publicity on a day-to-day basis. The single-minded determination of the early Thatcher years underpinned the tight coordination which was so essential for the successful promotion of Tory philosophy. But, as the clarity of the Conservatives' sense of purpose was diluted and their unity was dissipated, the command structure holding Downing Street, Conservative Central Office and Tory MPs together became weaker. Politicians are easy prey for the news media when party loyalty is at a low ebb or if they lack direction, and in these circumstances the wealth of experience gained during sixteen years in power is no safeguard. Even the Conservatives' safest self-publicists had become accident-prone. Major's government was running out of successful media practitioners. The casualties had started to outnumber the survivors.

Sir Anthony Meyer's unsuccessful challenge for the party leadership in the autumn of 1989 should have alerted Margaret Thatcher's government to the depth of rank-and-file discontent over unpopular measures, pre-eminently the poll tax. It should also have shocked the Tory hierarchy, because it exposed outdated publicity procedures within the party and underlined their failure to come to terms with the new and competitive pressures influencing the output of television, radio and the newspapers. Three general election victories had led to complacency where it mattered most, in the engine room of Tory headquarters. When polling day was in the offing, party fund-raisers found the necessary money. Central Office soon hummed with activity. But in between elections the party's own machinery for generating favourable publicity was effectively on care and maintenance. While Peter Mandelson was developing his well-rehearsed routines for promoting Labour, the Conservatives' communications department took a back seat behind the publicity initiatives of the government. Bernard Ingham's tight grip on the Whitehall information service was regarded as a sufficient bulwark against their political opponents. If ministers could command instant access to television and radio there seemed no point in the party trying to compete, or in the communications director and his staff remaining constantly at the ready just on the off-chance that they might suddenly be required to manipulate the media.

As long as Mrs Thatcher was successful there was a strong argument in favour of a low-key response. But alert soft-footedness is not the same thing as dormancy, and in allowing Central Office to wind down its activities between election times and party conferences, her government made a fatal error. When faced unexpectedly by the first challenge for the leadership, Mrs Thatcher and her supporters lacked both the organisation and the capacity to respond. Meyer was roundly defeated, but all told sixty Tory MPs had either voted against her or abstained. Meyer had effectively paved the way for Michael Heseltine. Long years of neglect, and the Conservatives' inability to overhaul their own internal structures, assisted Mrs Thatcher's opponents within the party and left the Prime Minister increasingly at the mercy of the broadcast media. Nor is this only a tale of five years and more ago: the almost limitless air time which her policies had helped to create proved equally troublesome for her successor. The nine rebel MPs who lost the Tory whip in November 1994 were, by and large, ruthless in exploiting the news media; Major complained plaintively that his tormentors were rarely out of the television or radio studios. Of even greater concern to him should have been the lack of a coordinated or competent response by his own party.

Throughout the 1980s the foot-soldiers of political journalism spent countless hours outside Labour and trade union meetings waiting for news of the splits and disagreements which repeatedly pushed back the party's chances of recovery. By the early 1990s the position had been reversed. Reporters began to find that the most newsworthy doorsteps were those of the Conservative Party and their splintering groups of supporters. Unlike Labour, Central Office did not even bother to redirect any of their public relations effort towards countering the slow build-up in potentially damaging news which was seeping out at Westminster, ready-made for the fast-moving deadlines of television and radio. When Tory backbench dissatisfaction turned to rebellion, the surge in unfavourable stories became a torrent. Party officials were literally swept aside as they fumbled to find ways of staunching the flow.

The Conservatives' vulnerability became evident as soon as Meyer stood against Mrs Thatcher, a full year before her eventual downfall after Heseltine's subsequent challenge. Amazingly for a party which had such strong links with the communications industry, there was no agreed procedure for briefing the media during Tory leadership elections. Central Office staff were simply nowhere to be seen. Political correspondents were left to their own devices. The internal affairs of Conservative MPs have always been the exclusive domain of their 1922 committee of backbenchers. Its then chairman, Sir Cranley Onslow, was a man of few words. He seemed to enjoy making it clear to all and sundry that it was not his job to act as a media mouthpiece for Tory MPs. Onslow's put-downs to journalists were in a class of their own. On one occasion, when politely asking for an interview, I reminded him that my name was Jones. He looked at me quizzically and then replied: 'That's a shame for you.' Without saying another word he simply walked away.

Onslow's successor, the loquacious Sir Marcus Fox, was far more obliging and seemed genuinely anxious to help reporters. But he too was restricted in what he could say. As party indiscipline increased, and Major's troubles worsened, Fox tended to stand back from the fray and lower his profile. Even the Tory revolt over the increase in Britain's contribution to the European Union, and the government's defeat in December 1994 over VAT on domestic fuel, failed to produce any measures to control or coordinate information on the collective anger of most Tory MPs about the conduct of the rebels.

The 1922 committee meets privately each Thursday evening. All backbenchers are invited to attend and those present are provided with a run-down of the following week's parliamentary business. Usually the meetings are routine. However, when there is tension in the party or a leadership election is imminent, the committee can exercise considerable influence. There is no established procedure for informing the news media about its proceedings; political journalists pick up what they can afterwards by talking to those who were present. An obvious precaution to prevent garbled or damaging reports would be to appoint an MP to act as a spokesman for the committee, or to delegate the task to one of the publicity staff at Central Office. But the committee's officers believed their principal role was to provide a link between backbench MPs, the chief whip and the Prime Minister and not to communicate with the news media. While their motives might have been worthy, they ignored reality. A divided party provides news stories, and the Conservatives' reputation for dissension and disunity was one factor which contributed to the haemorrhaging of Tory support.

The contrast with Labour could not have been more damning. As Neil Kinnock struggled to change party policy, the two regular focal points for dissent with which he had to contend were the Parliamentary Labour Party, representing the MPs, and the national executive committee, which included representatives of the unions and was elected by the party conference. Meetings of both groups were always considered of significance by political correspondents because in those years Labour, like the Conservatives under Major, had a powerful and vocal awkward squad who always made a beeline for the microphones and cameras.

Peter Mandelson hardly missed a meeting of either the PLP or the NEC when he was Labour's director of communications. If need be, he would provide a running commentary as the discussions proceeded inside so as to make sure that television and radio news bulletins gave prominence to the official party line as well as any criticism of the leadership. He would always try to get his version out first, before Kinnock's opponents emerged. Labour press officers would be assigned to doorstep duty. They would listen in to any interviews so that they could relay what was being said back to Mandelson. During all-day meetings he would monitor television and radio ouput. If he disliked what the broadcasters were saying, or detected inaccuracies in the stories which were being put out by the Press Association or the TV teletext services, he would immediately seek out the relevant reporter and make known his concerns.

Except for the odd occasion like the Prime Minister's end-of-session speeches to the backbenchers, Conservative press officers were rarely if ever in attendance at 1992 committee meetings. They did not even bother to hover in the vicinity to see what the reporters were up to once the weekly meetings had finished. I felt one reason for this indifference was that over the years the Conservatives' communications staff had always retained a closer affinity with newspaper journalism than with television or radio. Because the party knew they could rely on the loyalty and power of the Tory press, Central Office did not attach as much importance as Labour to the needs of the broadcasters; nor did they appreciate, as Mandelson did, that if their influence was to be really effective it had to be applied in time for the very first news summary, not just the main evening bulletin.

Of all the missed opportunities perhaps the most glaring were at weekends: while Labour remained firmly on the offensive, the Conservatives' response was invariably pitiful by comparison. Government press officers who were on weekend duty could be contacted by phone, and were able to supply background information, but most ministers, usually at home or busy with constituency engagements, were reluctant to be interviewed about unexpected news stories. The party ran an efficient distribution service supplying journalists with advance texts of weekend speeches by ministers, but these were frequently being delivered at private functions where there was no access for television and radio. Central Office was seldom of any help, even when broadcasters alerted the duty press officer to the difficulties they were experiencing in their attempts to provide balanced coverage. The communications staff seemed to have no understanding of the problems which the weekend news bulletins encountered in searching for Conservative MPs who were prepared to speak up in support of government policy.

Although the party establishment showed little inclination to exploit the introduction of rolling news programmes and hourly bulletins, the opportunities which had opened up proved invaluable to Michael Heseltine during his challenge for the leadership in 1990. With the help of his campaign manager Michael Mates, he adroitly played off one channel against the other, securing saturation coverage. Mrs Thatcher fell into the black hole which opened up when neither the government information service nor Central Office seemed to be in control. She was at her most exposed during the fateful weekend which preceded the first ballot and her departure to Paris for the summit of the Conference on Security and Cooperation in Europe.

Even when they realised that Heseltine had stolen a march on them, Mrs Thatcher and her advisers dithered. The challenger's campaign team had spent the final Friday preparing a weekend news blitz. Profiles were being written for the Sunday newspapers; arrangements were under way for interviews with the weekend political programmes; and information was being accumulated about the findings of last-minute opinion polls. As details leaked out of what had been lined up, panic spread through the Thatcher camp. Camera crews were tracking Heseltine's every movement; but there were no plans for a counterblast from the Prime Minister.

There had already been a succession of mistakes. A heavy-handed attempt to manoeuvre Henley Conservatives into disowning Heseltine's open letter to his constituency had backfired. The inept advancing of the closing date for the contest had damaged Mrs Thatcher. When nominations closed she was trapped. She had arranged to spend the weekend at Chequers before leaving for Paris. At first sight the timing seemed fortunate for the Prime Minister: she would be representing Britain at a European summit, well placed to get maximum television and radio exposure. But there was no fallback position if she found herself on the defensive or having to make a hurried appeal for support.

The Thatcher campaign team was divided over whether the Prime Minister should make herself available for last-minute television interviews. She was anxious to respond, but the option was rejected because it was feared she might appear worried by the challenge to her leadership. Enquiries were set in hand about a possible photo call to level up the exposure which Heseltine was securing. One of her advisers told me he checked to see whether there were any police or service personnel injured in hospital whom she could perhaps visit. Another idea that was looked at was the possibility of providing television crews with access to Chequers. In the end it was agreed she would pose for fresh pictures at her desk in Downing Street before setting off for Paris. Only one film crew was allowed in. The cameraman said Mrs Thatcher appeared rushed and preoccupied, saying she had a lot of work left to do in her study upstairs. At her hour of need she seemed to have been deserted by her many friends in advertising and public relations who in happier times had helped her become the arch-exponent of the photo opportunity.

The indecision continued after her departure for the summit. Heseltine alleged in an interview for that Sunday's *On the Record* that Thatcher had misled the Cabinet over the Westland affair by reading out the minutes of a meeting which had never taken place. By early evening her campaign team was in disarray over what to do. Norman Tebbit, who had been in the Cabinet at the time, was considered best placed to respond, but he was travelling back to London from the West Country. Norman Lamont was alerted and told to look at a video of Heseltine's interview. Lord Young was also put on standby in case he had to be called on to refute the allegations. With less than an hour to go Tebbit arrived at his London home, just in time to be interviewed for the main Sunday evening news bulletins.

Although Mrs Thatcher secured 204 votes in the first ballot, well ahead of Heseltine's 152, she had not won by a sufficient margin to avoid a second ballot: eight days later she resigned. Two of Heseltine's votes would have been enough to save her. She had made a grave miscalculation in letting him make the running. The failure of her advisers to campaign effectively on her behalf, when she was so desperately in need of some skilful promotion, seemed a fitting indictment of the Conservatives' casual disregard for party publicity and of the neglect of their own internal procedures.

In retrospect Tebbit's praise for Peter Mandelson, uttered only a few weeks before Mrs Thatcher's downfall, was all the more revealing. In being so effusive in complimenting Labour's communications director, at the conclusion of their 1990 party conference, about the effectiveness of Labour's promotional activities, the former Tory chairman was inadvertently inviting comparison and drawing attention to the inadequacies of Central Office.

Mandelson spent five years directing Labour's publicity department before leaving to become candidate for Hartlepool. He went through the 1987 general election and then stayed on to see the completion of Neil Kinnock's policy review. Compared with his opposite numbers at Central Office, he was an old stager. Conservative publicity chiefs tended to have a much shorter tenure. On average they stayed for only two years. Replacing the director of communications chosen by his predecessor became one the first tasks of each new party chairman. There rarely seemed to be any continuity or even any desire within the organisation to build up durable expertise.

Whenever I had the opportunity to discuss my theories about the deficiencies of the Conservatives' publicity effort, I found that Central Office staff were unimpressed and uninterested. Brendan Bruce was the communications director from 1989 to 1991, at the midpoint between two general elections. He had extensive experience in marketing and had run the Department of Trade and Industry's campaign to popularise the European single market. Bruce thought there was no validity at all in my attempt to contrast Tory and Labour media strategies during his period in office. A fair comparison, he thought, could only be made once a general election campaign was under way. Bruce said that as the Conservatives were the party in power, Central Office had no remit to push news stories, except in the run-up to polling day or at party conferences. The task of promoting ministers and their policies had to be left to the government's information service. He was equally dismissive of my argument that Mandelson's concentration on television and radio had exposed weaknesses in the ability of Central Office to respond to Labour's regular news offensives. In his opinion the former television producer and image-maker Sir Gordon Reece, who started advising Mrs Thatcher in the early 1970s on how to make the most of her appearances on screen, had performed precisely the same role for the Conservatives before their election victory in 1979 as Mandelson did for Labour in the 1987 election – except that, in promoting Kinnock, Mandelson had not turned out to be anywhere near as effective as Reece.

Bruce made no secret of what he said was his 'extremely close' working relationship with Conservative-supporting newspapers. In an interview on the *Today* programme after leaving Central Office, he expounded on his team's strategy for trying to manipulate the national press. He said that one of the political editors with whom they worked closely would be contacted and presented with certain new facts, research or statistics. If they were successful with their briefing, that story would make the front page of that paper's first edition. Other national newspapers would then see the front page of their rival and change their own second editions to include the story which Central Office had supplied. 'By the end of the night pretty well all the papers are running on the same issue. Now that's what you wanted.'

For most of his time as director of communications Bruce served under Kenneth Baker, Mrs Thatcher's last party chairman and subsequently Home Secretary under Major. While he could not promote ministers, Bruce believed there were many occasions when the party could help improve their performance. In his view, government information officers were not always prepared to be as candid as they should be. 'It is very hard to train a press officer to have the confidence to be tough with a Cabinet minister. My rehearsals with Baker were so strong that it terrified the research department. But I was in the self-confidence business. If I am nasty, nastier than an interviewer ever could be, then the minister won't be fearful and it is the fear of making a gaffe which causes most mistakes.' When Baker gave interviews during Crime Prevention Week, Bruce told him to avoid giving the shadow Home Secretary Roy Hattersley any further opportunity to accuse the Conservatives of shifting the blame for the crime wave on to the carelessness of the public. Bruce believed that because of his efforts the Home Secretary got the balance right, emphasising the Tory commitment to law and order while pointing out that motorists, for example, could assist themselves by remembering to lock their car doors.

Bruce was unable to put his own theories to the ultimate test of a general election. Early in 1991 Chris Patten, who had been appointed party chairman by Major, brought in Shaun Woodward, a former television producer and editor, as his new director of communications. Woodward was recruited largely because of his television experience: he had spent eight years at the BBC, working on *Newsnight* and *Panorama* before editing *That's Life*. He was thirty-three, and had recruited a team of assistants who were in their middle and early twenties. This 'young motley crew' was dubbed 'Patten's puppies' by *Today*'s columnist David Seymour, who was staggered that Major was prepared to allow his fate to be determined by 'a few clammy palms'.

Woodward's plan for the 1992 election was to portray the Prime Minister as 'Citizen John Major' in what would be a new television format for a politician. On the fifth day of the campaign, journalists were taken by coach to a village hall in Major's Huntingdon constituency. Surrounded by party members and their friends, Major perched on a stool answering unrehearsed, but definitely friendly, questions. The cosy intimacy of the first 'Meet John Major' session was underlined when he stripped off his jacket and continued in his shirtsleeves. John Simpson, the BBC's foreign editor, described the occasion as being 'desperately tame'. Woodward was mortified by this unflattering review, which coincided with internal criticism from some long-serving staff at Central Office who had become disaffected by a succession of rapid changes in the party's press and publicity departments. They took great delight in telling Woodward that when she was Prime Minister, Mrs Thatcher would never have allowed herself to be talked into sitting on a bar stool in the middle of a village hall. Major soon dispensed with the image which had been crafted for him so carefully and, in reverting to the soap box of his youth, showed his frustration with the advice he was getting and his preference for a more traditional style of campaigning.

Until the last two days before the poll the Conservatives were consistently behind in the opinion polls and, as the *Daily Telegraph* reported, had been plagued by criticism of the negative tone of their campaign and of the lack of 'staying power of the inexperienced young workers' at Tory headquarters. Three months after their unexpected victory Woodward left Central Office. Major thanked him for his loyalty and commitment; Patten said Woodward's experience in media communications, and in drawing up their advertising strategy, had been invaluable. However, within a few weeks of the election Patten's replacement as party chairman, Sir Norman Fowler, had announced his own plans for a fundamental overhaul of Central Office. Fowler said his aim was to establish the party as 'the best political organisation in Europe'. Tim Collins, who had been the press officer assigned to travel with Major during the election campaign, was appointed as Woodward's successor.

Collins always provided what I thought were extremely informative advance briefings of speeches by the Prime Minister. He started at Central Office in the research department and before becoming a press officer had been special adviser to Michael Howard as employment secretary. Two months before the election, on the day before Major was to speak in Glasgow to the Scottish Conservative Party, Collins gave me a full run-down on what he indicated would be an impassioned warning of the dangers of any breach in the union between Scotland and the rest of the United Kingdom. I doubted whether the speech would live up to the billing given it by Collins, but the Prime Minister turned in a heartfelt performance.

Major's concern about the risks involved in any move which might encourage Scottish independence was in fact one of the themes to which he had returned with considerable effect in the closing stages of the 1992 election. On the final Sunday before polling day he issued another passionate warning. He said Labour's plans for a Scottish parliament could undermine from within 'the walls of this island fortress'. The United Kingdom was in danger: 'Wake up. Wake up now, before it is too late.' None of the reporters covering the campaign could remember rhetoric like that from the Prime Minister. Major repeated his apocalyptic criticism of Labour's plans in December 1994 when giving his New Year's Eve interview on *Today*. He said Tony Blair's commitment to make Scottish devolution a priority for the first year of a Labour government was 'one of the most dangerous propositions to be put before the British nation'.

It was on the strength of the accuracy of his previous briefings that I went hard on Collins' guidance at the Conservatives' 1993 party conference that Major's ill-fated 'back to basics' speech reflected the Prime Minister's wish that the 1990s should be about 'rolling back the permissive society'. I used the phrase in several of my radio reports. I felt it helped explain the significance of Major's appeal for a return to basic Conservative beliefs: 'It is time to return to those old core values. Time to get back to basics, to self-discipline and respect for the law, to consideration for others, to accepting responsibility for yourself and your family and not shuffling it off on other people and the state.' When the 'back to basics' theme backfired amid ministerial resignations, attempts were made to withdraw the spin which was originally put on the speech. Gus O'Donnell, Major's press secretary, insisted shortly before his own departure from Downing Street at the end of that year that the Prime Minister had never intended 'back to basics' to become a moral crusade. But Collins could not have been clearer in his briefing at Blackpool that Major was referring to personal morality.

The Conservatives' 1994 conference was Collins' last as director of communications. He told colleagues he intended taking up a new job the following year. Despite all the difficulties facing the party, the atmosphere in Bournemouth was relaxed. The general consensus among party officials was that there was no point in trying to batten down the hatches to 'stifle the odd voice of dissent' because there were another two years to go to the next election. Collins said he remained convinced that the slump in the Conservatives' electoral fortunes bore no comparison with the nosedive in Labour's popularity during the late 1970s and their defeat under Jim Callaghan. He believed that the pull of political events was already going in the government's direction. Slowly emerging evidence of an economic recovery would eventually improve the news media's treatment of Major and his ministers.

Collins' laid-back approach and his optimistic briefings were at complete odds with an assessment which was being prepared privately for Major by the former MP and Treasury minister John Maples, who had been appointed a deputy chairman of the party after the July 1994 reshuffle. Within a few weeks of the Bournemouth conference, news leaked out of what became known as the 'Maples memo'. A copy of this document was published by the *Financial Times*. It was a devastating critique of the inadequacy of Conservative publicity and the lack of effective coordination between party machinery and government departments. Market research commissioned by Maples indicated that 'a failure in communications' was responsible for the disenchantment of Tory supporters.

Maples identified the economy as a key area of weakness. 'While we trumpet the recovery, the voters do not think the recession has ended. They still fear unemployment, have no more money in their pockets etc. What we are saying is completely at odds with their experience.' His most controversial idea concerned what the Conservatives should do about the new Labour leader. 'If Blair turns out to be as good as he looks we have a problem. . .Could we set some backbenchers on to this? Maybe a few yobbos of our own to try to knock him about a bit and another team to operate more subtly on the changes of mind and differences of view.'

In the published extracts of his report, Maples appeared to show no great understanding of the inner workings of television and radio or of the importance to the Conservatives of doing more to strengthen their contacts with those who worked in the broadcast media. He was far more concerned about the need for the party to rebuild its relationship with newspaper proprietors so as to ensure better press coverage. 'We need to feed our friends and potential friends in the press with good stories ... We should not just concentrate on political and specialist correspondents but on columnists, leader writers and editors.' However, my attention was caught by the small print of the 'Maples memo', because it seemed to confirm so many of the points which I had made previously when writing about the failings of Central Office. He acknowledged Labour's superiority in rapid-response news management, which Mandelson had always made his priority: 'The ability to react rapidly to events and Labour's allegations is vital. They are much better than us at this.'

Maples accepted without equivocation one of the central tenets of Mandelson's philosophy on party publicity: the desirability of keeping untelegenic politicians out of harm's way. He was categoric in his advice: 'For television and radio we should use good performers ruthlessly.' Unlike Labour's communications directors, who were consulted about how the opposition should field their front-bench team for the purposes of party publicity, staff at Central Office had no alternative but to grin and bear it when, under both the Thatcher and Major governments, ministers blundered on, blithely ignoring the damage they might be doing to the Conservative cause. As the government's difficulties failed to abate, and tension heightened within the party, the backbiting intensified and the unguarded insights became more colourful.

A year before the 1992 scandal of his affair with the actress Antonia de Sancha, David Mellor was already being mentioned as an unwise choice as a frontman for John Major, being singled out without any hesitation by Brendan Bruce, to whom I spoke shortly after his departure from Central Office early in 1991, as a minister who should 'be kept firmly in a dark box'. Mellor was then Chief Secretary to the Treasury, and Bruce had been watching his television performances for some months. He felt that the minister's manner tended to grate with the public and, because he had made so many elementary mistakes, it was obvious he should be 'kept under wraps'. On *Question Time* the previous week, Mellor had apparently implied that the programme's audience was unrepresentative. 'The golden rule on a show like that is that a politician should never annoy the audience. To suggest they are unrepresentative is a recipe for disaster.' Bruce congratulated Labour for having acknowledged that the shadow Foreign Secretary, Gerald Kaufman, who was 'their equivalent of Mellor' when it came to television appearances, was best kept off the screen because of the way he could 'alarm and annoy' viewers. As it transpired, Kaufman appeared to have reached the same conclusion himself because he did maintain an especially low television profile during the 1992 election campaign.

A fortnight after my conversation with Brendan Bruce, Mellor hit the headlines after getting involved in an unseemly row with the village postmaster at Strensall, near York. The chief secretary had been staying with the Ryedale MP John Greenway and had complained when his box of official papers was delivered two hours late, phoning postmaster Richard Horseman from his ministerial Rover. According to a local resident who was with the postmaster and overheard the call, Mellor branded the village post office a 'tinpot place with a Postman Pat-style operation'. Next morning the leader writers of the national newspapers were in their element, with the *Sun* declaring that Britain was full of tinpot villages and their posties. 'Postman Pat is a cheery chap who does a good job. We like him much more than Mellor the Mouth.'

Against this background it is perhaps not surprising that Major's choice of Mellor, who was then the youngest member of the Cabinet, to spearhead the government's pre-election attack on Labour's economic policy attracted mixed reviews. Simon Heffer, writing in the *Evening Standard*, said that although Mellor had been patronisingly cast as the Conservatives' 'Mr Nasty' he was 'an obvious next party chairman' because he was the only member of the Cabinet who remembered what politics were about and who was capable of 'putting on the hobnail boots and letting fly'. But Alastair Campbell, in his *Sunday Mirror* column, considered 'desperate Dave' to be a victim of 'over-the-top-itis' and that nobody was fooled by his claim that Labour's economic plans would require an extra 15p on income tax. Gillian Shepherd, who was serving immediately below Mellor as financial secretary, told me that the chief secretary had the best job of all in the Treasury: Mellor could be the 'ultimate nosey parker' and, if he wished, poke his nose into the business of every other government department.

Maples was careful in his report not to name names, but he could hardly have been clearer about the obvious negative effect on public opinion of the repeated television and radio appearances of the health secretary Virginia Bottomley. 'Zero media coverage' for the next twelve months was Maples' prescription for the health service. At the end of a long analysis of how the Conservatives might reduce Labour's opinion poll lead over the Tories on managing the NHS, Maples concluded: 'We can never win on this issue.' Labour had expected Mrs Bottomley to be moved in the July 1994 reshuffle and were delighted when Major kept her in place.

While the health secretary had many fans within her department she never seemed to have given a moment's thought to the possibility that she should perhaps have rationed her exposure on television and radio. Whenever she was challenged by programme presenters about the latest problems being thrown up by hospital trusts or GP fundholders, she gaily trotted out what became her mantra: the need to 'move forward' and press on with the government's health reforms. This emphasis on the importance of 'moving further forward' became a Bottomley cliché. Watching an interview for *On the Record* in November 1993 was quite disorientating. Mrs Bottomley outlined the options that 'we can take forward'; the new treatments that 'I want to go forward faster with'; the charges that 'should be taken forward in whatever way'; and finally what she thought was 'the right way forward'.

Mrs Bottomley did so many interviews that she ended up sounding like the Conservatives' answer to Gordon Brown, churning out the same answers which, through endless repitition, became meaningless. I was surprised by her failure to take heed of a highly public warning that her television and radio appearances had perhaps become counterproductive. Two months before her *On the Record* interview a Gallup opinion poll in the *Daily Telegraph* showed that her insincerity rating of 59 per cent was higher than that of any Cabinet colleague. In his assessment of Gallup's findings on the sincerity ratings of leading politicians, Anthony King said that although Mrs Bottomley invited the nation to think of her as its principal physician, a clear majority regarded her as its 'principal quack' and her prescriptions as 'placebos'.

Nevertheless her grip on NHS statistics was formidable. Programme producers spoke in awe of the way she would continue briefing herself right up until the very start of an interview. When she was accused in a Commons debate by the Labour MP Alice Mahon of never answering questions but just reeling off statistics, Mrs Bottomley complained that this attack on her should not have been reported by *Today in Parliament*. The reporter concerned told me she stood her ground when Mrs Bottomley phoned in immediately after the programme saying the item should never have been broadcast. As I knew to my own cost, the Bottomleys were avid radio listeners and complained regularly about items of which they disapproved.

The day after Mrs Bottomley launched a white paper in July 1992 which, as the *Sun* reported, was aimed at curbing the 'soaring number of teenage mums', the *Independent* stole a march on its tabloid competitors by revealing that the health secretary was herself a former 'unmarried teenage mum': her first son was born when she was a nineteen-year-old sociology student at Essex, three months before she married Peter Bottomley. In a state of high dudgeon the *Sun*, which claimed it knew of Mrs Bottomley's teenage pregnancy but declined to report it without her cooperation, lashed out at the invasion of her privacy by the *Independent*, 'a paper that a parrot wouldn't deign to have at the bottom of its cage'. Andreas Whittam Smith, the editor of the *Independent*, said he had an entirely clear conscience. Mrs Bottomley was speaking to the nation as a government minister and it was 'a significant fact worth recalling that she was once an unwed, teenage mother herself'. He said that if the Bottomleys had wished to make sure that their family remained totally anonymous, they should not have gone into public life.

The following Sunday, when the *People* published its exclusive about David Mellor's affair with Antonia de Sancha, I reported that a growing number of Conservative MPs were complaining about what they considered was unacceptable behaviour by the newspapers. They wanted the Mellor and Bottomley cases to be considered by Sir David Calcutt QC, who was examining the effectiveness of press self-regulation. Immediately after my radio report was broadcast I was reprimanded by Peter Bottomley in the strongest possible terms. He said the BBC had no right to describe his wife as an 'unmarried mother' without saying that he was an 'unmarried father'. He demanded an assurance that if my report was repeated it should be amended to say that 'Peter and Virginia Bottomley had their first child three months before their marriage'. I duly complied with his request.

Some of Mrs Bottomley's complaints were pursued with considerable vigour. She was furious on discovering that the news bulletins one Sunday morning in July 1993 were leading with a warning by the new chairman of the British Medical Association, Dr Sandy Macara, that unless the government changed its policies the health service would disintegrate. Dr Macara's remarks were taken from an interview he gave to the *Sunday Mirror* which appeared under the headline: 'The NHS Will Be Dead In Seven Years If We Don't Stop The Rot Now.' Mrs Bottomley believed the story should never have been the lead item. I was told next day by the health minister Dr Brian Mawhinney that his boss had complained personally to John Birt, the BBC's director general. 'Apparently Birt happened to be in the wrong place at the wrong time on Sunday afternoon. Virginia saw him and handbagged him. She really was very cross.'

Despite the ferocity of her criticism of news reports which she disliked, journalists were invited quite frequently to attend receptions at Mrs Bottomley's department and she was a most considerate host. At her 1992 Christmas party she arrived wearing a blue scarf decorated with the stars of the European flag and the motif of a lion. Apparently it was the ladies' scarf issued for guests attending the European summit in Edinburgh which formed part of the British presidency. I inquired rather gingerly about its origins. She said she had just been over in

Downing Street and John Major had asked her why she was not wearing her British presidency scarf. 'I told John I would go and put it on straight away.' The reporters I was with were mesmerised. It was like taking part in a *Spitting Image* sketch. Mrs Bottomley must have realised she was sending herself up. She blushed a delicate shade of pink and immediately changed the subject. She said her Christmas card that year was of a rowing boat on the Thames outside the House of Commons. 'The boat's rowing up the Thames, of course, from Poplar to Kew. It's just like dealing with the NHS really, you just keep going and it's jolly hard work.'

Eighteen months later, at the end of March 1994, she held an Easter reception, telling journalists it was her 'April fool's day party'. She was wearing a black suit and was obviously in fine form. More progress had been made with the NHS reforms than she and her colleagues had ever thought possible: ninety-six hospitals had trust status; 36 per cent of doctors were fundholders; a million more patients were being treated; and fewer hospitals were running out of money than the year before. Mrs Bottomley said she had given her little speech earlier than usual that evening as she knew that one of the guests, the *Today* presenter Jim Naughtie, would be wanting to go to bed early as he had to interview the new NHS chief executive next morning. She hoped her guests would carry on enjoying the refreshments and she was sure some 'cocoa could be found for Jim' if that was what he would prefer. Naughtie shuffled awkwardly at the health secretary's tease, which went down rather well with the assembled journalists. Even so, I sensed that this time she had perhaps had gone too far and that she might regret her rather proprietorial references to the *Today* programme.

Sure enough, Naughtie turned the tables on the health secretary four months later when he was challenged at a radio conference in Birmingham. He was asked whether politicians really wanted to be interviewed by *Today*. Naughtie cited Mrs Bottomley as an example, saying that 'every second morning' she rang up asking to appear on the programme. 'There's a dread in the office when you hear the words, "and now with me live is the health secretary." You think, "Oh no, not again." There are limits and we do have to say no sometimes – "we're a bit bored with you."' Under the headline 'Why The BBC Dreads Mrs Bottomley On The Line', the *Evening Standard*'s political correspondent Peter Oborne said that 'virtually any mention of health' on *Today* was enough to get her ringing up demanding air time to speak. Oborne recalled that when she was the guest on *Desert Island Discs*, Mrs Bottomley said the luxury she would most like to take with her was 'a constant supply of the *Today* programme'.

If Naughtie, or anyone else for that matter, thought Mrs Bottomley might take the hint they were mistaken. In the very week she was ridiculed publicly over her endless *Today* interviews she was planning a masterly publicity coup against another of her critics, the Bishop of Birmingham, the Right Reverend Mark Santer. In a strident sermon a few days earlier, Dr Santer had said the business model adopted for the NHS was deeply distressing to those who believed that health care was a fulfilling vocation. The reforms had reduced patients to the status of a unit of consumption and exchange. 'That, in the Christian view, must be wrong because it is treating people as means and instruments instead of ends.' Newspaper headlines about 'unchristian' health reforms must have infuriated Mrs Bottomley because she wrote off immediately to the Archbishop of Canterbury, Dr George Carey, enclosing a lengthy note setting out the government's aims in a way which she hoped would be 'helpful' to the bishops. The pursuit of 'value for money and efficiency' in the NHS was 'a perfectly legitimate, indeed essential, goal'. The only profit made by the health service was to be 'measured in the cure of illness'.

Mrs Bottomley's letter to Dr Carey was dated 13 July 1994. Copies of it were issued to the news media on 15 July under a strict embargo for use on the morning of Sunday 17 July. The health secretary had chosen the publication date for maximum impact. She knew there was every likelihood that her fierce note, signed simply 'V.B.', would be picked up by the Sunday newspapers, the television and radio news bulletins and perhaps even the Sunday morning religious programmes. Mrs Bottomley was interviewed that morning on *Breakfast with Frost* which provided her with an ideal platform from which to reinforce her rebuttal of the Bishop of Birmingham's sermon. She said the health service was not a business. 'It is not for profit. It is not for sale. It is about improving the health of the nation.'

As the weekend political correspondent I quoted her remarks extensively in my radio broadcasts. Out of interest I enquired if the Department of Health knew by any chance why the letter she had written to Dr Carey had not been released for publication until four days after it was sent. The duty press officer told me that Mrs Bottomley had made the decision herself on when it should be published. While journalists tried to make fun of the health secretary's bossy behaviour, she had demonstrated her own talent for news management and her undoubted ability to 'put the boot in' politically.

A readiness to shoot from the hip when taking on the government's critics had been instilled in ministers during Mrs Thatcher's years at No. 10. Kenneth Clarke was generally considered to have the fastest draw. Brendan Bruce said Clarke's great virtue as Secretary of State for health, and then for education, was that after having given a controversial speech at a conference for one or other of the professions he would happily go up to the delegates afterwards, whether it was teachers or nurses, and have a cup of tea or a drink with them. Bruce revealed that Clarke's advisers had the greatest difficulty persuading him to keep away from demonstrations. Clarke's instinct was always to go and meet strikers or demonstrators, insisting that as he was 'a lawyer, paid to advocate a cause, he should go and talk to them'.

On becoming Chancellor of the Exchequer, Clarke had to show self-restraint because of the necessity to avoid speculation about interest rates or the budget, or the danger that he might say something which could harm the economy. During the Eastleigh by-election campaign in June 1994 I could see that Clarke found it tiresome to be so restricted in what he could say. Nevertheless, perhaps mindful that his predecessor Norman Lamont had tripped up spectacularly at the Newbury by-election the year before, Clarke was on his best behaviour.

By-elections are great fun for journalists. The main political parties lay on news conferences each morning and, because of the need to give some credibility to their individual campaigns, and so as not to be out-done by their opponents, they each feel duty bound to put up a senior politician to answer questions. As far as the reporters are concerned these events are open house and an opportunity to ask about any issue which might conceivably be considered relevant to the by-election. For the journalists that can mean literally anything connected with politics. These news conferences can become something of an ordeal for nervous or quick-tempered politicians. While ministers and their opposition shadows try to stick to their departmental briefs, they cannot duck awk-ward questions altogether and they have to make at least a stab at replying, otherwise their refusal to answer could become a news story in itself. In a way, taking part in one of these morning news conferences is rather like a having a go at a political coconut shy and then seeing the game played out in front of the television cameras. A well-aimed ques-tion can dislodge even the toughest nut and produce the most unexpec-ted response.

Norman Lamont paid his ill-fated visit to the Newbury campaign early in May 1993, three weeks before he was sacked by John Major. His budget in March that year had provoked a barrage of criticism. His decision to levy value added tax in two stages on domestic fuel was by far the most controversial element in what the *Daily Mail*'s front-page head-line had billed 'Norman's Timebomb'. For the media, Lamont was ef-fectively a marked man. Any utterance he made, however innocuous, was likely to be turned into news. In a full-page editorial the *Sun* had declared it was time Lamont saw a doctor because he had 'gone off his rocker' in trying to take the credit for falling interest rates when it was his own needless defence of the exchange rate mechanism which had delayed the recovery and forced the devaluation of the pound.

Once Lamont agreed to front the morning news conference at Newbury he should have taken the precaution of rehearsing, or at least thinking through, how he would fend off any difficult cross-questioning over his record as Chancellor. When the inevitable enquiry came and he was asked if he had any regrets, Lamont stammered: 'I . . . *je ne regrette rien.*' In his report for the *Guardian*, Stephen Bates described how the Chancellor 'grinned with pleasure at his cleverness', and said that Lamont did not find out whether Newbury's voters had any regrets because the 'nearest he came to them was when his car swept down the high street'.

After the Conservatives lost the by-election on a swing to the Liberal Democrats of 28.4 per cent, Major acknowledged that the electors had been 'determined to give the government a bloody nose'. Lamont's visit to Newbury was regarded by Conservative MPs as having been the most insensitive event in the entire campaign. Sir George Gardiner said that whoever wheeled out the Chancellor should be 'presented with a revolver on a silver tray'. Lamont had built up quite a reputation for incautious asides. The one prediction which was continually being thrown back at him was his assertion at the Conservatives' 1991 party conference that the 'green shoots of economic spring are appearing once again'. In a speech the week after the Newbury defeat he tried desperately to explain away his remark about having no regrets. He said that after two and a half years as Chancellor he was reconciled to being misquoted but he still felt hard done by over what happened at the news conference. 'I was asked: "What do you regret more, singing in the bath or the green shoots of recovery?" It was a lighthearted question, and I gave a lighthearted response, quoting Edith Piaf. Of course, all you have seen since, in the newspapers and on television, is my answer and not the question which put it into context. As usual, the media were determined to do it their way.' But Lamont still had not learned even the first lesson of the coconut shy of by-election politics: it is not the question which matters, but the answer.

On the day Kenneth Clarke was the Conservatives' star turn at the Eastleigh by-election, he was determined to sound conciliatory. The government's position was precarious. Ministers were bracing themselves for heavy losses in the elections to the European Parliament. In response to reporters' questions, the Chancellor agreed that the recovery had 'to go a lot further' before the average man or woman enjoyed any improvement in job security or increased prosperity. As the news conference had been rather lacklustre I decided to interview Clarke separately at the end of the proceedings in the hope of getting some livelier responses.

One issue which had not cropped up so far that morning was the weekend news story about the Prime Minister's criticism of the way beggars had become an eyesore in some town centres, driving away shoppers and tourists. Begging, Major said, was 'offensive and unnecessary'. He thought the police and local authorities should 'be very vigorous with it'. His tough words were seen as a quite a fillip to the Conservatives' flagging campaign. When I suggested to the Chancellor that the Tories were getting pretty desperate if they had to make beggars the latest scapegoats for economic failure, Clarke sprang to life. He claimed there were now 'crowds of people' who were receiving benefit from social security and who thought it was perfectly acceptable to add to their income by begging. The shock and horror expressed in the media about the Prime Minister's remarks had not been reflected at all by the general public, who knew perfectly well that 'beggars in designer jeans' were not an acceptable feature of modern society.

Clarke seemed extremely chuffed with his soundbite. As I switched off my tape recorder he smiled at his political adviser Tessa Keswick who had been standing nearby and had moved in closer once I started my interview. The Chancellor's tirade against beggars was broadcast not only by the national radio networks but also by the local BBC station, Radio Solent. Simon Brooke, the Conservatives' chief broadcasting officer, who was assisting with the campaign, told me afterwards that the Chancellor had cheered up no end once he had delivered his crack about 'beggars in designer jeans'. On arriving that morning at the Conservatives' Eastleigh headquarters he had asked the campaign team if there was anything he could do to help them get some headlines. He was disappointed that the formal news conference failed to provide the necessary spark, so he was all the more pleased that one of his interviews afterwards had provided a story.

The two Chancellors were complete opposites when it came to the way they handled the news media. Lamont lacked Clarke's easy-going way with reporters. He often seemed to be deep in thought if stopped and asked something by a political correspondent, and he could be somewhat tetchy if thrown an unexpected question at a news conference. Clarke could not have been more approachable. He enjoyed jousting with journalists and seemed grateful for any tips or suggestions about possible storylines. Clarke also took abusive coverage on the chin and seemed to bear no particular grudge against reporters from the tabloid press. Although he got ratty with me once or twice when he was health secretary, at the time of the ambulance workers' strike, I was not aware of his ever having gone to the lengths of making a complaint about my work, and that also seemed to be the case with many of my colleagues.

Alastair Campbell was one of the few journalists I knew who had succeeded in really annoying Clarke. Immediately after he was appointed Tony Blair's press secretary, but while he was still writing for *Today*,

Campbell had a front-page splash with an exclusive story about the way the Chancellor had ridiculed the attitude which Margaret Thatcher took towards football. Clarke said she failed to appreciate 'why anyone would want to go to a football match at all'. He accused her of excluding ministers who attended matches from taking part in the government committees examining the proposals for all-seater stadiums. The Chancellor was especially scathing about the recommendations of the Taylor report on football safety, which had made not 'a jot of difference' but had cost the clubs 'huge sums of money'. When journalists asked the Department of National Heritage if these views indicated a change in government policy, they were promptly referred to David Ruffley, one of the Chancellor's political advisers. He was scathing about the way Campbell had interviewed Clarke for a charity book, *Football and the Commons People*, which was an anthology of MPs' writings, and then turned it into a front-page story. 'It's pathetic. The Chancellor gave his valuable time for what he thought was a book for children's charity.' Campbell told me he had nothing to apologise for. 'Clarke read through what he had said. He knew full well that his words would be used by the press.'

Photographers and television crews were perhaps Clarke's greatest fans. He would always oblige them by stopping for a picture or by turning to acknowledge the camera, however scruffily he might be dressed or potentially embarrassing his pose. Newspapers regularly ran features giving tips on how the Chancellor should smarten up his appearance, though the *Evening Standard*'s fashion editor, Lowri Turner, appeared to concede defeat: chiding him for continuing to wear 'wide-boy double-breasted suits', she admitted it would smack of desperation if he ditched his brown suede Hush Puppies. She concluded that the Chancellor was clearly a man who wore 'disinterest in his wardrobe as a badge of honour'.

Clarke was characteristically nonchalant in his demeanour after the government's defeat over VAT on domestic fuel in December 1994. Right up until the vote the Chancellor thought the government would survive, believing he had won over enough of the rebels with fresh concessions. The defeat, by 319 votes to 311, caught ministers by surprise. Newspaper photographs of the Prime Minister in a statuesque pose on the back seat of his car as it arrived in Downing Street captured the depth of his despair. He was downcast, his face drawn and his mouth tight-lipped. When Clarke turned up half an hour later and went into No. 11, the contrast could not have been greater. At no point did the Chancellor give even the slightest hint of being rattled by the day's events.

The arrival shots formed a significant element in the overnight television coverage. A BBC news organiser, Martin Levene, who was on doorstep duty in Downing Street, stood poised to shout questions as

Major and Clarke returned from the House of Commons. Chris Meyer, the Prime Minister's press secretary, was the first to arrive. He walked up Downing Street shortly after midnight and looked across momentarily at the waiting television crews and photographers. Fifteen minutes later Major's car turned in from Whitehall. It sped up to the No. 10 front door. Levene shouted: 'Mr Major, a humiliating defeat?' Major had got out of the car on the pavement side so was partly hidden from the cameras. He walked swiftly past the Downing Street Christmas tree without turning or responding to the shouts and went straight inside. He was in shot for precisely two and a half seconds. When the Chancellor's car pulled up Clarke got out camera side. He appeared rather awkward as he tumbled out with his briefcase. His suit was crumpled. But despite his irritation at being let down by some of the rebel MPs, Clarke was not letting it show in front of the cameras. He dismissed the government's setback as a 'defeat for common sense'. Levene then asked if it meant the government would have to change course. Clarke, walking casually round the car towards No. 11's front step, took the questions in his stride: 'No. It just means we have to find another way of keeping the borrowing down. We have an industrial recovery out there to look after.' By now the Chancellor had opened the front door. Levene got in one last question: 'What about the reasons for your defeat?' Clarke paused for a moment and then replied: 'I think they were the worst reasons I have been beaten by for a very long time.'

The television footage seemed to speak volumes about the brutality and danger of defeat. An injured Major retreated inside No. 10 as fast as he could. He had obviously made up his mind to dodge reporters' questions and get out of public view as quickly as possible. The Chancellor had no way of knowing how the Prime Minister had reacted half an hour earlier, but he could hardly have been surer-footed and he certainly did nothing which could have been construed as suggesting panic in the government or causing alarm in the city when the financial markets re-opened. Next morning Clarke was equally bumptious as he fielded questions on *Today*. He claimed several Conservative MPs had given him their word they would support the government but had then reneged. 'There is no point me doing anything but accept the word of parliament however annoyed I am with the rebels . . . We are in charge and being in charge means delivering while the political world is going dotty . . . Yes, the boys and girls are playing around on quite a scale at the moment.'

Clarke's ability to ride out the storm was second only to that of the Cabinet's ultimate survivor, Michael Heseltine. Like the Chancellor, the President of the Board of Trade was usually smart enough to look after himself. Whitehall's directors of information, who served Heseltine in his various departments, all said he was the one Secretary of State who did not need a media minder, as he knew more about manipulating journalists than the civil service would ever do. Nevertheless even the Conservatives' great Houdini could make mistakes. His most celebrated gaffe was the result of his own forgetfulness, or perhaps complacency. Rather like a cross-channel ferry captain setting off with the bow doors open, Heseltine started answering questions in a television studio without stopping to think whether any of the cameras or microphones around him might be picking up what he was saying. Mrs Thatcher never provided any political out-takes when she was Prime Minister because she stuck rigidly to her golden rule of never relaxing for a moment once she set foot inside a studio.

Heseltine arrived at the BBC's Millbank studios in January 1993 ready for a lunchtime television interview on the continuing turmoil surrounding his announcement about the closure of over half the coal industry. Earlier that morning interest rates had been cut to 6 per cent, the lowest for fifteen years. The President had not been told of this before leaving the department. While the studio was being prepared for Heseltine's interview on pit closures, he was asked by another correspondent, who was carrying a tape recorder, whether he could give his reaction to the interest rate cut for *The World at One*. Heseltine expressed surprise: 'What interest rate cut? I hope you are not setting me up. Are you sure there has been a cut?'

What Heseltine was unaware of was that although he was not actually being interviewed at that precise moment, the output of the studio could be seen on the television monitors which were positioned all around the Millbank complex. Usually the set-up procedure before an interview is pretty uninteresting. In normal circumstances all that would have been visible would have been shots of Heseltine perhaps moving his chair or straightening his tie. Often studio technicians can be seen adjusting the microphone or the lighting. On this occasion the picture was more eye-catching than usual because it looked as if Heseltine was about to be interviewed by a reporter with a tape recorder. Mish Tullar, Labour's broadcasting officer, was standing outside another studio when he suddenly caught sight of Heseltine on a television monitor. He immediately put on a pair of earphones, in time to hear the President of the Board of Trade disclose that he knew nothing of the interest rate cut which had been announced two and three quarter hours earlier.

Having been apprised so fortuitously of this sensational admission, Tullar lost no time in alerting political correspondents on the lobby corridor. Heseltine's gaffe made the West End final edition of the *Evening Standard*. As its political correspondent Peter Oborne suggested rather tamely, this 'bizarre episode' raised questions about whether or not Heseltine was 'totally out of touch with the Westminster political process'. Next morning the *Sun* was in no doubt about what the rest of the government had decided to do about 'poor old Hezza' after the disaster of his pit closure announcement. The only alternative left to the Cabinet had been to give the President of the Board Trade the mushroom treatment: 'Keep him in the dark and cover him with fertiliser.'

Labour were cock-a-hoop at causing Heseltine so much embarrassment, and Tullar was the toast of the evening at the farewell party next day for the party's outgoing chief press officer Gez Sagar. Although he was still a little reticent about answering my questions, Tullar confirmed that he was the source of the story. 'I was very lucky to be standing where I was that morning and yes, I did have rather a busy time immediately afterwards talking to journalists along the lobby corridor.' Heseltine's department tried valiantly to play down the story, insisting there was nothing sinister in what had happened. 'This is boring. He was in meetings all morning. No one had a chance to chat with him.' However, once the dust had settled, Heseltine's director of information, Jean Caines, acknowledged there had been a blunder: 'Mea culpa. We let him down.' From then on, information officers who accompanied Heseltine said that before he gave interviews he invariably checked with them to see whether there were any last-minute government announcements that he was unaware of or news stories which he might not have caught up with.

Jean Caines had proved to be a doughty operator on Heseltine's behalf. If the President was running into political trouble she knew exactly where to apply pressure in the news media. A hurried announcement just before the start of the 1994 Christmas recess appeared to indicate that Heseltine had been rebuffed by the Cabinet over a decision to purchase twenty-five American-built Hercules transport aircraft for the Royal Air Force. Immediately before the order was confirmed in a written parliamentary answer, political correspondents picked up what they considered were reliable reports that Heseltine was letting it be known that if Britain placed the £1 billion order with Lockheed, rather than investing in the European alternative EFLA, it could turn into a repeat of the 1986 crisis when the Thatcher government rejected Westland helicopters in favour of American Sikorsky machines.

When confirmation came through of the Hercules order, the defence secretary, Malcolm Rifkind, announced that Britain had rejoined the EFLA project and might be in a position to purchase forty to fifty of the new European transport planes by the year 2003. Even so, the initial purchase of as many as twenty-five of the American aircraft was still seen as a setback for Heseltine. My report for the *Six o'Clock News* explained the reasons for Heseltine's opposition to the order. I also pointed out that he would have liked the government to have bought fewer of the American planes so as to have improved the chances of the European alternative.

Immediately after the bulletin Ms Caines telephoned me to say that she felt the BBC had been very negative. Heseltine was a 'happy bunny' and the commitment to rejoin EFLA was 'terrific news' for British Aerospace. I said her version did not square entirely with briefings by the Ministry of Defence, which had stressed there was no commitment to purchase the European plane. Rifkind's supporters had described the decision as a 'stunning defeat' for Heseltine. Ms Caines must have realised she had failed to convince me because five minutes later a call came into the newsroom from Heseltine himself. He told me he was 'delighted' by the announcement. The Hercules order included offset work for thirty-six British companies and would secure 3,500 jobs. By taking the positive step of rejoining EFLA Britain was back 'level pegging' with the French and Germans on the European alternative. My report for the *Nine o'Clock News* reflected Heseltine's upbeat assessment and I quoted him directly. Once Heseltine had given me a statement expressing satisfaction with the deal it had to take precedence over off-the-record guidance from some of his opponents.

But next morning's *Daily Express* carried the headline 'Heseltine Defeated'. Jon Craig, the political editor, said Heseltine fought an 'Armageddon battle against Rifkind' but was 'shot down' by the Cabinet after being accused of 'letting a romantic notion about Europe cloud his judgement in the face of overwhelming support for the American plane'. Ms Caines just smiled when I congratulated her on shooting down my story so effectively. She said she realised the only way to get the BBC to accept that Heseltine was entirely satisfied with the Cabinet compromise over the RAF order was to get him to ring me himself and give the BBC an on-the-record quote. Her speedy intervention on his behalf had made all the difference, and she had exercised her influence in those vital moments midway between news bulletins.

While both Heseltine and Clarke were sometimes outmanoeuvred by journalists, they were rarely tripped up when being interviewed on television or radio. Their abundant self-confidence and long years of service in the ministerial front line made them more than a match for most presenters. Even if they ran into difficulties or were caught off guard by an unexpected question they could usually extricate themselves quite easily with a little fancy footwork. When it comes to live broadcasting there is no substitute for experience. Even the most hard-bitten politicians can be thrown by technical difficulties or the confusion which sometimes develops in a studio close to transmission. At a time of perpetual crisis for his government, John Major took a considerable chance in his July 1994 reshuffle when he appointed Jeremy Hanley as the new Tory chairman. As a middle-ranking defence minister Hanley had never had to face the kind of grilling which Secretaries of State have to contend with on a daily

basis when their departments are in the news. Despite having no established track record of withstanding the cut-and-thrust of live interviewing, Major had given his new chairman only a few weeks to prepare for
what would be a critical autumn conference.

Hanley's appointment was described by political correspondents as
the biggest risk of the reshuffle. Under the front-page headline 'Major's
Showbiz Gamble' the *Daily Mail* said the Prime Minister had made a
daring move in handing the job to a relative unknown who had immediately told the paper's political correspondent, John Deans, that he did
not mind if people asked 'Jeremy Who?' Much was made of Hanley's
showbusiness roots, his mother being the actress Dinah Sheridan, star of
the fifties film *Genevieve*, and his father the late actor and television celebrity Jimmy Hanley. Simon Walters, writing in the *Sun*, said Hanley
would be expected to use his family background to tell ministers when
they were turning off voters on television. But Boris Johnson's observation in the *Daily Telegraph* was the most prescient. Despite his experience in broadcasting, he said, Hanley had been 'occasionally wrong-
footed on TV'.

As politics began moving back up the agenda after the summer break,
and with only a month to go to the Conservative conference, Hanley
appeared on *Breakfast with Frost*, hoping no doubt to boost party morale.
There had been violence the previous evening during a world title boxing
match at the Birmingham National Exhibition Centre. Seven people
were injured after trouble erupted among spectators. Police in riot gear
broke up the disturbances, which were seen live on television. Two days
earlier John Major had delivered a well-trailed speech on the need to
build an 'anti-yob culture'. Sir David Frost asked Hanley if he thought
the ringside violence was an example of 'some of those British yobs at
work'. Hanley replied: 'Oh, I hope not. This is an anti-yob culture that
we've now promised. I think that sort of thing is just exuberance. I hope
there is nothing more serious about it. But it's the sort of atmosphere and
attitude which does spread to others. People do imitate that sort of behaviour. It is very depressing.'

Once his answer was picked up by the Press Association news agency,
and by television and radio news bulletins, Hanley was roundly criticised
for his failure to condemn the violence outright, and accused of under-
mining Major's initiative aimed at curbing yobbish behaviour. Later
that day he apologised on Sky News for having commented on the disturbances without having seen the television pictures. A report on the
violence was being transmitted while Hanley was moving into his seat in
the Frost studio, ready to be interviewed. 'All I could hear in the background was that there was some cheering and chanting, so when Sir
David commented upon it I replied as best I could. Quite clearly it was an

incompetent response. . . I was caught on the hop. I am new in this game. I have only been in the job a few weeks and I am certainly learning to make sure that I have seen the news completely before I go on any TV programme.' Hanley said that when he saw film of the violence he was he was horrified. 'It was exactly the sort of yobbish behaviour, indeed worse than that, that John Major was describing and condemning, quite rightly.'

Alastair Campbell claimed in his *Today* column that he feared he might unwittingly have played a part in Hanley's inept choice of the word 'exuberance' to describe the disturbances. Shortly before the party chairman was interviewed, Campbell and Sir Bernard Ingham had appeared together reviewing the Sunday newspapers at the start of *Breakfast with Frost*. Afterwards Campbell said it was hard to accept Hanley's excuse that he had not watched the news footage of the violence while it was being transmitted by the programme. It was impossible not to see it. They were after all in a BBC television studio which had 'more TV sets per square inch than anywhere outside Radio Rentals showrooms'. He said that in fact Hanley had been 'ignoring the tellies in favour of a flick through the tabloids' and was 'mightily disappointed' when he found that the *News of the World* had failed to publish an article which he had written. Campbell claimed that Hanley's attention was also diverted by a *News of the World* feature on the 'Saucy Secret of Blair's New Boy'. This half-page exclusive revealed that 'clean-cut Alastair Campbell, appointed this week as Blair's official mouthpiece, once wrote porn thrillers for the adults-only magazine *Forum*.' The Labour leader's new press secretary was quoted as saying there was no point him denying that he had called himself the 'Riviera Gigolo' when he wrote for *Forum*. It had started as a laugh with a bloke he knew when they were living in France. 'We had this bet about who could first get into print. And it was partly a way to make to some cash . . . It's what we call youthful over-exuberance.' In writing about Hanley's trip-up in *Today*, Campbell said he feared the word 'exuberance' got stuck inside the Tory party chairman's head just as he sat down on the Frost sofa. 'Up came the question, out came the word . . . I've felt terrible about it ever since. He's such a nice chap and I'd hate him to lose his job.'

Hanley's swift apology went some way towards ameliorating concern within the party over his damaging gaffe. But even usually loyal leader writers were concerned at the way the Tories were having to explain away their chairman's clumsy remarks so soon after his appointment. In its opinion column the *Daily Express* said the Prime Minister had personally picked Hanley as a safe pair of hands in which the party could avoid self-inflicted wounds, and therefore it was all the more galling for the chairman to have put his 'fist in his mouth' just as Major had seized back the initiative on law and order. 'The government cannot afford to let this happen again. Neither can Jeremy Hanley.' But the *Daily Express* had to eat its words, because the party chairman stumbled again that morning when taking his first news conference at Conservative Central Office.

The launch of the agenda for the party conference might not necessarily have produced a hard news story but for Hanley's inexperience when answering reporters' questions. He had already alerted political correspondents by his claim on *Today* that he had been given the job of leading the party 'for the next two and a half years'. His remark was immediately interpreted as being rather presumptuous, because it implied he would automatically be party chairman at the next election, whatever appointments the Prime Minister might make in a subsequent reshuffle. When asked at the launch of the conference agenda about that morning's rise in interest rates to 5.75 per cent, Hanley said he hoped this 'rate rise is it' and that there would be no need for a further increase. But along at his own news conference, the Chancellor Kenneth Clarke had said he could not rule out a further rise in interest rates if that was what was needed. Treasury officials made no secret of their surprise that Hanley had departed from the accepted formula which ministers were advised to adopt of 'not ruling anything in or ruling anything out'.

For the second morning running Hanley's 'clangers' were headline news in the national press. Paul Eastham, writing in the *Daily Mail*, said the latest blunder had left the party's hierarchy wondering how long the chairman could survive. When talking to Conservative media strategists, I found that their main criticism of Hanley was over his failure to stop talking. They felt that if only he gave shorter answers, and had, for example, dismissed the question about interest rates by saying that it was a matter for the Chancellor, then he might have had more time to listen to the alarm bells which should have been ringing in his head when he faced awkward questions. Hanley's misfortune was that by having attracted attention to himself through his misapplication of the word 'exuberance', and by then admitting that this questioned his own competence, he had placed the news media on gaffe-watch. As politicians have discovered to their cost, journalists tend to be judge and jury in deciding what constitutes a gaffe and whether it has registered a significant reading on the political gaffometer at Westminster. While wounded ministers and MPs might think they have just cause for complaint, the feedback from viewers, listeners and readers is that the public enjoy being told about occasions when moralising politicians have tripped themselves up.

David Mellor, who had developed a lucrative career as a broadcaster and columnist after his resignation from the Cabinet, commiserated with the embattled chairman. Writing in the *Evening Standard*, he said that in 'today's media-pressured world, a senior politician is only ever a soundbite away from destruction'. The easiest place to get it wrong was

'Sir David Frost's breakfast boudoir'. So affable was 'mine host' that a politician's defences disappeared under 'the illusion that you're just a couple of chums having a quiet chat miles away from any eavesdropper'. Hanley should not have been pilloried for his innocuous references about interest rates and his role as chairman. Mellor then gave this advice to Hanley: 'Never apologise, never explain, said the Iron Duke, and Jerry should bear that in mind next time. Today's media pack has a simple motto. Don't hit a man when he is down, it's easier to kick him.'

Hanley was given some far more practical tips by one of his predecessors, Kenneth Baker, who said he knew just how the chairman must have felt. All Conservative ministers had fallen into the same trap of appearing on Sunday television. Politicians could not resist the temptation; but it was David Frost, Brian Walden and Jonathan Dimbleby who set the agenda. 'In terms of the audiences which you have to reach, the viewing figures are not really significant. The trouble is that you can be sure the one group always watching is the hacks, and they are just waiting for a gaffe. So my first piece of advice is don't go on Sunday television unless you have specific proposals to announce.' Bernard Ingham, writing in the *Daily Express*, weighed in with what he said was his 'survival kit' for Hanley. 'His every utterance, and non-utterance, will now be inventively tasted for gaffes as the ratpack gnaws at his confidence.' Ingham's 'beginner's pack for conductors of the Tory orchestra' included the following suggestions: 'Learn the score . . . Identify awkward passages and rehearse them often . . . Do not get over-matey with the loudspeaker operators.'

None of this advice seemed to help much. The predictions of the assorted media pundits proved correct. Hardly a week went by without the tabloids chalking up yet another boob by hapless Hanley. On the eve of the party conference at Bournemouth, the *People* claimed the chairman had become 'a serial bungler' who had 'dropped more clangers than Big Ben'. Top of their list of his latest gaffes was that he had accidentally called the former transport secretary, John MacGregor, 'unscrupulous' instead of 'scrupulous' when defending his move to the merchant bank which was advising the government on the rail link to the channel tunnel. Nevertheless, Hanley's first conference speech as chairman was well received and was described by the *Daily Telegraph* as 'a witty and polished' address. His three-minute standing ovation was 'a huge vote of confidence by the party, signalling that his early gaffes in the job have been forgiven'. Hanley told the delegates at Bournemouth that on his constituency visits around Britain he had found the party determined to 'fight back and win'. He was convinced there was a 'Conservative revival, starting right here and starting right now'. But the show of conference unity had not impressed a former Tory party treasurer, Lord McAlpine. After the Conservatives' crushing defeat in the Dudley West by-election in December 1994, he used his column in the *Mail on Sunday* to deliver a savage attack on the chairman. Hanley's speech at Bournemouth 'might have been considered amusing at a masonic dinner or the annual gathering of the salvage industry' but it had failed 'a great party in its hour of need'. McAlpine blamed the Conservatives' rebuttal at Dudley West on the 'unremitting incompetence' of a party which was run by 'a man who is a pantaloon'. Hanley was 'totally useless' and it was time Major 'pulled down the curtain on this musical comedy'.

The year could not have ended more disastrously for the Conservatives. As the chairman toured the television and radio studios trying to explain away their by-election defeat, the only lifeline he could offer his battered party was that they were at the midway point of the parliament and that therefore there were two years to go to a general election. Major and his advisers referred increasingly to the likelihood of their legislative plans lasting for a 'full parliament'. This added weight to the view that the Prime Minister might delay an election until the last possible moment and leave it until the spring of 1997 before going to the country.

Any attempt to assess the Conservatives' likely media strategy for the future appeared futile. Central Office was simply living from hand to mouth, fending off each successive publicity disaster, doing no more, it seemed, than just hoping for a quiet life. John Maples' memo had suggested the outline of a communications plan; but, as the communications director Tim Collins pointed out, the deputy chairman had no policy-making role. As Collins was on the point of leaving himself anyway, and as the party chairman had yet to establish his authority, the last of all eventualities the Conservatives were prepared for was a snap general election.

Although the electoral odds seemed stacked against him, Major began assembling a team of publicity advisers whom he hoped might be able to mount an effective fight-back if the Conservatives were able to wait until the return of the much-vaunted feel-good factor before having to go to the polls. Hugh Colver, a former public relations chief at the Ministry of Defence, was chosen to be the Conservatives' new director of communications, taking over after the May 1995 council elections when Tim Collins left Central Office for Downing Street to become one of the Prime Minister's policy advisers; and, as part of a shake-up in his Downing Street staff, Major appointed Howell James as his new political secretary. Colver had risen smartly through the ranks of civil service information officers after a stint in the Downing Street press office, where he worked under Bernard Ingham during the Falklands War. Many of Ingham's protégés went on to become heads of information in Whitehall, and Colver followed a well-worn path. His five years as public relations chief at the Ministry of Defence took in the Gulf War. James, who had been special adviser to the former Cabinet minister Lord Young, had wide experience of handling the news media. His front-line experience in public relations included a period as press spokesman during the turbulent start of the television company TV-AM. After working as a ministerial adviser, he spent five years as Director of Corporate Affairs at the BBC before re-joining Lord Young at Cable and Wireless. Within a few weeks of his appointment as Major's political secretary he was being praised by parliamentary sketch writers for having injected some witty asides into the Prime Minister's replies at question time.

James and Colver had much in common. Their expertise in promoting Conservative policies was developed during the early 1980s when Mrs Thatcher was at the height of her power; and they had both worked alongside ministers during difficult periods for the government. Yet while they were seasoned campaigners when it came to managing the media downside of political crises, neither had a reputation among political journalists for the interventionist approach favoured by Labour, and were considered to be at a further disadvantage because they lacked the pro-active temperaments of Tony Blair's publicity duo of Alastair Campbell and Joy Johnson. In contrast to Labour's preference for pushy, publicity-seeking spin doctors, Major's new team took their cue from the Prime Minister's press secretary Christopher Meyer and made it their business to keep a low profile.

Hugh Colver's appointment came as quite a surprise. Tory party officials had admitted publicly that they were finding it difficult to persuade an experienced publicity director to take on the task of heading up an election campaign which appeared doomed to failure. Colver, however, was ready for a move. He had been standing in as head of public relations at British Aerospace since leaving the defence department in 1992, and when an outsider was brought in over him to become the company's communications director he accepted the job at Central Office with alacrity.

The need for fresh thinking at Central Office on ways to counter Labour's record lead in the opinion polls was being reinforced on an almost daily basis as the Conservatives lurched from one publicity fiasco to the next. Of all the Tory gaffes in the winter of 1994–5 perhaps the most celebrated was the admission by the Chancellor Kenneth Clarke that it might be another two years before there was a return of the feel-good factor. His acknowledgement that an economic upturn might come too late to benefit the government caught his Cabinet colleagues by surprise. There seemed to be no overall coordination or direction in what ministers were saying.

Perhaps on the principle that attack is the best form of defence, Jonathan Aitken, Chief Secretary to the Treasury, pointed an accusing finger at the BBC for its failure, in an 'age of soundbites and spin doctors', to report the 'solid good news' of economic recovery. Aitken further accused the *Today* presenter John Humphrys of getting involved in 'partisan politics' for having chaired a meeting aimed at promoting the teachers' pay claim. If the BBC's journalists were going to embrace 'open partisanship' then, Aitken said, their organisation would have to be renamed the 'Blair Broadcasting Corporation'.

Ironically, on the Sunday before Aitken's attack Humphrys' guest for *On The Record* had been David Hunt, the Cabinet minister responsible for coordinating the presentation of government policy. Under some astute cross-questioning Hunt agreed that if Britain was at 'the top of the premier league for growth in Europe', as the Prime Minister claimed, this was not much use unless the government were also 'top of the premier league for presentation'. Hunt conceded that the Conservatives were 'unfortunately halfway down the league table'. Yet his only prescription for avoiding relegation seemed to be that the Tory party should follow the Prime Minister's example of 'leadership, courage and vision'.

8

Trials of Strength

*T*HE STATE OF a governing party's relationship with the news media has always been a useful pointer to its chances of electoral survival. In the 1970s, in the darkest days of the Wilson and Callaghan governments, Labour despaired of ever getting fair treatment from journalists. During the mid-1990s, John Major and his ministers felt equally beleaguered. By the halfway point of his second term in office, the elation surrounding Major's unexpected success in the 1992 general election was a distant memory. But the Conservatives clung to their belief that they could still win back the approval of the Tory press in time to help them secure a fifth successive victory. Major's audacious resignation in June 1995, triggering a Conservative leadership contest, was intended to be a turning point, from which preparations could begin for the daunting moment when he would again have to go to the country. His bravery in throwing down the gauntlet and defeating his opponents within the party won new respect for the Prime Minister in newspapers which had been highly critical of his administration. For once, Major's closest colleagues proved to be particularly adept at marshalling favourable news coverage on his behalf. Some equally astute news management the following year helped the government withstand the damaging revelations contained in the fearfully anticipated report of Sir Richard Scott's inquiry into the export of arms to Iraq. While these occasional highs made little lasting impression on the deep-seated sense of foreboding among Tory MPs, becoming ever more entrenched as the government's parliamentary majority ebbed away, Tony Blair and his publicity advisers were alarmed at Major's hidden powers of recovery. In some respects the long-drawn-out wait for the Prime Minister to go to the polls was as destabilising for Labour as it was for the Conservatives.

Labour's recurring nightmare was that Major would find ways of making a fresh appeal to the electorate. Concern had been heightened by a distinct shift in the stance being adopted by some of the tabloid newspapers. Having apparently written off completely the Conservatives' chances of defeating Blair, their proprietors and editors seemed to have second thoughts. Hostility towards Labour, and the kind of personal attacks which had been an everyday occurrence under Neil Kinnock, once more became a regular feature of the political news coverage of the *Daily Express, Daily Mail* and *Sun*. Blair had enjoyed a long honeymoon in his relationship with the popular press. Now, more than a year after his election to the party leadership, it had finally petered out. New Labour, and all that it stood for, suddenly found that it could be subjected to the kind of savaging which Old Labour had endured for years. Conservative pre-eminence in negative campaigning had left deep scars in the Labour psyche, and fears about the cumulative damage which could be inflicted by the Tory press added to the unease of Blair's advisers. The spectre of Major repeating his 1992 victory on the back of yet more scare stories about Labour's tax plans was enough to bring out a cold sweat in the campaign team advising Blair on election tactics.

Not the least cause for concern was the possibility that, at last, Peter Mandelson might have met his match. Dr Brian Mawhinney was appointed Conservative party chairman in the July 1995 Cabinet reshuffle, after Major's re-election as party leader. Central Office was back under the control of a Tory politician who understood the importance of motivating political journalists; who knew how to exploit opportunities to intimidate the broadcasting organisations; and who could see the immense political gain which was there for the taking if only the popular papers could be persuaded to repeat the degree of malevolence towards Labour that they had shown in the 1992 election campaign. Dr Mawhinney straight away began a recruitment drive to strengthen the party's publicity department. In December 1995 Charles Lewington, political editor of the *Sunday Express*, succeeded Hugh Colver as director of communications. In one respect Lewington was the opposite of Alastair Campbell: he avoided personal publicity. But, like Blair's press officer, the Conservatives' newest spin doctor had political commitment and an intuitive grasp of what was really going on within the party for which he worked.

Dr Mawhinney's promotion from transport secretary to party chairman was fitting reward for the diligence he had shown in organising support for the Prime Minister during the leadership contest. Political correspondents were summoned to a news conference in the garden of No.10 on Thursday 22 June 1995 to hear Major announce his resignation as party leader. After nearly five years as Prime Minister, he had found he was being opposed by a 'small minority' of Tory MPs. He was having to face repeated but 'phoney threats' of a leadership challenge. 'I am not prepared to see the party I care for laid out on the rack like this any longer.' His words galvanised Major loyalists in the Cabinet, but caused consternation among his critics.

Michael Portillo, the employment secretary, was urged by his supporters to take up the challenge. He hesitated, failed to seize his opportunity, and allowed the chance to become the standard-bearer of the Tory right to pass to John Redwood, who resigned as Welsh secretary and immediately set about harnessing the growing tide of Euro-scepticism within the party. Redwood justified his bid for the leadership on the grounds that Major had left Conservative MPs 'in limbo' over Europe when firm leadership was needed to defend the nation 'from damaging constitutional change'. Crowding round Redwood as the announcement of his challenge was relayed live on television were the party's most prominent Euro-sceptics, including the former rebel MPs who had only recently regained the Tory whip. Standing immediately behind Redwood, holding on to the back of his chair, was Teresa Gorman. She was wearing a bright emerald suit and had pushed her way to the front of the picture. Alongside, almost brushing the challenger's right ear, stood Tony Marlow, whose bizarre attire added to the gaiety of the packed news conference. Marlow had felt that morning like having 'a bit of fun'. He was wearing his Old Wellingtonian blazer – black, decorated with yellow, light blue, orange and amber stripes. Unwittingly Redwood had given the Prime Minister's supporters a golden opportunity to ridicule what was, after all, a momentous political occasion.

The task of coordinating publicity for the Prime Minister had been entrusted to Tim Collins, Major's personal press officer during the 1992 general election campaign, who had joined the Downing Street policy unit after standing down as director of communications in May 1995. Shortly after Redwood's televised news conference had finished, Collins walked out of Major's headquarters in Cowley Street to brief waiting reporters. My assignment that day was to report for Radio Five Live on the Major camp's reaction to the Redwood challenge. Although I had heard the live broadcast of the Redwood launch, and had already described briefly on air how he had delivered what I considered was a stunning set of arguments for his challenge, I had not, from my vantage point in the street, been able to see the television pictures. I was therefore taken aback when Collins began to outline what he thought would be the devastating impact of the images which had been transmitted. He said the Redwood news conference was a shambles. 'Redwood's supporters looked as if they'd all just stepped out of ward eight at Broadmoor. Didn't you see the swivel-eyed Teresa? I expect you'll all be saying Major must have bribed Marlow to turn up in that ludicrous blazer.' In my next broadcast I relayed the colourful but vicious language which Collins had used in this classic example of negative spin; and although Collins' remarks about Redwood's supporters looking like a 'barmy army' had been given unattributably, I sourced them firmly to 'one of the Prime Minister's closest Downing Street aides'.

Vivid as it was, though, Collins' portrayal of Redwood's news conference was nothing compared with the invective of the sketch writers in
the next day's national newspapers. Under the headline 'Vulcan
launches from slopes of Gorman', Matthew Parris of *The Times* suggested this was the first Tory leadership campaign ever to be 'launched
from the bosom of Teresa Gorman'. Redwood's 'claque of Earthling
riff-raff' had delighted the television producers by forming a 'doughnut'
around their hero, but it was surely the 'whackiest doughnut in history'.
Simon Hoggart in the *Guardian* said the multicoloured striped blazer
worn by Tony 'Von' Marlow resembled a chair from the 'passenger deck
of the Hindenburg'. But Hoggart praised the good-natured way Redwood responded when asked if he minded the comparisons with Mr
Spock from *Star Trek*. 'His self-deprecating soundbite was worthy of
Ronald Reagan: "No, they don't hurt, now I can see the joke – though
as you know it took me a long time. The logic cells have finally worked it
out."' Next day Redwood's campaign manager David Evans acknowledged on BBC radio that it was an ill-judged photo opportunity and
that it would have been better if some of the challenger's backers had
stayed away. 'It was a very unfortunate launch. The nutty element, as
you call it, really should not have displayed themselves.'

Portillo's supporters were dismayed by the verve Redwood had
shown, and they were clearly rattled by the speed with which he was
attracting pledges of support. At a lunch with two lobby correspondents
Portillo indicated that he intended to wait until the second round before
launching his own challenge. In anticipation of a lengthy contest, extra
telephone lines were installed in his likely campaign headquarters. Portillo prevaricated when challenged about this on *Today*. Instead of brushing the question aside or brazenly denying he knew anything about it, he
came close to admitting his involvement. 'It's just fantastic. There are
telephone engineers all over London who can't go about their business
without all sorts of rumours like this.' David Hart, who had been a close
aide to Margaret Thatcher and had since become one of Portillo's closest
confidants, was said to have been responsible for installing the tele-
phones. After he had been identified in Downing Street briefings as
Portillo's likely campaign manager, Hart told me that he did not mind
being described as the 'scapegoat'.

Portillo's apparent disloyalty in secretly planning a leadership bid
while publicly pledging loyalty to the Prime Minister worked in Major's
favour; yet Redwood was clearly attracting more support than the
Prime Minister had bargained for. Instead of facing a discredited stalk-
ing horse, he was being opposed by a Cabinet colleague. After ten days
of campaigning a poll of voting intentions was conducted for the *Sunday
Express* by the former Conservative MP Robert Hayward. He was one of

the party's most trusted election statisticians and had got closest to predicting Major's victory in the 1990 leadership contest. I was given advance warning of the poll on Saturday afternoon. Early that evening, as the final figures were being prepared for publication, there was a sudden hint of panic in the voice of the paper's political editor, Charles Lewington. He said it was going to be touch and go whether the Prime Minister would retain the support of two-thirds of his parliamentary party: Major might have lost the backing of well over 100 Conservative MPs.

Lewington's tip-off came just in time for my report for the tea-time television news bulletin. I had intended saying in my script that this poll, by the 'usually loyal' *Sunday Express*, would be seen as a considerable setback for Major. Lewington bridled instantly at my suggested line of interpretation. 'You can't say that. The *Sunday Express is* loyal to Major.' Half an hour later I was given the figures. Hayward's canvass of nearly three-quarters of the 329 MPs suggested that Major would get 224 votes; Redwood had received the promise of 60 votes and 45 MPs were still undecided or likely to abstain. A BBC reporter, John Devitt, who went to interview Hayward, told me afterwards that Lewington seemed staggered by the revelation that Major looked like losing the support of 105 MPs. Lewington insisted that out of party loyalty the *Sunday Express* would play down the likely desertions and hammer home the fact that the Prime Minister would win. 'It's Major!' was the front-page banner headline over Lewington's assessment next day that Major appeared to have 'pulled off his dramatic gamble' and was on course to 'top the critical margin of two-thirds' of the parliamentary party. If the paper's prediction proved accurate, Major 'can confidently claim that he has a mandate to carry on'.

Lewington's instant spin on the likely outcome proved invaluable to Major's campaign team as they prepared the line they would take once the result was announced. Their nervousness had been heightened by the last-minute desertion of two newspapers on which Major had hoped to rely. Under the headline 'Time for a Change' the *Daily Telegraph*'s leader column urged right-wing Conservative MPs to abstain so as to force a second-round ballot: it was 'time for Major to go', because his leadership offered 'little hope of averting a Tory election defeat'. Alongside a front-page cartoon depicting the sinking of the 'Toryanic', the *Daily Mail*'s comment column warned that if Major stayed as Prime Minister the Tories faced the prospect of 'meltdown' and their 'most catastrophic defeat since 1906'. The Prime Minister's supporters realised that, even if he gained sufficient votes to avoid having to go to a second round, they would have to act fast if his authority was to be restored.

When Sir Marcus Fox, chairman of the 1922 committee, announced the result, the outcome was remarkably close to the *Sunday Express*'s prediction. Major had secured 218 votes, comfortably defeating Redwood with 89; but when abstentions and spoiled papers were added in, a total of 109 MPs had failed to back him as leader. Trusted ministers had been assigned to give interviews to each of the television and radio programmes providing live coverage. Their instructions were to minimise any adverse analysis of the figures and to insist that the vote was a triumph for Major. College Green was packed with outside broadcast equipment. Robert Hardman of the *Daily Telegraph* described the scene as a resembling a 'rock festival' with hundreds of 'T-shirted tourists clustered around watching countless MPs being interviewed'. But, however hard they tried, presenters from the rival channels found it difficult to cast doubt on the result because the loyal hit team which fanned out from Major's campaign headquarters got in first, claiming a decisive victory which they said put to rest any idea of another pre-election leadership challenge. The effectiveness of the gloss being placed on the figures irked the *Daily Telegraph*'s Simon Heffer. Interviewed on *The Week in Westminster*, he accused the broadcasters of allowing themselves to be 'hijacked' by the ministerial spin that this was a 'crushing victor'. An editorial in the *New Statesman* concluded that viewers and listeners had been subjected to the 'most effective piece of Conservative Central Office puff broadcasting' since the Gulf War. 'The television coverage had set the agenda: from then on, everyone else was responding to its euphoric tone.'

The next day's newspapers reflected the upbeat assessment which had been put about so forcefully by the Major loyalists. Most of the Prime Minister's erstwhile critics beat a hasty retreat. Congratulations were the order of the day in the *Daily Telegraph*, which had no wish to be 'ungracious'. It said Major richly deserved a 'broad smile at the expense of almost every Conservative newspaper, including the *Daily Telegraph*, which had argued that he should be replaced'. The same conclusion was reached by the *Daily Mail*, which agreed it would be 'ungracious' not to congratulate Major on his 'terrier-like tenacity' in retaining the tenancy of No. 10. Rarely since the 1992 election had the Prime Minister received such favourable coverage.

For an incoming party chairman, Major's victory provided a heaven-sent opportunity to start the fight back against Labour with a clean slate. The smile on Dr Mawhinney's face said it all. Under the headline 'Westminster snakes and ladders' the *Daily Express* put the new chairman at the top of the pack. Way down the list it said 'goodbye to The Gaffer' over a glum-faced picture of the 'gaffe-prone' Jeremy Hanley, who, after his own unhappy sojourn at Central Office, was demoted in

the Cabinet reshuffle to become a middle-ranking Foreign Office minister. Dr Mawhinney was praised for having played 'Mr Nasty in an
effective double act with Mr Nice Ian Lang' in the leadership contest.
Lang, another key lieutenant in Major's campaign team, was promoted
to President of the Board of Trade.

Brian Mawhinney's first major challenge as chairman was to organise
the party conference in October; but before that he had a little local
difficulty to deal with – and an opportunity to limber up for battle.
Because of boundary changes his Peterborough constituency was
thought likely to become even more marginal at the next election and,
after some deft footwork, he succeeded in winning the nomination for
the neighbouring, more rural seat of North West Cambridgeshire. Dr
Mawhinney was only the latest in a long line of Conservative MPs to
move to safer constituencies in what Labour had dubbed 'the chicken
run'. John Prescott, the deputy Labour leader, took delight in referring
to the chairman as 'Dr Macwhinney', but the tables were about to be
turned. As the *Guardian*'s profile of the new chairman had observed, his
'favourite pastime' was 'sticking the knife' into Labour politicians and,
in order to enliven the usually quiet political month of August, he
arranged a regional tour to expose the activities of 'loony left' Labour
local councils. His timing was spot-on, because the weekend before he
was due to depart for the West Midlands, the *Sunday Times* revealed that
'Citizen Dave' was about to declare the 'People's Republic of Walsall'.
David Church, the new leader of the Labour-controlled Walsall District
Council, was reported as being on the point of sacking the council's
heads of department and replacing them with fifty-four 'Soviet-style
neighbourhood committees'. As Dr Mawhinney made post haste for
Walsall, Labour tried ineptly to pre-empt accusations about 'left-wing
extremism' by suspending the Walsall District Labour Party. A hurried
announcement to this effect by Labour's environment spokesman Frank
Dobson, in an early-morning interview on *Today*, was a gift for Dr Mawhinney who arrived in Walsall claiming that Dobson's 'panic response'
revealed the hidden dangers of Labour's 'rotten boroughs'. Glowing
tributes were paid to the effectiveness of the Conservatives' new 'Mr
Nasty'. Boris Johnson, writing in the *Spectator*, complimented him for
going so quickly to Walsall where, like 'a rubberneck at the scene of some
great natural disaster', he had been able to crow over Blair's discom-
fiture. His performance had put 'flecks of indignant foam' back on the
lips of the Conservatives' natural supporters.

Labour's spin doctors bided their time as they plotted revenge. They
were determined to make sure that when they had an opportunity to
retaliate, Dr Mawhinney, like the rest of his party, would be made to
suffer. The opportunity was not long in coming. In the autumn of 1995,

after a series of highly confidential meetings with prominent Labour politicians, Alan Howarth, the Conservative MP for Stratford-on-Avon, decided to cross the floor of the House of Commons and join the Labour party. He had a private meeting at Blair's home in Islington during the week before the Labour conference in Brighton. Alastair Campbell knew that the timing of any announcement would be crucial if Labour were to succeed in destabilising Dr Mawhinney's plans for the latest relaunch of John Major. Instead of letting the news leak out at Brighton, where it could have been trumpeted as another coup for Blair, Howarth's defection was kept secret until the eve of the Conservative conference the following weekend. As Dr Mawhinney and his staff prepared to set off for Blackpool, Labour released their bombshell. The story was given exclusively to the *Observer* and it dominated news coverage that weekend. Boris Johnson, writing in Monday's *Daily Telegraph*, was forced to pay a back-handed compliment to Labour's spin doctors for the 'vicious timing' of Howarth's defection.

Dr Mawhinney, caught firmly on the back foot, insisted that Howarth's 'eccentric' decision to 'slide across the political spectrum' would not damage the conference, and, in an attempt to regain the initiative, set about trying to securing some favourable pre-conference publicity. I previewed his programme of events on *Breakfast News* that Monday and remarked that his one photo call of the day, visiting a Blackpool car factory, sounded rather lacklustre. When I interviewed him later in the day he was decidedly tetchy, and my comments prompted a sharp reprimand. Nevertheless most picture editors shared my opinion; his photo opportunity made little impact in next day's newspapers.

Dr Mawhinney's conference address was the highlight of the opening session and he received the first standing ovation of the week. His speech included the annual attack on the BBC, which had become something of a conference ritual for the party chairman. This year, staff at Central Office had spent September monitoring the output of *Today* and had concluded that the programme's motto must be 'their hands in your pocket'. In one week alone it had given air time to people calling for government spending to increase by £8 billion, but hardly once had its interviewers asked where the money would come from. He reminded BBC journalists that the government did not govern because it had won some 'broadcasting award' but because it had a mandate, and the *Today* programme only had 'a licence'.

Given the pasting which Labour had inflicted on the Conservatives over the Howarth defection, political correspondents were waiting with interest to see whether Hugh Colver, the party's director of communications, would have any influence on news coverage of the conference. He had made little impact since being appointed by Jeremy Hanley the previous May, rarely seeming to have any noteworthy information to offer journalists. During the leadership election he appeared to be stranded on the sidelines. Colver told me that on the day Major resigned, he had suspected something was afoot but he did not know precisely what would happen until he was briefed in Major's room at the Commons just before the official announcement. I was surprised to hear him admit so freely that he was not on the inside track and that his advice had not been sought. In the weeks leading up to the conference Dr Mawhinney had relied increasingly on Tim Collins, who had left the Downing Street policy unit on being selected Conservative candidate for Westmorland and Lonsdale but now returned to Central Office to become the chairman's media consultant. He was often seen briefing journalists while Colver hovered awkwardly in the background. Word soon got round among broadcasters at the party conference that Colver lacked clout. He seemed to be out of his depth in the cut-and-thrust negotiations which are inevitable at a fast-moving event where there is considerable competition for interviews and facilities.

Three weeks later Colver resigned; and, after failing to create even a ripple of excitement in his six months as the party's spin doctor, he took steps to ensure that his departure became the top political event of the week. Sky News broke the story, suggesting Colver might have been sacked. As reporters pieced together what had happened, the drama slowly unfolded. Sensing that Mawhinney might want him to leave, and having found that he disliked the role of political propagandist, Colver went to Central Office at one o'clock in the morning and cleared his desk. He prepared eight copies of his resignation letter and left them together with his mobile telephone and message pager – 'the two vital tools of the spin doctor's trade', as the *Sunday Times* was to observe. In a handwritten note to Vanessa Ford, head of news at Central Office, he said he intended to inform the press of his decision. Colver assured me he went of his own volition. 'I knew some MPs thought the party chairman should sack me but I am sure to this day Mawhinney would swear on a stack of bibles that he didn't want to get rid of me. Actually he might have wanted me out of the way but he hadn't said or done anything about it.'

I knew of no political journalist who could remember ever having been given a memorable quote by Colver during his brief period with the Conservatives, but he was about to become an eminently quotable ex-spin doctor. Instead of going quietly, perhaps in the hope of landing another top job, Colver decided to become a freelance public affairs consultant. He transformed himself overnight into a political pundit, ready with an instant opinion on the failings of his former employers. In an exclusive article in the next day's *Sun* he described how he sat day after day in meetings of the party's high command, where looming problems were identified and endlessly discussed, only to see experienced ministers appear paralysed once the crisis arrived. He cited the National Lottery as a prime example of what should have been a public relations triumph. It had created over a hundred millionaires in its first year and contributed £1 billion to good causes and another £1 billion to the Treasury; but the politicians had failed to keep a grip on their own agenda and allowed it to become a public relations disaster.

Colver had also engaged in some soul-searching on his own account. He found political propaganda distasteful. 'You have to be a zealot, a political zealot... I think the difficulty in moving from being a professional communicator in government or industry is that that sort of evangelism or missionary zeal is not there.' In an interview for *News at Ten* he said that as the election approached he realised that Central Office wanted a political street-fighter. He hoped the Conservatives would not necessarily 'get down to the gutter'. He followed up this warning in the *Sunday Times*, which contained further predictions about the likelihood of the Conservatives mounting personal attacks on their opponents. 'It is a descent into sleaze with a targeting of personalities like John Prescott and Clare Short to demonstrate that they are still leftist socialists under the Blair veneer. If you take that kind of policy to its logical conclusion then clearly you want details of their private lives.'

Colver's former colleagues at Central Office were relaxed about his departure. Alex Aiken, who was promoted to chief press officer in the shake-up which followed, said resignation was the only option. Colver had failed to accept that the Conservatives had to remain hungry if they were to win the election and that therefore their approach towards Labour had to be 'kill, kill, kill'. Sheila Gunn, a former journalist with *The Times*, who was recruited by Colver to liaise with political correspondents, and who coincidentally had only signed her contract with Central Office the day before his resignation, thought their departing director should have acknowledged his own failings. She had noticed herself that Colver rarely seemed to put himself about or suggest possible story lines. As Colver had readily acknowledged, he came from a civil service environment, and government information officers were used to controlling the dissemination of information rather than setting the agenda; Colver simply could not match the aggressive, news-driven approach being pursued by Labour's publicity staff.

Within a month of Colver's resignation an episode occurred which raised echoes of his cautionary words about the dangers of descending into the grubby world of manufacturing news headlines. Among the Cabinet papers which Dr Mawhinney discovered in his red box was the draft of a speech in which the Lord Chancellor, Lord Mackay, appeared intent on taking the unprecedented step of reminding judges that 'the courts were not superior to Parliament and should not overstep their powers in using judicial review to challenge ministerial decisions'. Sheila Gunn was told to fax the speech to the *Daily Telegraph*. It made the front-page splash next morning. Lord Mackay was furious. He wrote to the editor, Charles Moore, complaining about an entirely 'erroneous account' of a speech which he had not even delivered. The Lord Chancellor said he had never sought to challenge the independence of the judges. Although he had spoken at the Guildhall the previous evening, he had made only a few 'light-hearted comments'. Apparently Lord Mackay had rejected out of hand a speech which had been prepared on his behalf and which had been circulated in advance to the Cabinet. Labour took delight in attacking the Conservatives' 'dirty tricks' department. Donald Dewar, the opposition chief whip, wrote to Dr Mawhinney asking whether his staff were 'incompetent, malicious, or simply out of control'. Blair broadened the attack, accusing ministers of allowing Central Office to become the Tories' 'lie machine'.

Dr Mawhinney took full responsibility for what had happened. Interviewed that evening on *Newsnight*, he said there had been a 'genuine misunderstanding'. As party chairman he had 'broad shoulders' and had no intention of attacking his staff. Colver was quoted widely, blaming Dr Mawhinney's 'slip-shod' approach: the party chairman was too ready to 'cut corners'. If he had still been at Central Office, Colver said, he would have checked the story out much more carefully. 'You can't go around spinning away about a non-existent speech by a Lord Chancellor. There has to be some discipline.'

Several weeks were to elapse before Central Office announced that Charles Lewington had been hired as Colver's replacement. Ceri Evans, the chief broadcasting officer, told me that Dr Mawhinney had enjoyed head-hunting and was 'incredibly happy' to have secured the services of a top political editor. A profile of Lewington written by the Press Association's Chris Moncrieff suggested that the new director had the 'looks of a film idol'. Eve Pollard, formerly editor of the *Sunday Express*, was said to have addressed him routinely as 'darling Charles'. Although he was well versed in the art of promoting stories favourable to the Conservatives, Lewington had little experience of broadcasting. When I went to interview him for the tea-time news bulletins on the day of his appointment, he insisted he would do only one pooled interview for all the television channels and said it could not be used on radio. I protested at this stipulation and remarked that even Princess Diana could not impose restrictions of that kind on the BBC. Unless he agreed that his interview could be broadcast across all outlets, I said, I would have to tell the camera crew to pack up and leave. After a short consultation with his

colleagues Lewington backed down. Our spat amused the *Sun*'s Simon
Walters, who wrote next morning of the gaffes being made by 'Lord
Charles, John Major's new charm guru'.

Lewington's appointment was nevertheless generally regarded as a
clever move. Matthew Parris of *The Times* told me he thought the new
director was an 'intelligent tabloid journalist' and would have a calming
influence on the Central Office publicity staff. Lewington was also
highly regarded by the Liberal Democrats' former spin doctor, Olly
Grender, who had left politics to become communications director for
Shelter, the campaign for the homeless. She remembered Lewington for
his ability to pick up inconsistencies in what the Liberal Democrats were
saying. 'He was a sharp tabloid journalist. I certainly had respect for
him.' Certainly, having worked on a Sunday newspaper during most of
his time at Westminster, Lewington had usually stood back from the
daily fray of life in the lobby and had not developed the sharp elbows
which are sometimes needed by journalists and broadcasters when faced
by frequent deadlines.

Lewington's inexperience in handling the rough and tumble of
instant briefings was only too apparent on the night in February 1996
when the Conservative MP Peter Thurnham resigned the Tory whip.
There had been speculation for some days about the MP's possible
defection, but when it emerged that Thurnham and his wife Sarah were
on their way to meet John Major for a private meeting in the House of
Commons it looked as though there might be a reconciliation. Afterwards, when giving correspondents a rundown on what had happened,
Lewington was hesitant and appeared uncomfortable. Thurnham had
apparently promised the Prime Minister to think again about his position and to return to see Major the following week. Lewington then
added rather cryptically that previously government whips had been
rather gloomy about their chances of persuading the MP to stay his
hand. The conclusion reached by most journalists was that it looked as if
Major had failed to get Thurnham to change his mind, but the top line
to the story had to be Lewington's rather more optimistic suggestion
about Major persuading the MP to reconsider his position. An hour
later *Newsnight* reported that Thurnham had told his constituency
chairman that he had resigned the whip.

Lewington's earlier vacillation worked to the Prime Minister's disadvantage because the next day's newspapers all went hard in reporting
Thurnham's decision to sit as an independent MP as a personal snub to
Major. Campbell mocked his opponent's incompetence. He said Lewington should have sought to distance the Prime Minister from
Thurnham and left the rebel MP to his own devices. Ideally he should
have persuaded Major to cancel the meeting once news of it got out,

because there was always the danger it would be reported as a rebuff to the Prime Minister. By briefing journalists on it afterwards, Lewington had only compounded the problem by supplying further details of what had taken place. Lewington was upset at having floundered so badly but said his annoyance was as nothing when compared with the fury of the Prime Minister who felt Thurnham had 'taken him for a ride'.

Although Lewington had been communications director for only a couple of months he should perhaps have thought through the possibilities with greater care in view of the devastation which had been caused just after Christmas 1995, within a fortnight of his own appointment, when the Conservative MP Emma Nicholson announced she was defecting to the Liberal Democrats. Just as Labour had milked Alan Howarth's defection for all it was worth, Paddy Ashdown had ensured the maximum advantage for his party from the arrival of their new recruit. In a publicity blitz timed with military precision the Liberal Democrats gave the Nicholson story as an exclusive to the *Nine o'Clock News*. Two considerations had been paramount in planning the announcement. Ashdown wanted to get the best possible news coverage while at the same time giving the Conservatives the least possible warning, so as to minimise the chances of their rubbishing Ms Nicholson's motives for defecting. She wanted the BBC to be first with the news of her desertion from the Conservatives. By giving it exclusively to the *Nine o'Clock News* the party had ensured maximum impact but still allowed newspaper journalists sufficient time to write it up for the next day's editions.

As was only to be expected, the BBC led with the story. It gave Peter Sissons a graphic opening headline: 'A political bombshell tonight as another MP defects from the Conservatives.' After a report on the background to her defection, Ms Nicholson was interviewed at length. Just as the Liberal Democrats had predicted, the Conservatives were soon on the attack, claiming she had deserted the party in a fit of pique. Michael Heseltine revealed that Ms Nicholson had approached him twice, asking him privately what he thought were her chances of promotion. The Tory right were cutting in their abuse. John Carlisle said the party was well rid of her because she had been 'prostituting' her views around Westminster for some months. Michael Portillo accused Ms Nicholson of a 'history of disloyalty' since she decided to 'stab' Thatcher in the back by voting against her for the leadership. The Liberal Democrats were delighted at the way the story kept going for almost a week, right through the usually quiet post-Christmas period. Alan Leaman, the party's strategy director, thought the whole episode revealed the ineptitude of the Conservative Party in their approach towards women MPs. 'It was a fatal mistake of Heseltine and the Tory right to begin telling tales about Emma. Once they started that game there was no way they could win because it was obvious they would come across to the public as nasty lot of male chauvinists.'

Coordinating the response of ministers and party officials to a fraught internal issue like the defection of an MP can be one of the most awkward tasks for any political press officer. The difficulties facing Lewington were all the greater because of the strict dividing line between promotion of the government's affairs and party publicity. Marrying up the sometimes conflicting interests of Downing Street and Central Office can be an intractable problem. On occasion it can result in a broken chain of command, with the Conservatives' communications director ending up at arm's length from the Prime Minister. Michael Jones, writing in the *Sunday Times*, thought the odds against Lewington making any difference to the government's body language were 'daunting'. He compared the constraints under which Lewington worked with the untrammelled access which Campbell had as Blair's right-hand man. He concluded that Lewington, 'a substitute player with no spin-doctoring experience', had not run on to a level playing field. Nevertheless, from what I heard, Lewington had succeeded in sorting out some of the demarcation disputes which can bedevil contact between Central Office and the Prime Minister's press office. Major was said to be on the phone himself to Lewington as early as six o'clock some mornings, so keen were they to ensure that opportunities to hit out at Labour were not missed. Lewington was soon putting his skills to good use. He proved adept at spotting gaffes made by Labour's front-bench team and at thinking up ways to exploit them. Donald MacIntyre, writing in the *Independent*, agreed with my assessment. After an 'unobtrusive start' he considered Colver's replacement had turned out to be a 'highly thought of player'. However, Lewington eschewed the kind of badinage with lobby correspondents which Labour's spin doctors regarded as their forte, and he was clearly no match for the garrulous Alastair Campbell. The *Observer*'s political columnist Iain Macwhirter, writing four months after Lewington's appointment, said he still found the new communications director 'sleek and supercilious' and had yet to have an intelligent conversation with him.

Lewington had the advantage of being able to start from scratch in establishing a strong working relationship with Downing Street with the appointment of a new chief press secretary. Jonathan Haslam, who had been deputy press secretary at No. 10 in the early 1990s under Gus O'Donnell, was chosen in January 1996 to succeed Christopher Meyer, who left after two years with Major to become British ambassador in Bonn. Although Meyer had proved to be a particularly doughty defender of the Prime Minister, and was widely praised for the firm grip which he maintained on Downing Street's contacts with the news media, he had always hankered after a top Foreign Office posting. Whenever he was in the company of journalists he played strictly by the rules of civil service neutrality, and he took care to avoid the political pitfalls which might have damaged his chances of returning to the diplomatic service. In his final months with the Prime Minister, as speculation about the timing of the election intensified, he was at pains to keep his distance when dealing with Tory party officials. Haslam, who had nearly twenty years' experience as a departmental information officer, seemed to share Sir Bernard Ingham's unerring ability to negotiate a path through the conflicting demands of government and party business. He also appeared to have greater self-confidence than Meyer when dealing with Central Office, and his sure touch was soon attracting praise.

Haslam's first testing assignment was to help prepare the government's reponse to the three-and-a-half-year inquiry by Sir Richard Scott into the circumstances surrounding defence exports to Iraq after the Iran–Iraq war. The careers of two Cabinet ministers – the Attorney-General, Sir Nicholas Lyell, and the Chief Secretary to the Treasury, William Waldegrave – were thought to be at risk because of the criticism which Sir Richard was expected to make of their conduct. Ministers received their copies of the report eight days before it was published. A team of civil servants in the Cabinet Office immediately began assessing Sir Richard's findings. The Scott Report ran to five volumes and was highly complex. In terms of news management the priority was to prepare short, easily understood answers which ministers could use when responding to questions about the central issues examined by Sir Richard. In the event it turned out to be a text-book example of how to hold the line in the face of hostile coverage in the news media and a sustained attack by opposition parties. One departmental head of information told me afterwards that it was the most effective exercise in government news management he had ever been involved in.

Throughout the barrage of criticism to which ministers were subjected, their responses proved extremely durable. There were three headline answers of overriding importance. According to the government's interpretation, Sir Richard's report showed that there was no conspiracy to export arms to Iraq; that ministers had not conspired to send innocent men to prison; and that there was no subsequent cover-up by the government. While opposition spokesmen tried repeatedly to question and undermine the answers which ministers were giving, these three key conclusions appeared to be unshakeable.

From what I could discover, Major's new press secretary had played a significant part in coordinating the government's reponse. Haslam was singled out by the *Sunday Times* as one of the key advisers. He had been told to 'immerse himself' in the background to Sir Richard's inquiry so as to help ministers ensure that in the 'first crucial hours' after the report's publication, the media would be persuaded to take a 'sympathetic line'. David Willetts, a junior minister under the deputy Prime Minister, Michael Heseltine, was assigned the task of preparing the political spin which would be placed on Sir Richard's findings. He was supplied with a copy of the report two days before publication and then had to think through the implications for the Conservative Party of the assessment which had been made by the civil servants. Immediately the report was published, Willetts began briefing lobby correspondents on the likely political repercussions. Next day's front pages were ample reward for the combined efforts of ministers, civil servants and government information officers. 'Ministers go Scott free!' was the *Daily Mail*'s headline. 'Scott a load of rubbish' was the *Sun*'s verdict above a smaller headline which declared that the Prime Minister was 'off the hook as arms probe fires a blank'.

Willetts enjoyed his new-found role as a spin doctor, pounding the lobby corridor, bending the ear of political reporters. He told me that it was essential for a minister in the Cabinet Office to have undertaken this task. Conservative party officials had been forbidden access to the Scott Report, and therefore there was no way that either Dr Mawhinney or Lewington could brief the media on its contents. 'Once I had distilled what the civil servants were saying, and looked at it in a way a layman would understand, it was my job to work out the political interpretation and then pass it on to the journalists.' Willetts had a well-established reputation as one of the Conservatives' leading policy thinkers. After serving in the whips' office, he was promoted to parliamentary secretary for public service in November 1995 – a move which placed him across the despatch box from Labour's foremost spin doctor, Peter Mandelson, who had been appointed shadow public service minister the previous month when Blair reshuffled his front-bench team. Once it became clear that the government looked set to escape virtually unscathed from publication of the Scott Report, Willetts was so pleased with his handiwork that he started ruminating with lobby correspondents on the precise etymology of the term 'spin doctor'. He was further amused by what became a week of role reversals for himself and Mandelson. Willetts had expected tough competition when it came to pushing the government's line, but said he found that Mandelson was 'nowhere to be seen and instead had been trying to pass himself off as Labour's leading policy guru'. Willetts' swipe at his Labour shadow was a reference to a new book, *The Blair Revolution*, written jointly by Mandelson and Roger Liddle, which examined whether New Labour would be able to deliver on the promises made by Blair and his colleagues. Mandelson had been preoccupied for weeks by his attempts to promote the book, which he believed would reinforce his claim to be one of the most important political strategists among Labour's modernisers and thus – he hoped – convince journalists that he had a more substantial role than that of a mere spin doctor.

The task of marshalling Labour's attack on the Scott Report had been entrusted to the shadow foreign secretary, Robin Cook. He was infuriated by the eight-day advantage ministers had given themselves to work out of ways of minimising the impact of Sir Richard's findings. Cook claimed that press releases issued by the Cabinet Office and the Treasury were 'dishonest' and contained 'five flat lies'. He protested to Sir Robin Butler, head of the civil service, calling for the withdrawal of the government's press pack. Civil servants had been 'bullied' by ministers into becoming 'another cog in the Tory lie machine'. The BBC's reporting of the Scott Report had also become a bone of contention. Sheila Gunn told me that Dr Mawhinney thought the Corporation's journalists had 'gone overboard'. 'There's enormous criticism within the party about the way the BBC has kept on and on about the Scott Report when it's not attracting anything like the same attention in the newspapers or on ITN.' Alastair Campbell had reached the completely opposite conclusion about the government's success in closing down the row over the arms-to-Iraq investigation. Writing in *Tribune*, he accused the BBC of falling in 'fairly quickly' with the 'line being peddled by the government and Tory Central Office that it was "boring" and that the public was not talking about it'. Campbell acknowledged that the government's entire strategy was based on seizing a few sentences which it felt vindicated ministers and then using them to 'confuse press and public' in the hope that the mass media would lose interest. Martin Kettle, writing in the *Guardian*, agreed with Campbell. He considered the press and the broadcasting media stood accused of collective 'laziness' and had 'let the story go too quickly'.

Campbell's belligerence about the BBC was symptomatic of the panic which occasionally gripped the Labour hierarchy when the party faced unexpected media hostility or when publicity initiatives proved ineffective in gaining favourable coverage, usually after they had been squeezed out by other news. Setbacks were hard to take after the remarkably good treatment to which Blair had become accustomed. His news and imaginative approach to politics had excited journalists, and that enthusiasm was reflected in the way the party's affairs were being reported. This initial success had tended to heighten the rivalry among Labour's various spin doctors. Amid all the jockeying for position, and the continued uncertainty about possible dates for the general election, there were occasional harsh words. As Blair approached his second party conference as leader, strains were becoming evident among the party's publicity advisers. Discontent soon turned to internal feuding. Labour's competing spin doctors were again about to attract more attention in the news media than the policies and personalities they were being paid to promote.

Joy Johnson had devoted her first few months as Labour's director of campaigns, elections and media to the task of sharpening up the party's response rate to the news events of the day. She believed that Labour could not always rely on the Blair effect producing favourable coverage; therefore the party's publicity machine, like the newspapers, television and radio, had to be prepared, if necessary, to be driven along by the news agenda. Water shortages during the 1995 summer drought were exploited ruthlessly by Labour. Each day Ms Johnson worked with the environment spokesman Frank Dobson to think up fresh ways of capturing the headlines with new surveys and statistics. Water companies were taken to task over inflated boardroom salaries and for wasting water through their failure to mend leaks. The government's discomfort in the face of Labour's onslaught turned to high comedy on the day the environment secretary John Gummer visited one rapidly emptying reservoir. Gummer appeared on television looking helplessly towards the heavens as if praying for rain. Ms Johnson believed it was images like that which would be remembered by the voters and would help sustain Labour's attack on the incompetent way in which the water industry had been privatised.

Ms Johnson and her colleagues held meetings each morning to assess the opportunities for news-driven initiatives. The challenge was to engineer ways in which Labour's reaction might provide a fresh top line to one or other of the stories attracting the media that day. Ms Johnson began to compile a diary of news events for the year ahead so that they could plan their tactics. Her strategy was supported by the shadow Chancellor Gordon Brown and his press officer Charlie Whelan. Brown had a great aptitude for thinking up catchy phrases which encapsulated a political message and which might make a snappy headline or form the basis of a soundbite. He was said to have devised the wording of the pledge which Blair had made to the effect that Labour would be 'tough on crime, and tough on the causes of crime'. Another slogan which Brown coined was 'lurch to the right', which Labour used with growing frequency when attacking Major for appeasing right-wing Tory MPs. Brown's talent for 'kicking his colleagues into swift and effective responses' was praised by the *Daily Mail*'s columnist Simon Heffer, in whose view the shadow Chancellor had one of the 'best strategic brains' on Labour's front bench.

Despite Brown's encouragement, however, the approach being

adopted by Ms Johnson, of using the latest news stories as vehicles for promoting Labour's ideas and policies, appeared to find little favour with Peter Mandelson. A month after becoming director, she told friends that she rarely spoke to him. She discovered he did not always share her preoccupation with daily news, although she believed it was her wealth of experience with BBC and ITN in handling instant reaction to political stories which had made her so attractive to the party in the first place. Her work of necessity often required her to flit from one news story to the next, and she told me she was shocked to discover that Mandelson had spoken of her in contemptuous terms as 'having, like most journalists, the attention span of a gnat'. Ms Johnson came to the conclusion that he disliked allowing the party's publicity initiatives to be so dominated by the news events of the day because it weakened the party's control in deciding who should speak for Labour, making it harder to promote those high-profile members of the front-bench team who were favoured by Blair and Mandelson. Reliance on a news-dominated agenda could also exacerbate the presentational problems inherent in pushing through long-term policy changes.

The tension was only too apparent as party officials began assembling in Brighton for the annual conference. When I met Ms Johnson in the reception of the Metropole hotel, her first words to me were that she wanted to leave. 'You can't understand how awful it is. Blair won't take my advice. It's only Mandelson he listens to. I hate it. The backbiting is terrible, just like the BBC, only worse. I've got to look for another job.' Despite her evident distress she put on a brave public face. Unfortunately Ms Johnson could sometimes be her own worst enemy. She had, rather unwisely I thought, used the conference guide to mock the way Mandelson and Campbell cultivated personal publicity. In describing her work as campaigns director she said she had no wish to become a 'household name' with a profile as high as the politicans she served. 'I am not a spin doctor for the very good reason that we won't win by spin. We will win by getting our policies right and then organising in support of them.' She had mentioned no names, but it was obvious she believed the messengers were getting in the way of the message. Political correspondents interpreted her article as an implied rebuke to Mandelson and Campbell. It was also regarded as public confirmation of the infighting which journalists suspected was going on, behind the scenes, among Blair's closest advisers. Peter Oborne, writing in the *Evening Standard*, predicted that Ms Johnson's 'unprovoked attack' would precipitate open warfare among Labour's 'ubiquitous spin doctors'.

Television and radio journalists had to tended become rather wary of Ms Johnson. They knew that her intimate knowledge of broadcasting techniques meant she could usually work out fairly accurately how newsrooms would react to the day's political events. Her ability to plug in instantly to the sometimes baffling terminology which broadcasters used in everyday conversation was of considerable value to the party. Early on the second morning of the conference she picked up talk of the dilemma facing the evening news bulletins and programmes in deciding whether to lead on Blair's speech to the conference that afternoon or on the imminent verdict from the much-publicised trial in Los Angeles of the black celebrity, O. J. Simpson. Ms Johnson thought that whatever the newsrooms decided Blair could only benefit because of the large audiences which the news bulletins would attract that evening. Her advice was ignored, and Campbell set in motion a chain of events which ended in considerable embarrassment and dissipated some of the impact of Blair's speech. As is so often the case, exactly what happened remains a matter of dispute, but Blair's staff were clearly agitated at the thought that his conference address might not lead the evening news bulletins and could get swamped by coverage of the Simpson trial. If Mandelson acquired operational intelligence of the kind obtained by Ms Johnson, and he considered there was a likelihood Labour could be disadvantaged, he would not hesitate to apply pressure on editors and producers, but he preferred to do it informally. He knew that if there was the merest public suggestion of a heavy-handed attempt to influence television and radio coverage this could become a news item in itself and distract attention from the party's objectives.

Forty minutes before Blair was due to start speaking to the conference, one of his press officers, Tim Allan, surprised reporters waiting in the foyer of the Metropole hotel by giving them details of an urgent fax which he said was to be sent out immediately from the leader's office, reminding BBC and ITN of their 'responsibilities' as public broadcasters to report Blair's speech. In the event BBC television's *Six o'Clock News* opened with live shots from Los Angeles of Judge Ito as he prepared to announce the jury's verdict; but the first report, before the programme returned live to the courtroom, was a detailed commentary on Blair's address in Brighton and his vision of 'New Labour, New Britain' in which he promised to transform the nation into a 'young country again'. His speech topped the *Nine o'Clock News*. *News at Ten* led with the O.J. verdict, relegating coverage of the Labour conference to second place. Earlier, ITN had extended its tea-time bulletin in order to take in the 'not guilty' verdict live from Los Angeles.

Next morning, Campbell was delighted with the prominence BBC television had given Blair's speech. Seeing me standing with a group of newspaper reporters in the press room, he walked over, wagged his finger at me rather accusingly, and said the BBC should be congratulated for having shown 'excellent news judgement for a change'. He then turned to the other reporters and said their next headline should be: 'Blair praises BBC'. John Deans of the *Daily Mail* asked for a comment on a line in the *Daily Telegraph*'s report which suggested that Campbell had been in a 'tizzy' all day over the possibility the BBC might lead on O. J. Simpson. Campbell walked off without replying. However, word got round that he was particularly forthright when challenged about his fax by the *Today* presenter John Humphrys, who was said to have told him, in an off-air encounter, that Labour should be ashamed of engaging in such blatant news management. 'But it worked,' retorted Campbell. When Humphrys suggested Campbell should be sacked, Blair chipped in, saying he had thought of giving his press officer a pay rise instead.

Campbell's bravado was about to take a knock. The first edition of the *Evening Standard* splashed over its front page a report of what it said was a 'massive internal' row within the BBC over the way editors had 'caved in' to Labour's pressure. An immediate denial was issued by the BBC. It said the suggestion that the *Nine o'Clock News* had been influenced by political pressure was defamatory because the editor had decided that morning to lead on Blair, long before Campbell had faxed his letter. Nevertheless a spin doctor, and not the party leader, had suddenly become the focus of the news media's attention. In an attempt to convince journalists that his appeal to the BBC and ITN had been 'completely measured and non-intimidatory', Campbell released the text of his letter. It said that while he accepted 'news judgements' must be made in the light of the day's news, he wanted to make a personal appeal to both the BBC's director general John Birt and ITN's editor Nigel Dacre: 'I would implore you not to lose sight of the news value and of the importance to the country of Blair's speech.' The following morning's newspapers had a field day. 'Blair's henchman bullies the Beeb by fax' was the headline over the *Sun*'s report that Campbell had suggested 'Tony is bigger than O.J.'. The *Daily Mail* concluded that either the 'poor old state-funded Beeb bowed to pressure' or was 'guilty of a massive news misjudgement'. Campbell's action in putting his appeal in writing, and then releasing it to the press, was regarded as the height of näiveté by Ms Johnson. Blair's office, she told me, should have realised it would backfire. There was always a danger that any big political story might be dropped by the bulletins if news came in of a royal death or serious disaster. Once the conference was over, the BBC announced that Birt had informed senior party officials that he considered Campbell's attempt to influence the running order of the news bulletins 'crass and inappropriate'. Key editorial decision-makers had been assured of the management's determination to support the 'editorial independence' of the BBC's journalism.

Campbell used his column in the following week's *Tribune* to mount another scathing attack on the BBC. He complained of a 'ridiculous fuss' over his 'gentle little letter' to Birt. 'A temperate reminder' of Labour's concern that the O. J. Simpson trial might 'squeeze out' coverage of Blair's speech was 'perfectly in order' and he was not going to be stopped from 'lodging similar thoughts' in future. Warming to his theme, Campbell then berated the BBC for its 'absurd' decision to delay the start of the *One o'Clock News* on the opening day of the Conservative conference so as to continue live coverage of Dr Brian Mawhinney's first speech as party chairman. At the root of Campbell's tirade was his dissastisfaction with the BBC's structures for handling complaints. He wanted to know if there was a 'meaningful way' of seeking redress which did not involve 'buck-passing' and the BBC's 'ususal "How dare you attack our integrity?"' scatter gun'. Campbell must have regarded the BBC as an easy target following what was, after all, a pretty severe mauling. He had been nursing a bruised ego all week. A damning profile in the *Spectator* examined the 'explosive evasiveness' of Blair's 'most potent weapon'. Campbell's trademark was 'eyeball-to-eyeball confrontation' with 'unhelpful' political correspondents. 'He hectors, cajoles and shouts. . . to ensure that the browbeaten journalist thinks twice in future.'

Labour's top spin doctors appeared oblivious to the possibility that their conduct might become counterproductive. The menacing way they dealt with offending journalists was being aped by the party's younger press officers, who lacked both the knowledge and the experience to carry off intimidatory behaviour. Even before the conference had started I was rebuked about the way I was reporting a meeting at which delegates were deciding on the composite motions to be debated that week. Among those attending were representatives of the Leeds North East constituency who wanted to challenge the national executive's decision to deselect their candidate Liz Davies. Nigel Harris, chairman of the disputes committee, said he would resign if the committee was forced to reconsider its decision. My first broadcast that lunchtime went hard on the threat of a resignation. Immediately afterwards I was called over by Campbell's assistant, Tim Allan, who had joined Blair's staff after working briefly as a television researcher on leaving university. Allan said Blair's office wanted to know why the BBC had run the story. He asked me to explain why I had used someone he had 'never heard of' to speak on behalf of the Labour Party. I pointed out that Harris was on the executive of the Amalgamated Engineering and Electrical Union and, only the previous week, had backed Blair publicly by describing Liz Davies as a 'cancer eating away' at the party. At this Allan backed off. Paul Routledge, political correspondent of the *Independent on Sunday*, was highly amused. He told me he had clashed with

Allan at the previous year's conference. In response to a casual enquiry about whether Blair could sing 'The Red Flag' Allan told Routledge, as though he should have known better, that Blair had been rehearsing the words all week. 'Allan saw me writing this down and immediately got all hot and flustered. He ordered me to stop taking notes. He said: "You can't use that." I said "Yes, I can," and it went in the paper the next Sunday.'

Complaints were again the order of the day after I reported on the aftermath of a private gathering of union leaders in the shadow Cabinet room a fortnight before the conference at which Blair had 'emphasised the need for a good conference' in Brighton. A leaked copy of the minutes, obtained by the *Daily Telegraph*, revealed that Blair had stressed to the assembled general secretaries the importance of the public seeing a 'united party with a clear purpose and agenda'. Conservative Central Office was quick to exploit what Dr Mawhinney claimed was proof that Blair was 'still in bed with the unions'. Late in the evening, as soon as other journalists started hearing about the *Daily Telegraph*'s exclusive, Gordon Brown's press officer, Charlie Whelan, was one of those assigned to the task of damage limitation. His job was to persuade other political correspondents to ignore the story. 'I had to rubbish it as quickly as possible so as to make sure it wasn't followed up by the papers like *The Times*, *Daily Mail* and *Sun*. You'd be amazed how gullible political correspondents can be once they're all sitting round a table in a restaurant. At that time of night all they want to hear is that another newspaper's exlusive isn't really a story at all. Usually it's quite easy to convince them.'

The 'extreme lengths' to which Labour went in demolishing the story were discussed by Michael Jones in his weekly column in the *Sunday Times*. He said that 'trying to teach journalism to journalists' by saying a meeting was not news was the classic defence of a politician in trouble. Perhaps not surprisingly, in view of his success, Whelan tended to be quite brazen about his ability to lead journalists astray. If he wanted to get an unfavourable report dropped altogether he would often turn to his colleagues for help. After one of Campbell's rather tiresome complaints I began to cross-question him as to exactly what he thought my television report had contained. As it soon became obvious Campbell had not even seen the item he was objecting to, I suggested he might care to watch the news bulletins before complaining. Next day Whelan admitted he had asked Campbell to make the call, fearing that if he had rung me himself I would have told him to 'get lost'. Indeed, Whelan said he rarely complained directly to reporters or editors but instead asked Campbell or Ms Johnson to do it for him. On one occasion Judith Dawson, a political correspondent on Sky News, suspected that Ms Johnson, because of her familiarity with television jargon, was probably behind a complaint from Campbell. 'He rang to say I had taken the wrong grab from a speech. I said pardon, surely journalists can still decide for themselves what they think is the soundbite?'

Mandelson seemed determined to remain above the fray as the final preparations were being made for the conference. Despite being addicted to gossiping with journalists, he was going through a phase of reminding all and sundry that he should no longer be regarded as a spin doctor. However, he spent much of his time hovering in the Metropole's foyer and, like a moth drawn to a storm lantern, he appeared unable to pull himself away once he was engaged in conversation. I soon discovered from chatting with other reporters that he was especially incensed by my eve-of-conference report that some left-wing constituencies might force a vote on their demand that the party set a national minimum wage of £4.15p an hour. In the event the Edinburgh Central constituency withdrew its resolution, averting a confrontation. As the week progressed a succession of votes went the leadership's way. When I remarked on this to Mandelson he offered his commiserations, saying he realised I must be 'terribly disappointed'. Next evening, in an address to the Young Fabians, he launched his own attack on the BBC's coverage. Arriving at the platform before the meeting had opened, Mandelson took off his jacket, placed it carefully on the back of his chair for a moment and then put it back on again. I found his action rather puzzling. However, as soon as he was introduced as the guest speaker he provided the television crews with a meticulous sequence of opening shots. While the audience was applauding him, Mandelson stood up, reached across to pour a glass of water and then removed his jacket, placing it on the back of his chair. His rehearsal paid off. He had supplied some eye-catching footage for use in a television report. I was sitting on the front row and had my tape recorder on my knees. Mandelson acknowledged my presence in his opening remarks, dismissing me with a flourish: '. . . Nicholas Jones, our old friend from the BBC, who was busy manning the barricades on Saturday night, fomenting rebellion, revolt and a non-existent backlash on BBC television news'.

My 'offence' had been to report the aspirations of Old Labour. A campaign by some constituencies to persuade the conference to set the minimum wage at £4.15p an hour was seen as a potential danger by the party leadership because it could be used by the Conservatives to put a price on Labour's programme. I knew Mandelson's anger at the BBC's reporting of the delegates' demands chimed in precisely with Blair's views. At the TUC conference the previous month, when the unions were persuaded to hold back from putting a figure on the minimum wage, Blair had derided the work of journalists like myself who took an interest in trade union and employment issues. He ridiculed our 'old rituals of winding up the issues' at each union conference where 'those labour correspondents, eagerly snatching every bit of inside information from the bars and committee rooms, dramatise each event as if the destiny of the nation is at stake. It's like living in a time warp. For the country's sake, let us move on.' Next morning, when Blair was attending a working breakfast at the conference hotel, I had thanked him for his name-check for the dwindling band of labour correspondents. Campbell laughed. I guessed he had purposely written that line into Blair's speech so as to poke fun at the journalists covering the TUC conference. Blair shook his head at me in mock pity: 'It must be very sad being a labour correspondent, writing about all those meaningless union resolutions. I do wish you could find a different agenda.'

Blair's reproachful words kept coming back to me a month later as I compiled my reports in Brighton on the outcome of the various delegation meetings and the arguments about the wording of the composite motions. Over the years these events have acted as the traditional curtain-raiser to Labour conferences, but Blair's advisers were anxious to sweep away these images of Old Labour. Instead of filming noisy meetings in the smoke-filled rooms of the sea-front hotels, the television camera crews and newspaper photographers were being pointed by the spin doctors in an alternative, more attractive direction. Blair and Prescott, together with their wives, had gone to the races. Brighton racecourse was bedecked with posters for Labour's Rolling Rose membership campaign. The evening news bulletins, and the daily papers, all had pictures of the Labour leader and his deputy, binoculars at the ready, scanning the runners and riders from the directors' box. Next morning Campbell was at Blair's side for another stunning photo opportunity. Kevin Keegan, the Newcastle United manager, had teamed up with Labour to promote the party's proposals for a standard entry charge at football grounds. Blair went head-to-head with Keegan, keeping the ball in the air for twenty-seven consecutive headers. The camera crews and photographers joined in the applause. Blair told me later that it had required maximum concentration and had been potentially the most dangerous photo call of the week. 'I knew that if I missed that first header, you lot would have loved making fun of me.' In fact, if he had fluffed it, the resulting footage would have been in the same league as the ill-fated occasion when Neil Kinnock fell on Brighton beach and was caught by an incoming wave.

Labour's supremacy in gaining favourable publicity was a source of envious comment at the Conservative conference the following week. Lord Tebbit was among those who told me how much he admired the effectiveness of Blair's spin doctors. His one reservation was that the 'cohort of young men' who formed a 'presidential guard' around Blair were in danger of becoming a barrier between the Labour leader and his members. 'The trouble is, Labour's spin doctors are exceptionally pushy. They have been magnificently efficient in delivering the party to him but they might end up getting between him and the party and then damage his rapport with his colleagues. Spin doctors should take away the message they are given and then promote it, but if party leaders aren't careful they start to rely on the spin doctors' version of what's really happening in the world outside.' Tebbit's cautionary words had followed hard on the heels of an exclusive report in the *Guardian* which revealed that Blair had been urged to establish a 'unitary command structure' leading directly to the party leader. This was one of several recommendations in an internal memorandum entitled 'The Unfinished Revolution', written by Philip Gould, a former advertising executive who advised Labour on polling and strategy. Gould was a close friend of Mandelson and had become one of Blair's most trusted political advisers. His assertion that Labour was not 'ready for government' caught the attention of the newspapers, but the real interest for party insiders lay in his conclusion that Labour was still not a 'genuine one-member, one-vote party' and lacked the 'campaigning operation' needed to ensure victory at the general election. He advised that Blair should be the 'sole, ultimate source of campaigning authority' and chair campaign meetings. Gould assigned a role to each of the spin doctors: Alastair Campbell, message; Peter Mandelson, implementation; Joy Johnson, rebuttal.

Campbell's 'message' about the memo was that it was six months out of date. He told me it was just one of many documents which had passed across the Labour leader's desk, giving advice on future strategy. He was desperate to play down Gould's suggestion that Blair's advisers would take all the key positions in the campaign team. While a new command structure would be needed in time for the election, any organisational changes would not give 'uncontrolled power' to the spin doctors; political control would remain in the hands of elected politicians.

Campbell's briefings were taking place against a background of what was being described as 'seething discontent' within the parliamentary party. Elections to the shadow Cabinet were due to be held the following month, and Labour MPs who regarded themselves as traditionalists believed Blair had authorised his spin doctors to promote the modernisers at their expense. Gould's memo was being seen as final confirmation of Blair's disregard for the views of his colleagues. Among those seeking re-election was Ron Davies, spokesman on Welsh affairs, who was convinced he was the victim of negative spin. Davies took his complaints straight to Blair. 'I told him directly what I was hearing, that Mandelson and Campbell were briefing journalists against me. Apparently I was being criticised for having gone native over a Welsh assembly. Blair denied this. He insisted that if there were any briefings they were being done without his knowledge or authority. Blair said that all that Mandelson did was advise him on how things were likely to be treated in the news media.' Despite these reassuring words, Davies urged Blair to give Mandelson a front-bench job 'so that he wouldn't always be talking to journalists'. In the event, the shadow Cabinet elections, and the consequent reshuffle, turned out propitiously for both Davies and Mandelson. Traditionalists secured the largest share of the vote, with Davies taking fourth place. MPs who held unelected junior positions, and whose chances had been talked up by the modernisers, failed to achieve a breakthrough but, as widely expected, Mandelson was given a front-bench job.

The activities of the spin doctors had also been attracting the interest of one of Labour's elder statesmen. Lord Cocks of Hartcliffe, a former Labour chief whip who served in the Callaghan government, and now vice-chairman of the BBC's governors, had begun keeping a watchful eye on the way political press officers were seeking to influence BBC journalists. He had started his detailed investigation in the summer of 1995, taking advantage of the political lull provided by the parliamentary recess, and consulted widely among BBC staff. When Cocks discovered that Campbell had gone 'way over the top' in sending a fax to the director general, he felt the governors had at last been provided with the opportunity they had been waiting for to assert the editorial independence of the BBC. A fortnight after the party conference Tony Hall, managing director of news and current affairs, announced that the Corporation's political journalists had been told to monitor the telephone calls they received. Editors, producers and correspondents would have the BBC's 'full support in resisting intimidation or bullying of any kind'. The BBC had to steer a clear line between calls from political parties which were designed to provide information and those which amounted to an 'intolerable invasion' of the requirement for journalists to make 'impartial, independent judgements'. If necessary the BBC would have to divert calls away for an hour before transmission so as to make sure that producers had the best chance to get the 'most accurate, fair and authoritative' news programmes on air. In a debate in the House of Lords, Cocks defended the governors' action in trying to uphold the BBC's impartiality. He said the spin doctors had been using 'increasingly desperate tactics' to persuade journalists to favour their political cause. One ploy was to allege political bias in a particular news item and then, in what seemed to be 'intentional time wasting', make protracted calls at inopportune moments. By monitoring all calls, faxes and letters, and assessing their relevance and content at a weekly meeting of the

management, Cocks hoped it would be possible to sort out those complaints which were justified and pass on any lessons to the staff concerned.

Campbell appeared to be genuinely taken aback by the continuing
fallout from his Brighton fax. I had rarely experienced contrition on the
part of Labour's publicity staff, but I did detect signs of a recognition
that perhaps the 1995 conference had been something of a high-water
mark in their belligerence. Throughout the autumn there was a string of
unsettling developments. Newspapers predicted, quite regularly, the
imminent departure of Joy Johnson. Seumas Milne, writing in the
Guardian, said she had come under 'strong pressure' to resign. Gordon
Brown's continuing success in capturing the headlines seemed to provoke only dissent within the shadow Cabinet. When the shadow Chancellor announced that a Labour government would cut up to £17 a
week from the social security benefits being paid to workshy young
people, he was accused of treading on the toes of his colleagues. Campbell was forced to issue a statement to the Press Association explaining
why Brown sometimes ranged into 'other people's territory'. As the
shadow Chancellor chaired the daily news management meetings where
Ms Johnson and her staff discussed ideas for promoting the party's
policies, decisions had to be taken to 'respond to events as they happened'. However, Brown intended to make sure there was much closer
consultation and cooperation in the future.

Continuing unfavourable press comment about Blair's overtures
towards Rupert Murdoch began to unsettle Campbell in his parallel
charm offensive with reporters on tabloid newspapers, including the
Sun. Blair had been a guest speaker that summer at a conference in
Queensland attended by two hundred of the most influential editors and
managers in the Murdoch empire. Campbell said that Labour had
nothing to apologise for in taking the chance to put the case for left-of-
centre politics to one of the biggest media organisations in the world.
Blair told his audience that only a Labour government could complete
the social and economic revolution which Margaret Thatcher began
in the 1980s. The old battles between the market and the public
sector were over; the 'past should be behind us'. His speech had also
struck a conciliatory not towards Murdoch's British interests by not
specifying any precise limits on cross-media ownership, saying rather
that Labour believed the best way to achieve choice was to have an
'open and competitive' market backed by a 'proper framework of rules'.
Blair was congratulated by the *Evening Standard* for a speech that had
'dazzling style, panache and sheer chutzpah'. The Labour leader had
chalked up another 'big success with his Australian adventure'. Other
newspapers took a more jaundiced view. Robert Milliken, writing in the

Independent, said Blair had trodden the 'well worn path of rising political figures unable to resist the media magnate's flattery'. The *Observer* believed Murdoch's invitation was an 'insurance policy' for his news-papers and television services, just as Blair was hoping in return not to be damaged by 'scaremongering stories'.

As the months went by, some newspapers became increasingly suspic-ious of Blair's 'cosying up' to News International. After the *Independent* exposed Labour's reluctance to comment on allegations of tax avoidance by Murdoch's newspapers, the *Guardian* declared that the 'power of the Murdoch empire' cried out to be taken on. It said Labour appeared 'so mesmerised' by the prospect of Murdoch's 'rotten borough' being delivered to Blair 'on a platter' that the party's spokes-men had acquired 'frozen lips'. Cherie Blair had no such inhibitions. While in conversation at an official dinner with the *Sun*'s columnist Anne Robinson she was asked if she ever read Murdoch's biggest-selling news-paper. Robinson reported Mrs Blair's frank response: 'Certainly not. I wouldn't have it in the house.' Stephen Glover, writing in the *Evening Standard*, said that if Mrs Blair despised the *Sun* then one could be pretty sure that her husband did too. Glover considered the interests of Labour and the *Sun* were irreconcilable, and that therefore the 'love-in' between Blair and Murdoch was 'utterly bogus'. Mrs Blair's candour, moreover, paid scant regard to the long hours Campbell had spent ghost-writing her husband's many articles for the *Sun*.

Campbell's sharp news sense rarely let him down. There seemed to be no limit to his willingness to do what was best for the party. One blind spot, however, appeared to be his reluctance to come to terms with the way Blair and several other members of the front-bench team were rejecting their local comprehensives and sending their children to grant-maintained secondary schools which had opted out of local authority control in response to the government's efforts to widen parental choice. When the Blairs chose the London Oratory, a highly regarded Catholic school, for their eldest son Euan, Campbell warned that this would inevitably attract damaging publicity. In what was taken to be a sign of his own dissatisfaction with the decision, he left it to other press officers to field most of the calls from reporters. As one of the inner circle, Campbell would have been among the first to have been notified when the shadow health secretary Harriet Harman informed Blair's office just before Christmas 1995 that her son Joseph had been accepted by St Olave's in Orpington, an opted-out grammar school which operated a selective entry system. Although the Blairs' choice of the Oratory had provoked hostile banner headlines in the popular papers the previous year, just as Campbell had predicted, no action was taken to prepare for a similar onslaught when news of Ms Harman's decision leaked out a month later.

Despite all the plaudits Labour's spin doctors had attracted, they behaved as if they had been caught completely unawares by what turned out to be the worst public relations disaster since Blair's election as party leader.

It was the *Daily Mail* which broke the story about Joseph Harman, just as it had been first with the news on Euan Blair. Under the headline 'Harriet's Hypocrisy', it said the choice of 'one of Britain's most selective grammar schools' by Ms Harman and her husband Jack Dromey heaped embarrassment on Labour, 'making a mockery of its commitment to non-elitist education'. The story had emerged on a Saturday morning, and there seemed to be an expectation by Blair's advisers that it might not make much of an impact in the short weekend news bulletins. Anna Healy, who was Labour's duty press officer, told me Ms Harman would not be commenting or giving interviews. Reporters were referred to a statement she had given to that morning's *Independent* and *Daily Mirror*. Ms Harman said her son's success in winning a place at St Olave's had got 'absolutely nothing' to do with the fact that she was an MP. It was a state school, available to every other local child, 'irrespective of income'. David Blunkett, the shadow education spokesman, said Ms Harman's choice of school was 'entirely one for her and her husband to make'.

Having spent so many uncomfortable weekends enduring abuse from Labour, the Conservatives were soon scoring every political point they could. Gillian Shephard, the Secretary of State for Education, weighed in immediately, accusing Ms Harman of double standards for having chosen a selective school for her son when 'Labour's stated policy of opposing selection would remove those choices from everyone else.' Once news of Mrs Shephard's counter-attack emerged in mid-morning, Labour's spin doctors faced what in retrospect was the point of no return. If they had wanted to try to close the story down, this was the moment to have offered Ms Harman for television and radio interviews. She could then have explained that she and her husband had made their decision in the best interest of their child, which was what any parents would do, and it was not a matter of party politics. In the event neither Ms Harman nor any other senior Labour figure was available for interview that Saturday. Mrs Shephard had the news bulletins to herself. As the story took off, Labour failed to fight their corner.

Clare Short, the shadow transport secretary, was the first member of the front bench to be cross-questioned on television, having been booked previously for an appearance on GMTV's *Sunday Programme*. She was briefed the night before by Labour's chief media spokesperson, David Hill, and stressed that she was anxious to be as supportive as possible. Ms Short was as good as her word, making it clear that this was an entirely personal matter – but then, in an unexpectedly frank turn of phrase, she expanded on her answer: 'I honestly don't know all the details and why Harriet and Jack have made that decision, and they must make the decision for their child and must answer to Harriet's constituents for it.' Although she denied vehemently that her reply could in any way be construed as critical, Ms Short did seem to imply a mild rebuke. By suggesting that her shadow Cabinet colleague had something to 'answer for', Ms Short was acknowledging that a decision of this kind might attact criticism in Ms Harman's inner London constituency of Peckham. St Olave's was eleven miles away from the family home in the London borough of Southwark.

Ms Short's unintended prediction proved entirely correct. Several Labour MPs, including Tony Banks and Ken Livingstone, lost no time in criticising Ms Harman's decision. There was a fresh development the following Monday morning when Gerry Steinberg announced that as a mark of his 'disgust and outrage' he was resigning from the chairmanship of Labour's parliamentary education committee. Conservative MPs were cock-a-hoop. At last they had found a way to needle Blair. They believed their charge of hypocrisy was easily understood by the public: Labour leaders were saying one thing but doing another. Presenters of radio phone-in programmes were as keen on the story as the Conservatives. Ms Harman's decision, and the controversy it provoked over Labour's education policy, produced strong audience reaction. One producer told me that it was the kind of simplistic issue which they longed for because it attracted opinionated callers who enjoyed sounding off.

Peter Mandelson was outraged by the way the story was being reported. Instead of dying down, as he had hoped, it had remained headline news for three days. He was particularly incensed by what he claimed was the action of the BBC in 'driving the coverage along'. He told one correspondent he thought the Corporation had become the 'plaything' of the *Daily Mail*. Another reporter was quizzed on his motives and then told in no uncertain terms that journalists were mistaken if they thought they could force Ms Harman's resignation. On the fourth day of the controversy, amid reports that some Labour MPs were calling on Blair to sack Ms Harman, Campbell was suddenly at the forefront of the fight-back, telling journalists that the shadow health secretary had not been abandoned by the leadership, and the Labour leader had no intention of dismissing her. Until this somewhat delayed intervention Campbell had left the impression with some reporters that he was holding back, as though, during the weekend build-up of the story, he had somehow been sitting on his hands in protest. When it became obvious that Blair's own credibility was at stake, however, Campbell's forceful briefings were just what was needed to help take the heat out of the story. Blair acted decisively in Ms Harman's support. When faced by Tory jeers at question time, he hit back, saying Conservative MPs were deluding themselves if they thought they could 'ride back to popularity on the back of a decision about eleven-year-old boys'. In response to John Major's taunt about his inability to sack Ms Harman because she was 'playing follow my leader', Blair rounded on the Prime Minister, saying the difference between them was that he would not 'buckle' under pressure. Blair's steely performance helped Labour turn the corner. Campbell told reporters that Ms Harman, who was to speak in a Commons debate the following day, would have to tough it out, just as Blair had at question time. In the event, she stood at the despatch box with confidence. Earlier that morning she had apologised to the parliamentary Labour party, saying she deeply regretted the distress she had caused. Blair appealed to the party to stand firm. He said the Tories were not going to get his health secretary's scalp.

My own reporting of the Harman affair had attracted some criticism within the BBC. Senior editors disliked one sequence in the footage I had used to illustrate my television report on the day the story broke. After being informed by Anna Healy that Ms Harman would not be interviewed, or even take a telephone call from the BBC, I advised David Hill that I had been asked to approach her at her home to see if she would respond. I was filmed ringing the front door bell. There was a small twitch of a curtain but no reply. I felt this illustrated Labour's refusal to comment. After transmission it was deemed to be 'a shot too far'. While the exterior of the house was being filmed, from the opposite side of the road, a car stopped outside and a young boy got out and went inside. The cameraman said he thought he had caught a fleeting glimpse of the back of the boy. On driving past Ms Harman's house a second time, after filming at St Olave's, I called again, but without the television crew, and spoke to Jack Dromey. He said his wife would not give me an interview. I alerted him to the fact that we might have taken a shot of his son earlier that morning and enquired whether the boy we had filmed was his son. I knew that because of BBC guidelines on the filming of children I would need to advise the editor of the day. Dromey made it clear he had no wish to discuss this, but he reminded me of what he said were the rulings by the Press Complaints Commission about publishing photographs of children without the parents' consent. I readily acknowledged the position and said I was sure the BBC had no intention of using the film. I tried to be entirely open about what had happened and, as I recalled it, our conversation passed off quite amicably. After all, I had been interviewing Dromey on and off for twenty years; I first made his acquaintance during the long-running industrial dispute at the

Grunwick film processing works in 1977 and had been in fairly regular contact with him thereafter because of his position as a senior official in the Transport and General Workers' Union.

Although I appeared to have been the only television reporter to have visited the house that Saturday, and I did not go again, there was a much bigger media presence the following Monday morning when Joseph left for school. Ms Harman objected to the Press Complaints Commission about the conduct of the cameramen and photographers. She said they surged forward as her son walked out of the door and he had to run away when one stills photographer started 'chasing after him'. In the event no newspaper published a picture of Joseph, and most denied having sent photographers to the house. Because I was concerned as to whether my visit the previous Saturday might have caused offence I sought the opinion next morning of Labour's chief whip, Donald Dewar. He said he had seen my report that Saturday and personally did not object to it; what Ms Harman had complained about was the action of cameramen and photographers that Monday morning. However, the following day I was informed that Peter Mandelson had complained to the BBC about the footage I had used. On being told that Ms Harman considered that my visit to her house, and the filming outside, had upset her children I wrote to 'apologise unreservedly' for any distress I had caused. To my mind it was an open and shut case: if any mother felt my action as a reporter had distressed her children then I would be anxious to make amends as quickly as possible. I explained in my letter that I recognised that the 'robust treatment' which politicians do not always enjoy but have come to expect, 'must be tempered when a politician's children are involved and the privacy and sanctity of a politician's family home fully respected'.

I delivered the letter myself to Ms Harman's office. It was handwritten and the envelope marked 'personal'. The following day Jon Craig, the political editor of the *Daily Express*, asked me to explain why I had thought it necessary to apologise. He said he had been tipped off about it and my letter had been read to him. He would not say who had supplied the information. Next morning the *Daily Express* reported that I had apologised after claims that I 'harassed' Ms Harman's family; Craig said that Ms Harman and her husband were out when I was filmed ringing her door bell but 'their three children were inside, being looked after by a friend'. Once I had sent my apology I naturally hoped it would be accepted. I did not mind it becoming public knowledge. Nevertheless I was naturally interested to discover more about how it was leaked. I knew that Mandelson had taken a close interest in the story from the start, and therefore I thought he was probably responsible for engineering the tip-off to Jon Craig. I assumed the *Daily Express* had been chosen because it would not usually publish a story sympathetic to Ms Harman and also because it was a newspaper which would probably take an anti-BBC line. Mandelson seemed pleased by the way it was reported and had no compunction about discussing it with my colleagues. He said the contents of my letter had been released to the *Daily Express* because it had only been marked 'personal' and was not stated as being 'private and confidential'. Mandelson confirmed that the story had been given to only one newspaper but said it could have been 'put up in lights for the Sunday papers' if that had been what was wanted.

Some days elapsed before my next encounter with Mandelson, which followed the publication of an opinion poll in the *Guardian* showing that a majority of voters felt that Ms Harman was right to let her son go to a grammar school and that she would have been wrong to resign. Mandelson said he hoped I had taken due note of the findings, which he felt justified his assertion that the BBC had 'over-stepped' the mark in its reporting of the story. I broached the question of my apology but he did not respond. However, he did discuss Labour's tactics in handling the story. He felt that even if Ms Harman had given a television and radio interview that Saturday morning it might well have fuelled the coverage rather than closed it down. He thought the most important lesson from the whole saga was that it illustrated the wisdom of his advice that the Labour leadership should hold their nerve when faced by a runaway news story. He said this was exactly what Blair had done. There was always a danger in such circumstances that the party could exaggerate the likely damage and take panic measures. If faced by a similar situation again, he would play it in exactly the same way.

Mine was not the only wry footnote to the Harman affair. Joy Johnson took advantage of the furore to announce her resignation. It had been common knowledge for several weeks that she was in the process of discussing her departure with the party. These negotiations had apparently taken some time, it was assumed because she was insisting on some kind of agreement to ensure that neither side discussed publicly what was clearly an irreconcilable clash of personalities. Ms Johnson believed the timing of her announcement illustrated her professionalism. Her resignation attracted some coverage but it was overshadowed by news about Ms Harman. Ms Johnson stuck rigidly to her side of the agreement, steadfastly refusing to enlarge on her short formal statement.

Mandelson's confident assertions about the effectiveness of Labour's handling of the Harman affair were not widely shared. From what I could discover, both Campbell and Hill and wished it had been dealt with rather more rigorously. There was a general feeling that Ms Harman should have explained her position on television and radio straight away, perhaps through a short, controlled interview on the doorstep of her home that Saturday morning. Alternatively, the party should have ensured that senior shadow Cabinet members spoke up firmly in her support, right from the start. Labour's ineptitude heralded a rethink, especially by some newspaper reporters, of the way they were tackling other stories about the party. The tone of the coverage did seem to become far tougher and more personalised. Cherie Blair became a regular target, and Mandelson was particularly annoyed with the conduct of the *Daily Mail* and *Daily Express*, which he felt were engaged in a 'vicious' pursuit of the Labour leader's wife. A constant theme of the coverage was the suggestion that Mrs Blair was influencing party policy. In an attempt to compare her with the wife of the President of the United States, she was dubbed 'Britain's would-be Hillary Clinton' by the *Daily Express* correspondent Peter Hitchens. After a highly publicised trawl Hitchens unearthed a copy of her election address when she stood, under her maiden name of Cherie Booth, as Labour candidate for Thanet North in 1983. Hitchens justified his investigation on the grounds that Mrs Blair was a public figure in her own right: she was a leading barrister and made frequent speeches on legal reform. In a letter to the *Guardian*, Hitchens said it was 'absurd to imagine that this intelligent and highly political woman never discusses major issues with her husband'.

As the attacks increased, Mandelson challenged me to investigate why some of the tabloids were already engaging in the kind of distortion which was usually only seen in the final days of an election campaign. In an interview recorded for *Today*, Mandelson told me he believed the *Daily Mail*, *Daily Express* and *Sun* were reverting to type because of 'pressure from a handful of owners at the top'. Their 'Labour bashing' was the result of 'collusion between Central Office and the Tory press'. Campbell also thought there had been a 'definite change' in the way the tabloids were treating Labour. He agreed that the intensity of the abuse had increased in the wake of the Harman episode. 'It's not as bad yet as it was under Neil Kinnock but we are worried about it. . . if the *Sun*, *Daily Mail*, *Daily Express* and *Daily Telegraph* all went against us that would be one hell of an attack. If it gets really nasty it could become a political issue.' Jon Craig replied for the tabloids. Writing in the *Guardian*, he accused Labour's spin doctors of developing 'acute paranoia' after being 'rattled by the Harmangate affair'.

Usually Mandelson would insist that he was anxious to avoid excessive personal exposure but he threw caution to the wind in order to promote his and Roger Liddle's book, *The Blair Revolution*. Almost every other day for several weeks there would be either a new profile in one of the newspapers or yet another mention in the gossip columns. When I complimented him on his success in gaining so much publicity, he

looked at me reprovingly. I assured him that I had read with great
interest his ideas on how Labour intended to strengthen the political role
of the back-up staff in Downing Street so as to ensure greater support for
Blair if he became Prime Minister. Mandelson had singled out the No.
10 press office as definitely needing a stronger political presence. I took
this as yet further confirmation of Campbell's likely appointment as
Downing Street press secretary should Labour win the election. Joy
Johnson's departure the previous month had left Mandelson reigning
supreme over Labour's newly commissioned media centre at Millbank
Tower, a short step from the House of Commons. Some of the newspaper
stories about Mandelson's book referred to the fact that he had finally
been installed as chairman of the group planning Labour's election campaign, an appointment first mooted publicly a year earlier at the time of
Blair's front-bench reshuffle. Although relishing the attention, Mandelson was getting drawn into rather dangerous territory. He had told me
repeatedly that his appointment as shadow public service minister,
together with the publication of his book, marked the 'end of his role as a
spin doctor'; yet this hardly accorded with his new responsibilities for
election campaigning and his new-found predilection for policy pronouncements.

Mandelson had always prided himself on his self-discipline; having
rebuked others for their loosely worded answers there had seemed no
danger that he might be lulled by a television interviewer into giving
incautious replies. When questioned on *A Week in Politics*, Mandelson
returned with a vengeance to his attack on the proprietors and editors of
Tory newspapers. He accused them of 'malice aforethought' in their
'premeditated decision to try to smear Labour' by 'dripping the poison,
distorting the image'. He then went on to warn the press that if their
'uninhibited exercise of commercial corporate power' amounted to
'direct political intervention' and affected the outcome of the next election then the 'pressure for change, for some sort of reform, will be almost
unstoppable'. If the electoral process was going to be 'constantly abused
and undermined' then 'parliament will have a duty to stand up and take
some action on behalf of the democratic system'.

Mandelson insisted that he did not support regulation of the press, but
media commentators interpreted his attack as a clear warning that
Labour was contemplating some form of legislation. Blair was urged by
the *Daily Mail* to repudiate 'every bullying word' which Mandelson had
uttered. It claimed no Labour leader had 'ever enjoyed anything like the
level of press support' given to Blair, who had won 'a substantial reputation as an intelligent, civilised, reforming leader'. Mandelson was taken
to task over his remarks by John Diamond, presenter of *Stop Press*, who
said it sounded as if a Labour government would establish 'a ministry of

truth'. Andrew Neil, one of the commentators interviewed by the programme, claimed the implicit threat in what Mandelson had said was that Labour would set up a statutory press authority if the newspapers did not behave. When Mandelson sought to reassure listeners that Labour did not support 'statutory curbs which limit freedom of speech in the press', Neil said that what they had just heard was the sound of 'gears going rapidly into reverse'.

The endless machinations of Labour's spin doctors were a source of encouragement for Conservative Central Office. The freedom which Blair allowed them, and the growing boldness of some of their interventions, were regarded as perpetual weak points in the Labour leadership's command structure. Lord Tebbit's conclusion that they formed an 'exceptionally pushy presidential guard', which might end up damaging Blair's rapport with his colleagues, was given unexpected backing by the experiences of the shadow transport secretary, Clare Short. While several shadow Cabinet members had complained before about having their reputations traduced by the spin doctors, Ms Short's contribution to the touchy topic of Labour's tax plans produced a spectacular display of savage backbiting. Her 'offence' was to express a willingness to contribute more of her earnings towards the state, should this be required by a future Labour government. She told GMTV's *Sunday Programme* that under a 'fair tax system' people like her 'would pay a bit more tax'. A few days earlier, on a trip to Washington, Blair had appeared to suggest that anyone earning up to £40,000 a year would not pay more tax under Labour. As Ms Short's annual salary as an MP was around £35,000 there was consternation among Blair's advisers. Her remarks were seized on by the Conservatives as confirmation of what they claimed was Labour's real intention to put up tax rates. Ms Short tried immediately to clarify her remarks, insisting that Labour had 'no intention of adding to the tax bills of middle-income families', but the damage had been done. She was seen to have ignored Blair's directive that Shadow Cabinet members should refrain from speculating about Labour's tax and spending plans. When asked by reporters to comment on this 'gaffe', Blair's press office responded with a blunt but chilling statement to the effect that Ms Short's 'colleagues were now questioning her competence and professionalism'. Some reporters told me they were instructed not to attribute this directly to Blair's office. A party press officer said she had been 'leant on' and asked to issue the same, unsourced comment.

Ms Short was deeply wounded at the way a statement attacking her judgement had been issued to the media without any consultation or warning. So angered was she by what had happened that when she was interviewed on the *Today* programme the next morning she could hardly have sounded more defiant. She defended her right to speak out: 'Someone like me, who says what I really think, is supposed to be quiet and not speak the truth. . . I will not be silenced.' She then hit back at the party's anonymous briefers: 'There are these unknown, so-called highly placed sources. . . I don't know who they are. . . I don't respect people who hide behind those kind of descriptions.' After a hurried telephone conversation with Blair, Ms Short withdrew from the rest of her scheduled television and radio interviews. She had been expected to comment that day on the government's plans for the flotation of Railtrack. When challenged by reporters at a news conference later that morning about the spin doctors' conduct, Alastair Campbell blamed the whole episode on the 'appallingly low standards of British journalism'. If it had not been for the original distortion of Ms Short's remarks there would have been no need for the statements 'clarifying' her remarks. Next morning, under the headline 'Knifed by the Blair enforcers', the *Daily Mail*'s political editor David Hughes analysed what he described as Ms Short's 'bruising twenty-four hours at the hands of Tony Blair's henchmen'. Her punishment had been a 'sly flash of the political switchblade', designed to teach her a lesson and demonstrate to the rest of the shadow Cabinet what would happen if they stepped 'out of line' under New Labour. Within a few days Ms Short was her usual buoyant self. Amid the trials and tribulations of railway privatisation she was soon redirecting her fire towards the government. Nevertheless her forthright retaliation when attacked by the spin doctors had drawn warm, private words of encouragement from some other aggrieved members of the shadow Cabinet. From what I discovered she regarded the character assassination being authorised in Blair's name as tantamount to political thuggery.

Just as the reverberations over Ms Short's brush with the authoritarianism of Blair's aides began to subside, Campbell suffered the ultimate indignity of having doubts cast on his own veracity in a forum where political spin counted for nothing. By an unfortunate twist of timing, no sooner had the media spotlight started to turn away from exposing the practices of Labour's 'anonymous briefers' than it suddenly refocused on the journalistic standards of Blair's principal lieutenant. In a throwback to his days as the *Daily Mirror*'s political editor, Campbell found himself in the High Court, where, together with Mirror Group Newspapers and another political journalist, Andy McSmith, he was being sued for malicious falsehood by the Conservative MP Rupert Allason over an article published in 1992. Allason said it was 'untrue in every material respect' to state that fifty MPs had signed a parliamentary motion calling on him to give Mirror pensioners the £250,000 in libel damages that he had just won from the paper. The judge, Sir Maurice Drake, ruled that the story was false and had been published with malice, but he dismissed the action because Allason had failed to show he had suffered financial damage. One of Allason's witnesses was the Labour MP George Galloway, who had a long history of antipathy towards Blair's press secretary and said he had kept a 'weather eye' on Campbell's activities ever since the days when he was the 'hired character assassin' employed by the late Robert Maxwell, the former *Daily Mirror* proprietor. In giving judgement, Sir Maurice said that on the balance of probability Campbell had played no part in the story but he was not 'by any means a wholly satisfactory or convincing witness'. The judge found Campbell 'less than completely open and frank', adding: 'He did not impress me as a witness in whom I could feel one hundred per cent confidence.' Outside the court Campbell said the case should not have been brought. There had never been a 'shred of evidence' against him and all three defendants had been cleared 'on every limb' of Allason's case. When challenged about the damage the judge's remarks might have done to his own credibility, Campbell brushed reporters' questions aside. By a happy coincidence he was able to spend the evening celebrating Labour's successes in the council elections.

Blair's advisers were so self-disciplined when they were in the company of journalists that there were few real insights to be gleaned into their precise relationship with the Labour leader. However, I knew from my own experience that he would have few qualms about allowing his staff the licence they judged to be necessary when policing the press statements and interviews of those shadow Cabinet members who were considered to be less than wholly reliable. Blair's objective in calling on his colleagues to observe a self-imposed silence on sensitive issues like tax was to prevent Labour inadvertently supplying ammunition to the Conservatives. He believed the tactics which were being deployed by his spin doctors, and their sometimes fractious relations with one another, rarely counted for much outside the confines of Westminster.

Labour continued to hold a commanding lead in the opinion polls as the government careered from one disaster to the next. And of all the cries to have beset John Major, the débâcle over the March 1996 announcement about 'mad cow disease' best symbolised the disarray which can ensue when ministers find themselves at the mercy of the news media. On receiving fresh advice from the government's spongiform encephalopathy advisory committee, ministers believed they had to make the information available to the public immediately, although no attempt had been made to think through the consequences for farmers or consumers. Once the health secretary, Stephen Dorrell, told MPs that the 'most likely explanation' for ten new cases of Creutzfeldt-Jakob disease was that they were linked to exposure to BSE, panic set in. Beef sales collapsed amid a welter of scare stories. Late on the fourth day of the crisis I was on duty in the radio newsroom. Just before midnight that Saturday evening, there was a frisson of excitement when the news came through that McDonalds were about to announce that their restaurants had stopped using British beef in their beefburgers. The effect was catastrophic. European farm ministers hardly needed any further justification for their decision to impose a worldwide ban on beef exports from Britain. The government was in chaos. Next day the agriculture minister, Douglas Hogg, told *On The Record* that one option would be to remove from the human food chain all cattle aged over thirty months. Although Hogg did not enlarge on what this meant, the obvious implication was that millions of older cattle would have to be slaughtered. Four hours after the interview I was told by a Ministry of Agriculture information officer that this was precisely what was being considered: four and a half million dairy and beef cattle, aged over thirty months, might have to be destroyed. Next morning Hogg denied that selective slaughtering was an option; yet within days this was the policy adopted by the government.

Hogg seemed to have no concept of the need for clear and effective communication with the news media. His nonchalant approach to the disaster engulfing the cattle industry seemed to be exemplified by his headgear; he started turning up at crisis meetings in Brussels sporting a low, soft felt hat known as a fedora. Alice Thomson, writing in *The Times*, was struck by Hogg's inability to come to terms with 'modern media madness'. She concluded that this 'self-effacing old Etonian' would no more spend his time 'dreaming up soundbites and posing for the camera than he would give up his Sunday roast and Yorkshire pudding'. Indeed, there could hardly have been a greater contrast in style than that between Hogg and his predecessor at the Ministry, John Gummer, who became increasingly distraught at the cult status which was being afforded to the infamous photograph of the occasion on which he fed a beefburger to his daughter Cordelia at the height of the 1990 'mad cow' scare. The frequent re-use of this picture was a constant reminder of the government's inept handling of this whole sorry saga. Gummer's gullibility in having connived in such an ill-advised photo opportunity in the first place was cited as one reason why he should be sacked in a pre-election Cabinet reshuffle.

Major's hopes of a revival in his fortunes were dashed again in April by the Conservatives' crushing defeat in the South East Staffordshire by-election. Labour took the seat on a 22 per cent swing, chalking up a majority of well over 13,000. Yet again, Major faced speculation that he might be unable to hang on until the spring of 1997 and could be forced into an early general election. With his parliamentary majority down to one, rumours resurfaced about another challenge to his leadership. Again, too, Major was savaged by the *Daily Telegraph*. Its editorial could hardly have been more damning: 'Overall this government is a disas-

ter. . . People have no belief in the men or the measures, no expectation
that they will be told the truth, no impression of competence, no faith or
hope or charity.' The *Sun* was equally pessimistic. It would take 'one
heck of a feelgood budget' to wipe out voters' disillusionment with the
Tories and perhaps, come election day, it would not matter anyway
because 'people will just want a change'. Even so, the *Sun* believed that if
Major was going to lose, he should 'at least go down with a fight'.

Labour were taking no chances. Blair and his advisers were still tor-
mented by the fear that their careful election planning could all unravel
if they were caught defenceless by a deadly round of negative campaigning. Deep inside the new media centre at Millbank Tower, publicity staff worked away, firing up their secret weapon. In order to
accelerate the party's ability to retaliate and, they hoped, neutralise
damaging allegations by the Conservatives, Labour were establishing a
new computerised database, which would allow the instant retrieval of
information from a vast array of documents. Both the Democrats and
Republicans had operated rapid rebuttal units during the 1992 US
presidential campaign. Labour's spin doctors were determined to usher
in another first in British electioneering. However, within a matter of
weeks of this development, Conservative Central Office evened the score
by revealing that it too had acquired the same computer software and
would therefore have a comparable database on contradictions in
Labour's policies. In the long months of pre-election skirmishing, tit-for-
tat retaliation remained the order of the day.

Index

KNEE DEEP IN DISHONOUR
The Scott Report and its Aftermath

Richard Norton-Taylor, Mark Lloyd & Stephen Cook

Established by John Major in 1992 in the wake of the collapse of the trial of three businessmen accused of selling weapons to Iraq, the Scott Inquiry mounted a raid on the corridors of power, prising open locked filing cabinets and hauling government ministers and Whitehall mandarins into the interrogation room.

But when the Report was eventually published in February 1996, its 1800 pages of dense legalese presented a daunting prospect for anyone wanting an accessible account of what had really taken place.

In KNEE DEEP IN DISHONOUR three senior journalists who have followed the 'Arms to Iraq' affair from its outset extricate the hidden story of the Scott Report – what it really means, what its implications are for the governance of Britain, how the government reacted to its publication – to provide a lay person's guide to the hottest political event of 1996.

£9.99   0 575 06385 8

A Gollancz paperback original

SECRET SOCIETY
Emma Nicholson

'The Conservative Party has changed so much whilst my principles have not changed at all. I would argue that is not so much a case of my leaving the party but the party leaving me.'

Emma Nicholson's defection from the Conservative Party to the Liberal Democrats in December 1995 came as a bombshell to John Major's already tottering government. Long admired as an articulate and concerned politician, she represented the human side of Conservatism which was rapidly being drowned in a cascade of scandal, sleaze and a growing conviction that the Tories had been in power too long.

Now Emma Nicholson gives her own account of what led to that momentous decision – how lack of leadership, arrogance, tiredness, corruption and a pervasive lack of principle had corroded the soul of the party and reduced it to no more than a secret society.

Emma Nicholson's defection drove another nail into the coffin of a discredited government. SECRET SOCIETY tells how and why.

£7.99   0 575 40072 2

INDIGO

HONEST OPPORTUNISM
Peter Riddell

What is it that attracts people to politics? And of the 651 men and women who represent us in Parliament, why will some become ministers and a few climb to the heights of the Cabinet, whilst the majority remain on the back benches?

HONEST OPPORTUNISM – first published in 1993 and now updated to take account of the findings of the Nolan Committee's inquiry into standards in public life – describes the rise of the career politician, charting meteoric successes, spectacular failures and committed nonentities with equal relish for detail.

'Essentially a guided tour of the way Westminster politics works by one who's been buried deep in them over the years and appears to have spotted everything. This book is the best available substitute, on every level from gossip to academic inquiry, for spending countless hours in the place talking to politicians for yourself'

David McKie, *Guardian*

'Peter Riddell is an exceptional political commentator . . . His book should be read with care, if only to warn us that we can expect much more of the same kind of politician in the future'

Robert Rhodes James, *The Times*

£8.99   0 575 40039 0

INDIGO

ANATOMY OF DECLINE

The Political Journalism of

Peter Jenkins

Edited by Brian Brivati and Richard Cockett

Introduction by Polly Toynbee

'In a career spanning more than 30 glorious years, Peter Jenkins established himself as one of the leading political journalists of his generation. Within this collection of his columns . . . are many of the memorable turns of phrase, predictions and analyses that were the trademark of a man who cared passionately about the state of the world and the actions of those with the power to change it . . . For any fan of political journalism, and certainly for anyone who misses Jenkins' unmistakable flair, wit and insight, this book is an absolute must'   *Time Out*

Peter Jenkins, who died in 1992, was widely regarded as the finest political journalist of his generation. His regular columns in the *Guardian*, the *Sunday Times* and the *Independent*, as well as his essay-length contributions to a wide variety of journals and maga-zines, set the standard for commentating on current affairs.

This extensive selection of his journalism encompasses British, European and American politics since the late 1960s, and covers, in addition to the cut and thrust of domestic politics, the high drama of general elections, the condition of British Rail catering, and many of the turbulent events and issues of the period.

£8.99   0 575 40051 X

INDIGO

THE HIDDEN WIRING

Peter Hennessy

'Hennessy's discussion of his separate themes is . . . brimming with scholarship and erudition. He writes, as he speaks on both radio and television, with pace and verve'　　　　Anthony Howard, *Spectator*

Peter Hennessy is a demystifier who for twenty years has been searching for the concealed codes of state power, and in THE HIDDEN WIRING he unravels the mysteries of the British constitution to expose the true nature of the relationships between the five institutions at the core of public life: Monarchy, Premiership, Cabinet, Whitehall and Parliament. This paperback edition is fully updated and includes a new chapter on the constitutional implications of the Scott Report.

　　With the conduct of public affairs under scrutiny as never before, Peter Hennessy's characteristic wit, zest and incisiveness have never been deployed to better effect.

'The vibrant tones of the author's infectious enthusiasm ring from every page'　　　　Julia Langdon, *Glasgow Herald*

'Characteristically timely, lively and provocative'
　　　　David Cannadine, *Observer*

£7.99　　　0 575 40058 7

INDIGO

BALKAN ODYSSEY
David Owen

In 1992 David Owen, former Foreign Secretary and co-founder of the SDP, was appointed European negotiator charged with bringing the conflicting parties in the former Yugoslavia around the conference table to hammer out compromises that could then be implemented on the battlefield. For three years he and his counterparts – first Cyrus Vance, then Thorvald Stoltenburg – strove both to contain the various wars in the region and to impose a peace plan on a political impasse which consistently defied solution. BALKAN ODYSSEY is his personal account of these turbulent years and of the most traumatic event of recent European history.

'BALKAN ODYSSEY is the detailed diary of a man who was at the centre of international debate, negotiation and hesitation in perhaps the most crucial episode in the early life of post-Cold War Europe. His energy is unflagging, not only in the sheer hours devoted to shuttle diplomacy but also in the formidable detail with which his thoughts, words and deeds are recorded . . . As a source for future historians this book will be invaluable'   Robert Fox, *Daily Telegraph*

'Important and revealing . . . will be a tremendous resource'
William Shawcross, *Sunday Times*

£8.99   0 575 40029 3

INDIGO

Out of the blue...

*IN*DIGO

the best in modern writing

FICTION

Nick Hornby *High Fidelity*	£5.99	0 575 40018 8
Kurt Vonnegut *The Sirens of Titan*	£5.99	0 575 40023 4
Joan Aiken *Mansfield Revisited*	£5.99	0 575 40024 2
Daniel Keyes *Flowers for Algernon*	£5.99	0 575 40020 x
Joe R. Lansdale *Mucho Mojo*	£5.99	0 575 40001 3
Stephen Amidon *The Primitive*	£5.99	0 575 40017 x
Julian Rathbone *Intimacy*	£5.99	0 575 40019 6
Janet Burroway *Cutting Stone*	£6.99	0 575 40021 8

NON-FICTION

Gary Paulsen *Winterdance*	£5.99	0 575 40008 0
Robert K. Massie *Nicholas and Alexandra*	£7.99	0 575 40006 4
Hank Wangford *Lost Cowboys*	£6.99	0 575 40003 x
Biruté M. F. Galdikas *Reflections of Eden*	£7.99	0 575 40002 1
Stuart Nicholson *Billie Holiday*	£7.99	0 575 40016 1
Giles Whittell *Extreme Continental*	£6.99	0 575 40007 2

*IN*DIGO books are available from all good bookshops or from:

> Cassell C.S.
> Book Service By Post
> PO Box 29, Douglas I-O-M
> IM99 1BQ
> telephone: 01624 675137, fax: 01624 670923

While every effort is made to keep prices steady, it is sometimes necessary to increase prices at short notice. Cassell plc reserves the right to show on covers and charge new retail prices which may differ from those advertised in the text or elsewhere.